Joan Metge was born in Auckland, New Zealand, in 1930. An anthropologist by training and a teacher for many years at Victoria University of Wellington, she is particularly well-known as a researcher in Māori communities. She is a leading scholar on Māori topics, noted for her outstanding promotion of cross-cultural awareness, and has published a number of important books on Māori society and cross-cultural communication. They include *The Maoris of New Zealand* (1967; revised 1976; and later republished by Routledge as *Rautahi: The Māori of New Zealand*), *Talking Past Each Other* (1978/1984), *In and Out of Touch* (1986), *New Growth From Old* (1995), *Kōrero Tahi: Talking Together* (2001) and *Tuamaka: The Challenge of Difference in Aotearoa New Zealand* (2010). She was created DBE in 1987. Dame Joan was awarded the Royal Society of New Zealand's inaugural Te Rangi Hiroa Medal in 1997 for her outstanding scientific research in the social sciences and in 2006 she received the Asia-Pacific Mediation Forum Peace Prize.

TAUIRA

Māori Methods of Learning and Teaching

Joan Metge

AUCKLAND UNIVERSITY PRESS

First published 2015

Auckland University Press
University of Auckland
Private Bag 92019
Auckland 1142
New Zealand
www.press.auckland.ac.nz

© Joan Metge, 2015

ISBN 978 1 86940 822 0

A catalogue record for this book is available from the
National Library of New Zealand

This book is copyright. Apart from fair dealing for the purpose of private study, research, criticism or review, as permitted under the Copyright Act, no part may be reproduced by any process without prior permission of the publisher. The moral rights of the author have been asserted.

Royalties from this book go to the Kōtare Trust for Māori purposes.

Cover design: Johnson Witehira

The design on this cover draws on a form called poutama, which has a symbolic connection to learning and knowledge. Generally used as a tukutuku pattern, poutama is said to allude to Tāwhaki's / Tāne's ascent to heaven to gain the baskets of knowledge. Its symbolism also encompasses ideas of family, whakapapa, aspiration and dynamism. As Pakariki Harrison wrote, 'the steps of the pattern indicate the genealogies (heke) descending to the people now alive from the main genealogical line (tāhuhu). They also symbolise various lines of achievement.' In this design the pattern has been rotated away from its traditional upright form, thus offering new insights and meanings.

Printed in China by Everbest Printing Co. Ltd

Contents

He Mihi	vi
Chapter 1: Voices from the Past	1
Chapter 2: Learning as Part of Living	14
Chapter 3: Teaching and Learning	46
Chapter 4: Spirituality and Values	96
Chapter 5: Learning in Maturity as Part of Living	137
Chapter 6: Storehouses of Knowledge	143
Chapter 7: Wānanga	189
Chapter 8: Storytelling	211
Chapter 9: Learning in the School System	238
Chapter 10: Educational Practices and Principles	252
Glossary	267
Ngā Kai-whakauru/Biographies	291
Bibliography	302
Index	305

He Mihi

He mihi aroha tēnei ki ngā Maunga Kōrero katoa o te Motu. Mīharo ana te ngākau ki ngā Māngai Kōrero o ngā iwi whānui i homai nei i ō rātau whakaaro ātaahua hei kākahu hei tautoko hoki i ngā kupu kōrero o *Tauira*. Kei te tangi atu hoki te ngākau mō Sonny Wilson mā, mō Hapi Potae rāua ko Akuhata Tangaere, mō Priscilla Manukau mā, kua wehe atu ki te Pō. E koutou mā, moe mai i roto i te Ariki. Moe mai hoki rā i Paerau. Tai pō ki te hunga kua hinga ki tua, tai awatea ki te hunga e takatū ana i runga i te mata o te whenua. Nō reira, tēnā koutou, tēnā koutou, tēnā koutou katoa.

Wiremu Kaa, Rangitukia, 2015

He Mihi

From conception to publication, this research has been a collaborative enterprise, Māori and Pākehā working together to record aspects of the past for the generations to come. Now that this waka is launched, I pay tribute to the kai-whakauru who helped build it. Returning aroha for aroha, I thank them for their friendship and support over many years and for their generosity in sharing their names and memories with the readers of this book. I mourn the loss of those who have died, and thank their whānau for supplying details for the biographies.

I am grateful to the readers who made helpful comments on the draft text: Wiremu and Jossie Kaa, George Parekowhai and Haare Williams representing the kai-whakauru, and Alison Jones, Jane McRae, Wally Penetito, Charles Royal and Lynne Tito as educators. I acknowledge my debt to the Royal Society of New Zealand for the award of the Cook Fellowship (1981–83) which made the original research possible. For their patience and understanding in realising our vision, the kai-whakauru and I give grateful thanks to Sam Elworthy, Anna Hodge, Katrina Duncan and the workers behind the scenes at Auckland University Press, and also to copyeditor Ginny Sullivan and cover designer Johnson Witehira. Kia ora koutou katoa.

Joan Metge, Auckland, 2015

All my relatives lived just over the fence. That was the pā. We played in each others' backyards or we'd go to the river to swim. We all had jobs to do . . . Up at 5 a.m., light the fire, feed the chickens, milk the cow . . . After school, we came back, we were going to look for kai, picking pūhā, peeling potatoes . . . Especially on Sundays, everyone would take food and go to the gardens. There were acres and acres of it. We weren't taught what to do, we learnt by watching them do it. When you are four or five, you water the plants. — HONE PIRIHI

Finding kaimoana was our fun. We knew when we got home we'd get a hiding for not saying where we were going. So the thing was to bring home a kit of crayfish or kinas . . . If they had a big hui coming up they wouldn't go to a section of the beach till the hui was near and everyone, fifty to a hundred people, would go down and get it all in one day. — TE AOMARAMA MATETE

We didn't have a lot but what we had we shared and we never went without. Money just wasn't around, but we were never hungry. Because if they knew our rua was empty, well, 'Haere mai, come and get something to eat.' — MATEOHORERE KAA

I remember starting out at school, my koroua taking me to the side of the puna, doing a karakia there; . . . and the iriiri or sprinkling of water on my head, and sending this child to school, a sort of dedication for the purposes that he wanted me to have in life. And one of those was this idea of being a repository of information for the people.
— HAARE WILLIAMS

When they would plant, they would say, 'Aa, this is for us, this is for the marae.' My mother's uncle would say, 'Aa, mō ngā mea pani', for the orphans. So there would be main crops for the family, some for the marae and some for the orphans. — WIREMU KAA

The old people live on the marae. There's about three kaumātuas – real kaumātuas with tokotokos – and old kuias, sitting around with us, and there's oodles of kids, and they're telling us stories. How people got to Pawarenga, how the local mountains were named. And we are sitting on the marae and we are looking out at these mountains. — NIKORA ATAMA

In my childhood it was the accepted thing, when we went to Karepōnia church [on the hill], afterwards we came down to Karepōnia marae. On their way to church everybody dropped in a plate of meat or whatever as their contribution to the communal lunch. When we came down to the marae there would be the usual whaikōrero as lunch was prepared by the women. We'd all sit down to a meal. If there was any take [issue] that concerned the tribe, after lunch it was discussed and resolved. About milking time, people began to disperse. — MAORI MARSDEN

CHAPTER ONE

Voices from the Past

The voices from the past that light up the pages of this book are the voices of Māori adults recalling what it was like growing up in Māori rural communities over fifty years ago. I recorded them on tape in the early 1980s in the course of collaborative research on the whānau in the modern world. Aspects of that research were published in *In and Out of Touch* (1986) and *New Growth From Old* (1995). Completing the series on that research, this book focuses on Māori methods of learning and teaching in whānau and community.

Background: The Research in Context

As a Pākehā child living in small rural towns with teacher parents, I was exposed to constant discussion of teaching methods, caught tantalising glimpses into the Māori world through Māori friends, and developed an enduring interest in the problems and rewards of cross-cultural communication. In the 1950s, as a newly qualified social anthropologist and with the support of Māori mentors, I spent two and a half years carrying out research into Māori urban migration by talking face to face with Māori living in Auckland city and a rural community in Northland, and another two years writing up my findings as a PhD thesis at the London School of Economics. Those years established a pattern of collaboration that endures to this day (Metge, 2010, pp.107–22).

Returning to New Zealand in 1958, I renewed friendships with colleagues working in Māori education and read a succession of educational reviews, conference reports and media articles as they were published during the following years. I was shocked to find that the phrase 'Māori education' was invariably used in these publications to refer to the education of Māori children in the formal school system, a usage that implicitly denied the very existence, let alone the value, of the learning and teaching taking place in Māori homes and communities. Moreover, the reported underachievement of Māori children in state schools was commonly attributed to deficiencies in the children's home environment, a conclusion based on non-Māori assumptions about Māori communities and reinforced by the 'deficit' theories then in vogue overseas.

Rejecting such views, I worked with like-minded Māori and Pākehā colleagues to advocate the development of national educational policies better attuned to the needs of Māori children. In particular, we fought for increases in the availability of Māori language and other aspects of Māori culture in school curricula and teacher training programmes. These ideas had actually won the backing of senior adminstrators in the Department of Education in the 1970s and were being translated into action (albeit within funding constraints) when young Māori, angry at limitations on access to their cultural heritage, combined forces with Māori leaders in a campaign that led eventually to the establishment of kōhanga reo and kura kaupapa Māori (see Glossary). Meanwhile, in the late 1970s the Maori and Islands Division of the Department of Education initiated a series of conferences and workshops on policy-making to which I was invited to contribute (Metge, 1990, 2008).

In 1981 and 1982, during research on 'The Whānau in the Modern World' for the Royal Society of New Zealand as Captain James Cook Research Fellow, I recorded lengthy interviews with Māori participants about their experience of learning and teaching in the Māori rural communities in which they grew up. A preliminary report I wrote based on these interviews was published and distributed to schools by the Maori and Islands Division of the Department of Education in 1984 under the title *Learning and Teaching: He Tikanga Maori*. Later I included quotations and insights from the interviews in *In and Out of Touch: Whakamaa in Cross Cultural Context* (1986) and in *New Growth From Old: The Whānau in the Modern World* (1995). In the years since, I have continued to explore the subject in discussion with colleagues and research participants.

Re-reading the transcribed interviews again in 2010, I was forcibly struck by the richness and variety of the speakers' accounts of their learning experiences as children, the individuality and liveliness of their voices, and the light they shed on a neglected period of New Zealand history. With the encouragement of Māori friends, including many of the speakers, I set out to make these riches available through this book to relatives, educationalists and historians in the speakers' own voices. To that end *Tauira* gives pride of place to extracts of varying length from the interviews recorded in 1981 and 1982. Published with the permission and under the real names of the speakers, these extracts are ordered and linked within a narrative framework based on a close study of the full interviews.

Foreground: The Speakers

In the following pages thirty-nine speakers talk about growing up in Māori rural communities in the middle of the twentieth century with special reference to their learning outside school. They were recruited originally as participants in a research project on 'The Whānau in the Modern World', which included Māori methods of learning and teaching as part of the whole. Twenty-five speakers talk about their early experience of learning and teaching at length and in detail; another fourteen contribute occasional pertinent comments. As a group and individually I identify all thirty-nine speakers as 'ngā kai-whakauru', participants in this research on Māori methods of learning and teaching (see Ngā Kai-whakauru/Biographies).

The core group of twenty-five kai-whakauru comprised fourteen men and eleven women. Most of them were in their fifties at the time of interview and had grown up between 1930 and 1960; some were older. They were affiliated with iwi from many parts of the North Island, came from both senior and junior lines of descent, and occupied varied roles in their whānau and hapū (see Glossary). They combined their particular childhood experiences with achievement in adulthood as community workers, kaumātua,* teachers, social workers and ministers of religion. While most were living in urban areas at the time of interview, they all had rural roots and kept in close touch with their home communities.

The sessions I recorded with the kai-whakauru lasted between one and two hours and took place in a variety of contexts: in participants' homes and in mine, in offices and conference rooms, and on marae between hui. Eighteen took part in interviews that included spouses and colleagues, including six Itinerant Teachers of Maori who set aside a session at one of their meetings for the purpose. Twelve were interviewed several times, on their own and with others. The interviews were recorded with participants' permission in notebooks and on tape. I transcribed the tapes myself as soon as possible after the event, checked my transcriptions with the speakers and gave them copies of the typescripts.

While I have referred to these sessions as interviews, they would be more accurately described as kōrerorero or discussions. They were typically free-flowing, relaxed and informal. While I normally opened the discussions with a question, I did not control the ensuing conversation but engaged in it as an equal participant, contributing observations and stories from my own experience and presenting

---

* Note that 'kaumātua' is a gender-free term, and in the plural it includes both men and women of senior age and status. In certain areas and among some age groups it is used to identify male elders, while the term 'kuia' is used to identify female elders. See Glossary.

hypotheses for testing and development. Far from simply responding to the questions I asked, the kai-whakauru entered into lively debate with me and each other, initiating and pursuing lines of enquiry, analysis and interpretation, and often taking the discussion in (to me) unexpected directions. They emphasised some aspects of the subject more than others at different stages of the research and according to their interests and experience. In order not to interrupt the flow, I sometimes failed to ask intended questions or to follow up on questions of detail. For these reasons some topics are explored in more depth than others. Because our discussions took place in informal contexts in homes and offices and on marae, the extracts display the characteristics of informal conversations as regards grammar, vocabulary and explanatory detail.

In these discussions the kai-whakauru shared their own particular memories of childhood learning, looking back over at least four decades. On the evidence of these interviews these memories remained vivid, undimmed by the passage of time, while maturity and wider learning had enhanced the capacity of the kai-whakauru for discerning patterns and identifying episodes of particular importance. Spouses and colleagues who were interviewed together capped each others' stories with complementary and contrasting detail. And comparison of the transcribed interviews established both the common features of the speakers' learning experiences and a wide range of variation.

This book is specifically focused on the experience and reflections of the thirty-nine kai-whakauru. The commentary that links the interview extracts was checked by the kai-whakauru with whom I keep in touch. In this commentary I concentrate attention on the categories, distinctions and ordering principles used implicitly and explicitly by the kai-whakauru themselves and refer to other works mainly to help explore and elucidate difficulties. Both extracts and commentary involve the frequent use of Māori words and phrases. These are briefly explained in the text on their first appearance. A full exposition of meanings and the use of macrons in spelling may be found in the Glossary (p. 267).

In the main text the speakers' own words are reproduced from the transcripts with minimal editing. Pauses of increasing length are indicated by commas, dashes, semi-colons and fullstops. Three dots indicate the omission of words and phrases, repetitions and digressions from the subject in hand. The length of the omission varies from a word to a sentence to a paragraph, the details of which can be checked on the original transcripts.* Within the extracts I enclose translations of Māori words by others than the speaker in square brackets. And I preserve unaltered non-standard usages typical of Māori speech at the time of interview, such as the addition of an 's' to Māori words to indicate the plural and the intermixing of past and present tenses. The mixing of tenses reflects the fact that tense is not built into Māori verbal forms but is indicated by the addition of particles and adverbs.

A number of quotations appear more than once in the following pages. This happens for good reason, usually because the quotation in question relates to more than one aspect of learning and teaching and thus is relevant in different contexts.

Talking about Education: Key Words

When talking about education it is important to remember that the Māori and English words commonly matched as 'translations' belong to and are defined within two different linguistic and cultural systems. Rather than being a perfect match, they often differ significantly in the range of meanings they cover and where they place the emphasis.

---

* The unedited interview transcripts may be accessed for research purposes on application to Joan Metge (via Auckland University Press) during her lifetime, and subsequently to the Curator, Māori, at the Alexander Turnbull Library, Wellington.

Tauira/teacher, learner: In *A Dictionary of the Maori Language*, which favours classical Māori usage, 'tauira' is credited with the related meanings of 'teacher; pupil; pattern; copy' (Williams, 1975, p.398). Within its small compass it embraces four aspects of education that English identifies as separate. In the twenty-first century, 'tauira' is used mainly to refer to students at secondary and tertiary level.

Tikanga/methods: English–Māori dictionaries agree in translating the English word 'method' as Māori 'tikanga' and vice versa. Both words indicate 'a way of doing (something)', but 'tikanga' covers a wider range of meaning. The dictionary definition of 'method' emphasises procedure and orderliness, the *how* of doing something (Allen, 1990, p.746). 'Tikanga', formed by adding a noun ending to 'tika' (right and fair) (Williams, 1975, p.416), emphasises the group's values and goals, the why that underpins the how. However, although the word 'method' does not refer specifically to the purpose behind use of a particular method, that purpose is usually easy to discern.

Since the late 1980s the phrase 'ngā tikanga Māori'[*] has replaced Māoritanga and Taha Māori[†] as the approved translation of 'Māori culture'.

Ako/learning and teaching: In English, 'learning' and 'teaching' are distinguished as separate activities. In Māori the two are encompassed in the word 'ako', a transitive verb that dictionaries credit with meaning both 'learn' and 'teach' (Williams, 1975, p.7). Since at least the 1980s, the English words 'learner', 'pupil' and 'student' are generally referred to in Māori as 'ākonga', while 'teacher' is commonly referred to in Māori as 'kai-ako' or 'kai-whakaako'.

---

[*] Note the plural form, acknowledging that a group's culture comprises multiple parts, some of which are contradictory.

[†] 'Taha Māori' (the Māori side or dimension) began to be used in the 1970s as synonym and sometimes alternative to 'Māoritanga' and was used as the title of the curriculum development adopted as policy by the Department of Education in the 1980s (Scott, 1986, pp.14–15).

Mātauranga, whakaakoranga/education: The English word 'education' covers a broad field, encompassing learning and teaching carried out in a variety of ways. In practice it is often used to refer to formal education in schools and tertiary institutions, sidelining informal, experiential processes of knowledge transfer. When the interviews were recorded in the 1980s, 'education' was rendered into Māori by the word 'mātauranga'. Thus the Department of Education was (and is) Te Tari o Te Mātauranga and the New Zealand Council of Educational Research was (and is) Te Rūnanga Whakawā Mātauranga. Education as process rather than institution was sometimes referred to descriptively as 'whaka-akoranga' (making to learn).

'Mātauranga' is formed by adding a noun ending to the verb 'mātau', which means 'know, understand, feel certain of' (Williams, 1975, p.191).* As a result, mātauranga was (and is) also used to mean both knowledge and understanding (Allen, 1990, pp.656 and 1332). In this work I use mātauranga as the kai-whakauru did to mean education, knowledge and understanding – all three; and mātauranga Māori to mean distinctively Māori ways of knowing and understanding.

Tohunga, pūkenga/specialist teacher, expert: In Māori the word 'tohunga' is used to identify a person who is highly qualified in a specialised field. This word has so wide an application that it should properly be qualified by an adjective identifying the special field involved, for example, he tohunga whakairo (a carving expert). Because tohunga has lingering associations in the popular mind with expertise in occult lore and practice, I prefer to use its synonym 'pūkenga'. This word is defined as 'repository' by Williams (1975, p.307) and given the modern meanings of 'lecturer, professional, skilled person, storehouse of knowledge' by Ryan (1995, pp.200 and 560).

---

* In Māori the word 'mōhio' is very close to 'mātau' in meaning, but opinons differ on exactly how they should each be used.

Tuku iho nō ngā tūpuna/handed down from the ancestors/ traditional: 'Handed down from the ancestors' is a word-for-word translation of 'tuku iho nō ngā tūpuna', failing only to convey the full significance of 'tuku', the word used when giving something of value. The English word 'traditional' is 'based on or defined by tradition' (Allen, 1990, p.1293). Like the two previous phrases it refers to inheritance from previous generations but without specifying genealogical links. The beliefs and practices described in these terms may have their beginnings in pre-European times or at any time in the years since; many incorporate elements appropriated from non-Māori sources. Whatever their origin, they have typically undergone a degree of change, in particular through adaptation to changing needs and circumstances.

The Community Setting

The kai-whakauru on whose recollections this work is based grew up in households several of which constituted large extended families (whānau), which together formed a community (pā or kāinga) with a marae at its heart. Participation in these groups – household, whānau and local community – involved children in a variety of daily, seasonal and occasional activities including household chores, combined gardening and fishing enterprises, and gatherings at the marae.

Most of the kai-whakauru lived with parents and siblings in households that typically included other relatives (grandparents, aunts, uncles and cousins) for shorter or longer terms. Three lived with several related nuclear families in large old homesteads, while one spent his first nine years living in a one-roomed raupō (bulrush) whare remote from other settlements with grandparents who kept in touch with their whānau by travelling to hui.

In general, the households comprising a community were located within easy access of one another, scattered on small land development farms or clustered around a marae. Because of close kinship ties between households, children moved easily between them.

> While we related more easily to our parents than to others, at the same time we enjoyed an easy and close relationship with grand-aunts and grand-uncles, my father's cousins – they were all regarded as grand-aunts and grand-uncles. If we were too far away from home when lunchtime came, we went into the nearest house. We accepted that as our right. More often than not our own table at home had a lot of visitors. We children tended to gather at a particular place, especially after I started school. At weekends we would turn up at one of the relations' home, about twenty children, and we'd play together there as a group. When it came to meal times, then the burden fell on the particular auntie at the time, whoever she was. Sometimes at night we just bedded down with these other people, too. While every nuclear family had their own home, at the same time everyone from Ngāi Takoto would entertain others from the tribe. Your home is my home and my home is your home is the attitude we had.
> *(Maori Marsden)*

With the exceptions noted above, houses in these communities were typically small wooden boxes with washing and toilet facilities located separately 'out the back'. Lighting was provided by candles and kerosene lamps and cooking was done in wood-burning cast-iron stoves and/or on open fires.

> I was brought up in Te Kūiti right below the pā. We had one of those houses made out of ponga [tree-fern] logs with a raupō top and iron on top of that. We had two houses like that. One had a wooden floor where we slept, the other one [the kitchen] had an earth floor and a beautiful chimney that took up one whole wall . . . To clean the floor you sprinkled water on the floor and swept it with a tea-tree

broom. Because it was an earth floor we had a hole in the floor for cooking rēwena [leavened] bread. We put ashes in and ashes on top, buried it for an hour. *(Priscilla Manukau)*

Nikora Atama was one of nine children. The house their father built for them in Pawarenga comprised one sitting-room, three bedrooms and a kitchen.

One bedroom was Mum's and Dad's and their bedroom was the smallest in the house and you could just fit their bed in their bedroom. In the [second] bedroom we had one double bed and a single bed. We had about three or four of us [boys] in one bed and a sister in the other bed. In the other room we had one big bed just about from wall to wall, so one end of the room would be clear for the drawers for our clothes. These drawers hold the clothes to everyone in the house. *(Nikora Atama)*

The households that occupied these houses were effectively kin-based production units tapping a variety of resources and supporting not only themselves but also community goals associated with the marae. Many adult males in these households were farmers nominated as 'owner-occupiers' of small farm holdings developed by the Department of Maori Affairs under the Native Land Development Schemes initiated by Sir Āpirana Ngata; other adult males found employment on a contractual and often seasonal basis in such jobs as fencing, shearing, draining, droving, general farm labouring and bridge-building. Very few women were in paid employment because it was rarely available anywhere close. Since the farms were usually small (40 acres or less) and heavily loaded with development debt, the farmers too had to take up short-term employment, leaving the women and children to carry out the routine tasks on the farm as well as in the house. Income from the farms and paid employment was supplemented by vegetables and fruit from extensive 'gardens' (māranga kai) and orchards, and foodstuffs, medicines and materials gathered from the bush, rivers and sea.

> My father didn't have a regular job. When I look back on it there was no real need, the only thing we needed money for was clothing, because we had everything planted, we had our own pigs and cows and there was always something from the beach . . . We cured our own hams and preserved pāuas [abalone shellfish]. We were self-supporting. (*Hineari Babbington*)

In many communities, related households worked together to do their planting and harvesting communally.

> The planting of the garden, . . . when they planted it was ten acres . . . The men did the ploughing and the discing and the women came along behind and did the planting. They were always together, so I wouldn't say it was just the parents; no, it was the whānau that did it. They planted all in the same place. They'd decide how many rows they'd have, how many acres, how much they'd plant, and they all did it. They knew the time to plant, they prepared for that and did it together . . . The harvest was awkward, usually it was shearing time. But there was always someone there . . . The men would be out shearing and it was left to the womenfolk. (*Joe Matete*)

The marae so frequently referred to by the kai-whakauru is more accurately described as a marae complex. Sited on a marae reserve, it comprised the marae ātea (an open space set aside for encounters between the haukāinga/the home folks and manuhiri/visitors from elsewhere), a whare hui (a meeting-house, fronting on to the marae ātea), a dining-hall (whare kai) with an attached kitchen or detached kāuta (open-sided shelter over cooking fires), a toilet block and sometimes a small wooden church (whare karakia), all enclosed by a fence with a front gate facing the meeting-house across the marae ātea and a back gate giving access to the amenities 'at the back'. In most communities this complex of land and buildings was referred to as 'the marae', especially on the East Coast, but in the Far North it was sometimes called 'the hall'; in both cases the name of a part of the complex was used to identify the whole. The array of basic elements, their interrelationship and functions were everywhere the same but they varied widely in the form they took. Some of the whare hui were large rectangular wooden structures distinguished by gabled porches adorned with carvings, but others were much smaller buildings that lacked these distinguishing features. The former were typically associated with equally large rectangular dining-halls with attached kitchens, while the dining-halls of the latter were much smaller, with detached kāuta.

In the rural settlements where the kai-whakauru grew up, parent–child and extended families operated within a web of relationships that linked households with each other and with the marae. Whatever its physical location, whether its buildings were large or small, carved and painted or unadorned, the marae was the emotional and spiritual heart of community life, a gathering place where old and young worked together, mourned their dead, and welcomed and cared for visitors.

CHAPTER TWO

Learning as Part of Living

Reflecting on their recollections of growing up in Māori rural communities, the Māori contributors to this book – ngā kai-whakauru – all agreed that most of their learning outside school and much of their most important learning as children had taken place as part of their ongoing lives at home and on the marae. Because it was shared and pervasive in their experience, the kai-whakauru took this way of learning for granted and saw no need to give it a name in either Māori or English. In *Learning and Teaching: He Tikanga Maori* (1984) I described it as 'learning by exposure'. Unable to find a widely accepted alternative, I have settled temporarily on the phrase 'learning as part of living'. What the kai-whakauru had to say under this heading is set out in this and the following three chapters.*

Typically found in all human societies, learning as part of living is of particular importance in the formative years of childhood and adolescence but continues through life, waxing and waning in influence with changing circumstances. In the Māori communities where the kai-whakauru grew up, it covered a wide range of activities, encompassing both those that took place in the context of daily living (tending house and garden, farmwork, childcare and so on) and on dramatic occasions such as the communal planting and harvesting of crops, religious services and festivals, and hui (formal gatherings) on the marae. Because these communities were predominantly Māori in

---

* More specialised ways of learning are explored in Chapters 6, 7 and 8.

membership and culture, learning as part of living was of basic importance in developing the speakers' identity as Māori.

Work and Play

Talking about their growing years, the kai-whakauru had a lot to say about the 'work' they were required or chose to do, more than they did about 'play'. In general, work and play were not clearly differentiated: many activities involved elements of both. While they resented some of the work tasks required of them, the kai-whakauru recalled finding others enjoyable and were proud of making a contribution to family and community wellbeing.

As children the kai-whakauru contributed to the household economy by working in the house and household garden and on the farm, and by gathering in the bush and on the sea coast. The details of what they did varied with age and the location of the settlement.

Hone Pirihi (Whakatōhea), who grew up in the Bay of Plenty, recalled:

> We all had jobs to do. Up at 5 a.m., light the fire, feed the chickens, milk the cow . . . After school, we came back, we were going to look for kai [food], picking pūhā, peeling potatoes. Even the boys partook in that. *(Hone Pirihi)*

Priscilla Manukau (Ngāti Maniapoto), who grew up inland in the King Country, had similar memories.

> We had a spring. We [children] each had a duty to cart the water before school and at night. We used to use bark for firewood; each one of us was to get a sack, we got it from the bush further down the Waititi road. We all helped with the planting of potatoes. We had a shed at the back and in it a place where we put fern, then potatoes,

then fern. I never knew why, I didn't question. They had little potatoes set aside for next year. One of our duties was to split each in half with an eye on each side. We carted water from one spring for the house, from another for the washing [of clothes], otherwise we had to wash down at the creek. We rubbed the clothes with soap and hit them with a stick. My mum used to make the soap.
(Priscilla Manukau)

Nikora Atama (Te Aupōuri) summed up his early years in Pawarenga on the west coast of the Far North as:

Hard, not hardship. Physically, you had to work hard for what you had to do . . . We were taught to cook. I was baking bread at the age of seven or eight. We all had to learn . . . We were taught to do housework, every one of us. Scrub floors, wash clothes, cook breakfast, cook lunch, cook tea, bake bread. The only thing I never learnt to bake was cake but all my other brothers did . . . And on top of that we had sports, we had time for everything. We had acres and acres of gardens. We would use one whole paddock, say about three or four acres, for gardens . . . We had the old plough, horses pulling it, and we would go about a mile away to get our supply of water, in 44-gallon drums, on our sledges . . . Dad, he was a bridge-builder. He worked for the Hokianga County Council and his job was all over [the county] . . . He was a bridge contractor in the end . . . On school holidays we used to go with him on his jobs and be billy boys to cook their meals. And the people there who used to work for him, it was the family again. It was Dad, Uncle P, Uncle D, practically everyone from Pawarenga that he took with him was his gang. And the people that they left behind, to do the chores on the farm and in the home, was the eldest son, my brothers, and we had to cope with what we had at home, never seeing Dad for months, for weeks. There's certain nights we go fishing. Mum would go out practically all night and fish and come back. We'd live on fish,

shellfish and all the things we get from the bush . . . Everything we had was livestock; we had ducks, poultry, pigs. I think that is how we survived, on food . . . We used to milk our cows [by hand] and take the cream down on horse and sledge from the cowshed to the creamstand, and we used to catch the cream truck, because the cream truck came from Broadwood to pick it up.
(Nikora Atama)

Maori Marsden (Ngāi Takoto) lived with his family on the shores of Rangaunu Harbour in the Far North. His father combined roles as an Anglican minister, farmer and rangatira of the iwi. Māori himself was one of the youngest in a large family.

We were farmers. We milked quite a number of cows. The older children went off to milk and we were allowed to sleep in until we became a bit older. Then we were expected to milk, come home [from the cowshed], have a rushed breakfast and rush off to school . . . Back home in the evening, we had various duties but these were seasonal. During the harvest – we had an extensive orchard, a hundred and one different varieties of peaches. As soon as we arrived home [from school] the knife was put in our hands, we had a bite to eat and we were expected to peel peaches. Mum preserved hundreds and hundreds of bottles of preserves. We were expected to peel all the peaches after school. And in the evenings, after Evensong, preserving began. *(Maori Marsden)*

In these communities children also contributed to the economy on forays to seaside, river and bush with adults or on their own, to fish and gather shellfish and to garner materials for rongoā (herbal medicines), crafts and construction. These expeditions often involved hard physical work that they sometimes found miserable and sometimes enjoyable, and sometimes both at once.

We go fishing. We fish from the rocks or sometimes we have a dinghy and we row the dinghy out into the middle of the river and then we fish. I didn't like fishing but Mum used to take me and my brother [at night] and she come back all hours of the morning and that is what we live on. She goes fishing and sometimes she goes musselling. When she goes musselling she takes the older boys with her and they come home with sacks of mussels for us.
(Nikora Atama)

We only went to the bush for two reasons . . . We went a lot to get posts; it was usually to split fresh pūriri posts, or someone would be contracted to split them for us and our function was to snig them out of the bush, either as partially cut logs or as completely cut posts. We used to snig them out of the bush into the stream and all the way back to the farmhouse, which was quite a way, about three miles along the beach. We did a lot in winter. I remember being miserably cold. Snigging means dragging it along the ground. Sometimes we'd use the spring cart but it was heavy work in the spring cart in the sand. It was heavy snigging them as well. It was an incredibly miserable life – we were always bare-footed. [The other reason we went to the bush was] to hunt for pigs and so Dad could get tāwhara, the fruit of the epiphyte kiekie. The other thing was to shoot pigeons – don't you write that down! We knew where the pā miro [stands of miro trees] were. At the time of the miro season we used to go there with a pea rifle. We used to get whekī too, from the dried stalk of the ponga tree. We'd also get nīkau – we made nīkau houses for the scrub-cutting gangs. We also went to the perimeters of the bush where there were fallen logs to rob beehives of wild honey. [A mate] and I have robbed in our lifetime ten or so hives. He'd locate one – I was still at primary school but he had left school, he was sixteen or so . . . We put sacks on our hands, raincoats on our bodies, balaclavas on our heads – we weren't very successful. We waited until it was raining, built a fire and smoked

it, then chopped the log up, split it open. We were able to take whole wedges of honey home in kerosene tins. His mother rendered it down... In the case of the honey it was just devilment.
(Wiremu Kaa)

Expeditions to bush or coast might involve siblings only or draw in cousins from neighbouring houses. Joe Matete (Te Aitanga-a-Hauiti, Rongowhakaata) recalled frequent visits to 'the beach' with other children.

Finding kaimoana [seafood] was our fun... I learnt to eat raw pāuas, crayfish, kinas [sea urchins], learned how to cook them, out at the beach. When it was decided we were going to the beach, everyone had to bring a potato in each pocket. The main problem was matches – everyone brought some matches, waterproof ones. We'd go out [to the beach] and spend the weekend. The parents would call others and ask if we were there. Someone would have seen us going to the beach. There were two little creeks and plenty of eels in it. It was easy to me at that time. *(Joe Matete)*

Going to get eels became a game for us. Different pās had different ways. We used to use hīnakis [woven eel traps]. *(Hone Pirihi)*

Maori Marsden, on the other hand, preferred his own company on fishing expeditions.

Weekends were regarded as a holiday for us younger ones. During haymaking we were expected to pitch in but on Saturdays we were fairly free. Early Saturday morning I'd be off to Rangaunu Harbour, most of the time by myself. *(Maori Marsden)*

Beyond their own household, children were involved as workers when their whānau or community gathered for some collective purpose, such as communal planting, the celebration of religious festivals or caring for visitors to a hui on the marae. Nikora Atama's whānau included his father's brothers, his mother's brothers and sisters, and all their children. While its constituent families lived in their own houses, they planted communally.

> Gardening, the older people, like my uncles, they did the ploughing, because there was no way we could handle that plough as it is too heavy for us, but they would make sure that we followed behind them, picking up the stumps and watching them, and we'd hitch up the horses for them, hitch the plough up, and then they do the ploughing. And when it comes to the rakaraka, the harrow, the kids do that. We catch the horses, slip it on, the kids sit on the platform, and away we go breaking the soil up, and that is our job. Once that is done, they plough it again, go back over it again, so we do the rakaraka again, and then they set the gardens up . . . They planted communally. They worked together as families, and they put their gardens down as families. *(Nikora Atama)*

Whether the participating families had separate 'gardens' or planted defined sections of a combined 'garden' on suitable land, the work was done as a group. The kai-whakauru had happy memories of these communal work groups, proud to be included and to contribute at the level of their ability. Sharing her experience with other Itinerant Teachers of Maori, June Tangaere of Ngāti Ruanui commented:

> One of the things that I loved the best when I was little was how we used to gather all our lunch, go down to whoever's paddock was going to be ploughed or planted, and we'd put all our kai under the walnut tree, and away we'd go. And in my mind it was one of the best days when we were all there. And if we were old enough, to carry a kete [kit] full of planting kūmara [sweet potato], potatoes or whatever, or if you were too little, well, you were

allowed to play. Singing, and calling out to one another, and the humour, ... all in Māori, going across the paddock to each other. And I can remember being so happy. And again when everything was ready to be harvested, we'd go back again. It was the joy that seemed to be between all the families, being all together.
(June Tangaere)

Another Itinerant Teacher of Maori, Hapi Potae (Ngāti Porou), added his experience to hers.

Talking about harvesting, it was an enjoyable day alright. It wasn't a drag, ... it wasn't considered work in those days, planting kūmaras. And even kids, the involvement of the kids, this was something I used to enjoy, because I used to have to get the horse and put it to the sledge, because you had a 44-gallon drum – and take it down and fill it up with water and take it up into the kūmara patch. You had that little task. *(Hapi Potae)*

Those managing these communal plantings typically set aside several rows for each widow and elder living on their own.

It was real communal involvement. So and so had a few rows of kūmara. The old man [the kaumātua in charge] would ring them up and say, 'Kei te one maroke, te one parareka' [the ground for the potatoes, the ground's dry] and they would come and they would have their own [rows]. And they would tend them and when they dug them they generally didn't turn up, so you had to dig them for them. *(Hapi Potae)*

Whenever community members gathered at the marae, whether to discuss community matters or to host visitors, the children gathered with them, engaging in work and/or play according to age and competence. Those who were old enough were given tasks to do before, during and after the hui, beginning in the kitchens and moving on to the dining-hall and even the meeting-house as they proved worthy.

> If there was a [Ringatū] Twelfth [see Glossary] at the marae, we all helped getting things ready for people coming from all over the place, preparing the food, preparing the meeting-house.
> *(Hone Pirihi)*

The younger children played round the marae, making their own fun and a lot of noise, but when the ceremonial began they were sent off to play elsewhere or were taken home to bed.

> We played round the marae, and when there was any occasion, this big group of kids, we used to have a ball of a time. Running round the meeting-house and chasing right until about this time of night. And then our grandparents, my grandmother in particular, would gather us together and take us off home, wash us, feed us and put us off to bed. And then she would go back again to the meeting-house. *(Hapi Potae)*

If adults were not available, older, responsible children were deputed to supervise the younger ones as a group.

> If there were too many visitors, the kids were in another part [of the marae] but they had their meal at the same time as everyone else. There is a table set aside especially for the children. They always had a wahine pakeke [adult woman] standing around – she supervised your eating. No one talked on the table . . . When the meal is finished, even their play was supervised, by the older kids, girls about fifteen or sixteen, senior kids. That left the elders in the meeting-house doing whaikōrero [speechmaking]. Most of the games were very competitive, usually in a spare paddock away

from the marae – things like horse racing, using a pig's bladder blown up and tied with flax as a football. There was a Māori way of playing softball, knucklebones, hopscotch and competitions [using] spinning tops. When we went to the river [for diving and other water competitions], it was always supervised... by an adult who was available or... boys about seventeen or eighteen, always someone older than you... There could be thirty to eighty kids at a time, every Twelfth. They had to have someone to control the children while the rest were doing other things – having karakia [prayers] and meetings. *(Lena Pirihi)*

Whether it was a matter of work or play, a gathering at home or in the wider community, music accompanied every activity.

Every home had music. I was about twelve before we got our first radio. A great event that was. But, you know, there were violins round the place, and ukeleles, and there was always singing, and the cousins were always around. *(Hineari Babbington)*

Learning Practical Skills

As children, the kai-whakauru acquired a range of practical skills in the context of real life. The main emphasis was on demonstration, observation and imitation. By comparison, verbal instruction was limited and questions discouraged, at least until the task was done.

It really wasn't learning, it was living, wasn't it, Liz? I wasn't conscious of learning things. You just accepted it as part of living. *(June Tangaere)*

We were shown physically more than talked to, talked to about how to do these things... Everything we were taught wasn't by word of mouth, it was picked up. Or they took us to a place and we'd watch them do it. *(Nikora Atama)*

Mavis Tuoro (Te Arawa) summed up her experience of growing up in Rotorua in these words:

In one way, you really learnt indirectly. You learnt by seeing and hearing what was going on. They didn't really sit down and teach you certain things. They did things and you as a young person just looked on, and listened. And because you were in a situation where it happened over and over again, you probably got to understand. They never said, 'You do this and you do that.' They'd just do it . . . When I was young I just accepted what happened and I didn't dare ask why . . . There were little things I felt that I didn't understand about things at home but I never asked about them.
(Mavis Tuoro)

Keri Kaa (Ngāti Porou) told me that her grandparents and elders rarely set out deliberately to teach anything.

They never called a youngster aside especially to teach something and they didn't accompany what they were doing with verbal instruction. I was never taught to make bread and things like that. I just watched my mother and other women doing it for years. Then one day my mother passed over the bread and said, 'Knead it! I'm going to bed!', and I did it. I would sit and watch my grandmother making kits. If I asked Granny how and why she did something, she would say, 'Hōhā i te pātai!' [I'm tired of questions] and point at me and then at my eyes. *(Keri Kaa)*

Merimeri Penfold (Te Aupōuri/Ngāti Kurī) and Nikora Atama confirmed this practice of discouraging questions.

The thing was to observe. I can remember a kuia saying, when people start asking questions they have lost the thread of what you have established; they have been distracted and broken the thread. It weakens your teaching point for that person and interferes with the follow through for others in the class. You make the point with the child early that he holds his peace till the take [subject] is complete. In storytime questions were never allowed. The old lady said, 'Questions can come when you come away from the session, not at the time.' *(Merimeri Penfold)*

We never asked questions any time we were working. It is at night that we'd ask questions and they'd answer our questions there and then. *(Nikora Atama)*

Growing up with his widowed mother's relatives in Ahipara, Wiremu Hohaia remembered being pushed into doing some tasks without any instruction at all after he had watched adults doing those tasks for years.

They ploughed the gardens – there was no such thing as rotary hoes. They had ploughs and discs, and chain harrows to level it out, and they also had a scarifier, that's to make ridges ... Actually I was one of the ploughers. I just went into it, got going – nobody taught me. The old people, they said to me, 'Oh, you'll have to try and plough our garden.' It finished up we did quite well. We had a good pair of horses, draught horses. *(Wiremu Hohaia)*

But when it came to the planting and care of crops, the senior generations made sure he knew not only what to do but why.

They tell you, they tell you as you plant – that's the old people, they tell you as they go along. They say that memorising is a good thing, don't forget. It is far better to forget anything else but the main

thing is, anything to do with eating, you never want to forget that
... They show you that because that's the most needed thing, is the
kūmara, the corn and the potato ... That is the only time they talk
to you, show you how it is done. Of course, if they see you doing it
wrong, well, look out, they really pounce on you then. But once they
see you doing it right, they'll never say a word. *(Wiremu Hohaia)*

Wiremu went on to share his knowledge of growing kūmara and potatoes and preparing karaka berries in a great deal of detail.

Tawhao Tioke (Ngāi Tūhoe) was born and spent much of his childhood living in settlements in the Urewera bush. He and his mates learned bushcraft and hunting skills from Manuka Ereatara, who was one of Rua Kēnana's physicians (Binney, 1979, p.78).

Ereatara, Granddad's nephew, took us for bushcraft ... Bushlore
was taught in the bush. It included how to find water in the bush.
We were taken to a rātā vine, told to look for a dark red vine, not
a white or green one. You cut a vine eight feet long, carry it, put
it up against another tree on a slant, put a billy under it and wait
until the water flows down into the billy. If you can't find a rātā
vine, look for a tōnui, a member of the ponga family – it could be
dead for forty years. Push your butcher knife in two feet from the
ground and put a billy underneath. But you couldn't patch it, so
you waste all that water. That's why you look for a rātā vine first ...
The hunter must do things respectfully. He must not go hunting for
the sake of killing. He must not litterbug or pollute ... Instead of
talking about something, our teacher showed us. He would always
take us up to the subject he wants to talk about. If he stopped, we
know it's something he wants to teach us. If there are manono trees
around, he'll say, 'He manono tēnei. Ko tana mahi, te whakaora i te
poroiwi, hei hono i te poroiwi whati.' [This is a manono tree. Its job
is healing bones, joining broken bones.] *(Tawhao Tioke)*

Lena Pirihi (Ngāi Tai) identified situations involving verbal instruction as 'teaching' and contrasted this with situations where learning was absorbed by osmosis.

> The only time I know when we were taught was weaving and knitting. When it came to planting, it just came automatically. Where we walked along the road they didn't tell us 'Look for pūhā', but we'd watch out for pūhā spots. *(Lena Pirihi)*

Looking back on growing up in a settlement located on a dangerous sea coast, Hapi Potae and Hineari Babbington remembered learning how to keep themselves safe but not how or when they learnt.

> Just below the school there was a strong rip but nobody got drowned there. I can still read the water. But I can't remember being told in so many words. *(Hapi Potae)*

> I have wondered how we ever learned to read the tide. We lived right along the coast. We used to walk right round the coast and there was a certain spot that you had to know – you had to leave the bay and the township at a certain time to get past. It took you about three hours to walk there and you got past this spot and you had your swim right at the end of the bay, then you walked back and you had better have got past that point again, otherwise you were cut off. I can't remember to this day [how we learnt this], except that it must have been through everybody just going, time after time, with older people. And reading where you could swim – there were certain places around the bay that you just didn't swim. Below our school was one of the spots. You just didn't swim there. You had to read the tides. And I don't remember anybody ever telling me how you could tell, but we just didn't . . . There must have been a sort of family teaching that went along with you as you grew, the older ones taught the younger ones, and those ones taught the next lot. *(Hineari Babbington)*

Sometimes adults took the initiative, attracting children's attention and showing them what to do.

JOE: I learnt by imitation. My uncle said, 'Come and stand by me; now, you watch.' I wasn't told how to do it. **VI:** That's how we learnt too. **JOE:** We watched and we acted. My uncle would say, 'You come here and hang on to this line. Don't go to sleep or a shark will come and haul you out to sea.' *(Joe and Vi Matete)*

Where my dad was concerned, he didn't distinguish the functions of different pieces of equipment [by naming them]. He'd say, 'This is how you do it', and I would need to observe as closely as I can and it would probably follow that he'd repeat the same process, of using the equipment, and then at some time, generally from about the third viewing of it, it's 'You do it.' And, man alive, if you flunked it, he'd get angry. He'd assume that you as the learner would have established the order in which the equipment is arranged and the process as the technical skills were acted through for that part. *(George Parekowhai)*

At other times adults simply presented the opportunity and waited for an expression of interest, aware that the uninterested would not persevere if hard work was involved.

Old Granny M, my grandmother's sister . . . was always doing it [weaving]. We were never chased out but neither were we encouraged to sit down and learn to do it. Granny used to sit there, and she was always weaving. *(Hineari Babbington)*

Using the flax for kete or whāriki [woven flax mats], they didn't teach you, but they were there and 'Haere mai, e moko, kei konei!' [Come here, grandchild!] They didn't force you. *(Jossie Kaa)*

More often, the children took the initiative without prompting, watching and copying what went on around them. Maori Marsden said he learnt to fence as a child while holding a can of staples for his father. As important as the skills he learnt was his father's attitude to all he did.

> In everything he was very meticulous . . . He was an expert on the adze and axe and many other tools. All the pūriri posts we used were bevelled. When he fenced, if from strainer post to strainer post there was one post out of line, then that post had to be dug up and set so that if you looked from one end of the fenceline to the other you could see naturally only one post. That was the type of person he was. This was the example he always set us. He was a perfectionist in that regard. *(Maori Marsden)*

Hone Pirihi remembered copying the adults in the family who always kept a lookout for wild greens.

> You know tōihi, the curly ends of the kamokamo? They grew among the maize. When I was little, about four or five, I said to my nanny, 'Is this tōihi?' She said, 'Here is one.' It was a game. She'd say, 'Now our kit is nice and full, we are going to have a lovely tea.' They always looked for greens – watercress, pūhā, tōihi, poroporo – that's deadly nightshade. It's alright to eat if picked at the right time. *(Hone Pirihi)*

Adults resorted to direct verbal instruction mainly in order to ensure the children's physical and/or spiritual safety and in cases of community need.

> Going to the bush and getting firewood, we were told the type of wood of the tree we had to chop down and not to chop down certain trees because of their sacredness. *(Nikora Atama)*

> During the [Second World] War all of us kids, we were made to sit down with knitting needles and a ball of wool and knit socks for the Maori Battalion. All the young girls... and the boys, they had to do it too, knitting vests and balaclavas. *(Lena Pirihi)*

> The only thing I can remember being consciously taught, that was tukutuku [lattice work on the inside walls of the meeting-house]. That was for the specific purpose of adorning their dining-room [at the marae]. Remember when we used to go in the afternoon, after school, and take turns at making panels for that place? But apart from that, I didn't ever get to learn to make a kit or any of those kind of things. *(Hineari Babbington)*

Hone Pirihi included poroporo in his list of the wild greens they kept a lookout for. He and his mates were explicitly taught when these plants were safe and when they were poisonous.

> They said, 'When they have berries, don't eat the leaves.' We ate the leaves when they were young and there were no berries.
> *(Hone Pirihi)*

In settlements where there were no doctors, children soon learnt to make use of plants that were readily available and the healing properties of salt water by a combination of observation and direct instruction.

> We used to go out and get milkweed for warts and dockweed, you know those big leaves, for poultices, or lilies, because we had a lot of lilies around. We used to heat that up for poultices, to draw the boils. It was just a sort of practical lesson, of being told to go and get this or to get that. When we used to have hakihaki [a rash or other skin disease] on our backsides... they used to take us down to the sea, we used to make a special trip to be immersed in the salt water

and left with our pants off so that the sun would get in to dry all the salt. Oh, it used to sting. It took the heads of the hakihaki off and it sort of dried. It's amazing how quickly it heals after it has dried. *(Hapi Potae)*

There was only one rongoā we ever used, taught to us by the old lady: koromiko, the narrow-leaved koromiko. It might have been when this young boy had an upset tummy from the raw honey. She actually demonstrated for us – three or four leaves, bite them and then chew them. I know of an uncle who went to the bush to get pikopiko [a type of fern] fronds. Apart from that there was the harakeke [flax] but we didn't have to go to the bush for that. In the case of the boils we had as children, our parents actually told us to use the kopakopa, the lily, or the runa... kopakopa, that's the wide-leaved plaintain; runa, dockleaf. They just went and did it [put it on the boil or sore] and when it was time for taking the whatu [core] out, you sat there and they did it. You screamed but it didn't matter, they cured you. *(Wiremu Kaa)*

A great deal of experiential learning took place in the context of groups larger than the household.

Learning was part of the whole family network rather than just the nuclear family... There's always a third party, and the third party plays a very important role in the transmission of knowledge. Sometimes it is by the uncle, sometimes by an auntie and sometimes it is by the grandparent. *(Wiremu Kaa)*

Hone Pirihi remembered children playing their part when the related families gathered to plant, weed and harvest their gardens.

Especially on Sundays, everyone would take food and go to the gardens... We weren't taught what to do, we learnt by watching them do it. When you are four or five, you water the plants as they went along. They didn't direct us – you just followed suit, you mimicked the adults . . . You'd get tired of playing and start following them around. *(Hone Pirihi)*

Children of all ages were involved in the large work parties that assembled for the key events of the agricultural year. Hineari Babbington and Hapi Potae had complementary memories.

> **HINEARI:** A classic example of learning that I recall in the olden days was at the planting time; you know, when we got together, we kids had to count out those tipu [kūmara shoots] into bundles of a hundred . . . I could count and do those kind of things before I went to school, that was our thing. And each hundred was bundled up and tied with flax and put into those tubs of water, so many bundles in each tub. And of course they knew exactly how many tipu went into each furrow . . . And then, when the actual planting started, we little kids, we had the jugs, a bucket with water, and we put the water in the holes. I tell you, it was hard work planting in those days. **HAPI:** You knew exactly what quantity, what amount of water [to pour into each hole]. I suppose you learnt through experience: you were reprimanded if you put too much or not enough. **HINEARI:** The water was put into those coppers at the end of each furrow. And the water had to be brought up from the creek. There were no hoses. Somebody else had that job, but we kids had the job of filling those holes with water. *(Hineari Babbington and Hapi Potae)*

Remembering similar learning experiences, Wiremu Kaa commented on the wide range of things learnt by these inclusive and practical processes.

> We knew all that, weeding, planting, ground preparation, from kids. Even preparing the bedding for the plants, the tipu, we did

all that, we helped in that, we were part of the workforce. It is later [in the year] in Rangitukia, the kūmara cultivation. [By being involved we learnt] the time of the month, whether the moon was right for planting, the signs to look for, for the blight, for an attack by insects, what you must do when you are weeding, turning the leaves out, the runners out. That kind of thing was all part of our upbringing. Because Nanny or Auntie would go and turn them, you'd watch them doing it, then you would go and turn them, you'd watch them doing it, then you join in, and probably about halfway through one row you'd take off and go and have a swim or something and leave them to it still. But it was all part of learning, being a part of all that activity. *(Wiremu Kaa)*

It was in the context of the planting and harvesting of kūmara that Joe Matete acquired what knowledge he had of the most important phases of the moon.

[It was] the same thing again – we listened, we weren't actually taught. A week before, a fortnight before they'd plant the kūmaras, they'd go to the bed [where the tipu were growing] and lift the plants. We'd say, 'Why now?' 'In ten days' time, the full moon, we'll plant our kūmara then.' 'What is full moon?' 'Rākaunui.' You were told there are three days you can plant kūmara, just about full moon, full moon and just as it starts to wane. There are three nights the moon is at a standstill. There were other nights too, but these are the ones I remember. You are told to take your plants up on those nights or days, then seven days, nine days after, you can plant them. *(Joe Matete)*

Joe absorbed much of his knowledge of the prime locations of kaimoana when the community prepared to host important hui. As part of the preparations, a rāhui (ban) would be placed on a section of the coast for three or four months beforehand.

If they had a big hui coming up they wouldn't go to a section of the beach till the hui was near, and everyone, fifty to a hundred people, would go down and get it all in one day. One of the uncles would say, 'Go to so-and-so rock, the crayfish will be ready.' *(Joe Matete)*

Learning Mātauranga Māori

Looking back on their childhood, the kai-whakauru realised that they had taken in considerably more cultural knowledge than they recognised at the time in the context of daily life in the home and through participation in whānau and community activites. The transmission of such knowledge involved more verbalisation than was the case with practical skills, more explicit teaching and a greater emphasis on listening. However, they were still left, and sometimes directly challenged, to work much of the meaning out for themselves. Just how much they learnt and what it meant they did not appreciate until many years later.

Typically, parents preoccupied with making a living and running the household concentrated on ensuring their children acquired necessary practical skills. Most parents were too young (in Māori terms) to have much conscious grasp of mātauranga Māori. Those older parents who were knowledgeable in such matters did not usually embark on a planned course of instruction but took advantage of what opportunities household arrangements presented. A busy farmer with a large family, George Parekowhai's father shared aspects of his knowledge from time to time after the evening meal, when the family gathered together.

> [Dad] never actually had formal sessions in the sense that he'd say, 'You sit down and I want you to listen to this.' He'd simply get interested in a particular subject and off he'd go... From an idle remark he may give a proverb, and the proverb would reflect on a family

incident. By our response – and I was always interested – he would start off and he'd tell a story, and it would relate to this proverb and it would relate to historical facts. And he would also connect that incident with himself by line of descent. *(George Parekowhai)*

However, he would avoid anything too profound and stopped when it was apparent that the children were not following him.

These sorts of stories would vary in length of names in a descent-line from about ten names, sometimes fifteen. Much more than that was taxing even myself. My brothers would sit, outwardly absorbed in the story; they were clearly interested and so was I. We didn't ask questions. We didn't try to direct the story into a particular line of development, even though I for one was interested in pursuing, say, a particular ancestress . . . Dad would just tell a sentence or a section until he felt he'd had enough. Whether he was judging the concentration of my brothers [I don't know] – I always felt I would have liked to hear more but accepted pretty automatically the end of the session. *(George Parekowhai)*

Where older relatives were part of the household, children were regularly exposed to patterns of behaviour that were much more traditional than those of their parents.

As kids we used to sleep with our grandparents; I can remember as a ten-year-old, even younger, well, older too, I'd climb into bed with them. In the early hours of the morning, three o'clock in the morning, they would start talking and singing and doing their waiatas [songs]. They would sit, and they would discuss a lot of happenings, at this time of the night or of the morning. I'd go to bed and they'd be asleep, and then they would wake up and naturally they would wake me up too. This used to happen quite frequently. *(Hapi Potae)*

My own family, there were three of us [children] . . . but Mum had a lot of adopted children [as well]. The most enjoyable time we had was at night. We had an uncle staying [with us] and after tea they would take turns telling stories. It was spooky. The uncle was a cousin, I'm not sure where he fitted in, he was not my father's brother or my mother's brother . . . He was the one, every time we went to bed, he'd come in and tell us stories. If they got too spooky, we'd pull the covers up and go to sleep and he'd pull faces, disgusted because we'd gone to sleep . . . In the bedroom kids had only one bed; just below us our uncle had his. The other thing he used to do was make us sing a lot. He'd say, 'If you go to a hui, be prepared to stand up and sing.' Māori songs, pātere, pao, the old ones . . . he just kept singing them over and over and we had to try and pick it up. He corrected us by making us repeat it . . . He would just sing, he would just start up . . . always at night when we went to bed . . . Most of the time when he tells a story, there is a song, the song is connected to the story. To me he was the best uncle out.
(Priscilla Manukau)

Because their home was crowded, Nikora Atama and his siblings often went to stay for a spell with their maternal grandmother. It was in her house that Nikora first encountered aspects of mātauranga Māori.

Her teaching was very, very old, very tapu, very Māorified . . . Whatever she did, she would karakia: you could hear her mumbling, doing her thing . . . She tells a story every night about the old days; every night she talks about our history, our tūpunas, teaches us a lot of things, like marae protocol, how you should do this, why you should do that . . . She used to take us on the marae and show us what it is all about . . . It's a different way of bringing up from Mum and Dad. *(Nikora Atama)*

This grandmother was deeply knowledgeable about the local landscape and weather conditions. She did her best to share this knowledge with her mokopuna (grandchildren), despite a lack of interest on their part.

> She used to tell us a lot about the weather. She would sit on her verandah looking out to the harbour and she would say . . . 'Could you see the change in the land?' [We couldn't see the difference] and we just would say 'Yes.' It is a beautiful day and she would say, 'Do your washing today, because it is going to rain tomorrow.' And it rained – she would never miss a beat. Right up to this day I can look at the same hills, I couldn't see the difference . . . She would try to teach us but we weren't interested . . . We would go to the coast [for kaimoana] and everything was lovely. She would say, 'That's enough, come back.' We say, 'No, we get some more.' 'No', she would say, 'No, come back, that's enough.' In about an hour after you leave that rock, you see the place is pounding. We never got to ask her why this, why that, but there is a lot of landmarks that we sort of use a heck of a lot [now]. *(Nikora Atama)*

Children living with older relatives in the same household took for granted such behaviour as early morning karakia and waiata and let teaching they did not understand pass over their heads. But experiences like these seeped into their subconscious where they lay dormant until adulthood.

> As I'm getting older I'm starting to see what my grandmother sees, . . . the different colouring in the paddocks and the ranges and the swirling of the clouds. She pointed it out. She used to go out when it's cloudy, and especially on dusk, when it's about to get dark, you see a cloud swirling; and when a cloud swirls, she used to point up . . . when she used to look at the clouds, it used to turn, whipping it out, out towards the ocean, and she reckons in

our place it's good for diving because it [the wind] is keeping the shores really clear, because it's taking everything out to sea. If the cloud's coming round from the back hills, coming in this way, it's bringing everything in, the dirt right in to shore. *(Nikora Atama)*

Children often encountered important aspects of mātauranga Māori when they participated in the seasonal round of food production but such encounters were rarely accompanied by detailed explanation.

At the time [when we were children] we never thought of the Māori calendar because we still had the old people at home. They were the ones that were passing on those things to Mum and Dad. 'Tonight is the night to go out [to plant or fish], tomorrow is not a night to go out' . . . They didn't explain why tonight, they just said, 'Tonight's the best night to go out.' When we go out crayfishing, the sea is nice and calm, they'd say, 'Oh no, no! It's no good now. Don't go out', and then they say to us, 'Now is the time to go!'; especially at the time when it is cold and raining, they say, 'Go!' You think, 'Oh my goodness!' but you go; man, you soon catch them. They probably used that calendar: they know it. We never asked them why. *(Nikora Atama)*

Although he did not pay attention at the time, Nikora found out about the importance of the Māori lunar calendar as an adult. When he and his wife and children went to live inland at Broadwood, they missed their seafood. At first they would go to the coast when they felt the craving and find that the tide was in, covering the rocks. That was when they learnt about the Māori calendar and began to use it, so that they would catch the tides at the right time.

In the course of acquiring practical skills, children often picked up cryptic sayings tossed off in their hearing. If asked, the adults might or might not explain the full context and meaning. They were more likely to supply a mere snippet of information which made no sense until the children had learnt more about the context.

> My people fished for shark when the karaka berries were ripe. You had to ride over the hill, you rode past the karaka trees. They'd gather karaka berries, go down [to the beach] and stay the night, cook the karaka berries during the night while they were fishing. So they got the fish and the berries at the same time. One of the hardcase uncles would say, 'When the karaka berries are ripe, the mako shark [arrives]. Then the Māoris lift their hāngīs [food cooked in earth ovens], great big puku kai [stomach full of food].' I never forgot it. Even now, when I see the karaka berries, it naturally flows through the mind . . . When the kōwhai blooms, you start getting your garden ready, or when the grey warbler sings, you get the whakataukī [proverb], 'Where were you when the grey warbler was singing?' By the time the shining cuckoo is there in October our garden should be ready to plant. When I say garden, I mean the main crops to plant. If you plant kūmara around Labour weekend in October you should harvest them at Easter, give a week or two.
> *(Joe Matete)*

The association of the grey warbler with the spring planting was used to rebuke the lazy, comparing them to dodgers who wanted a share of the harvest without sharing the hard work of planting.

Wiremu Kaa had a similar experience to recount.

> My grandmothers, they used to say things we couldn't understand, and the grandfathers too . . . I remember we found a centipede among the kūmaras and he said, 'O! Te mokopuna a Tangaroa!' [Tangaroa's grandchild]. And we called it Tangaroa for a long time until we went to school and then we found what it is. It was a game. Later he told us about Tangaroa, but it had nothing to do with that centipede. Tangaroa is the moana [sea]. *(Wiremu Kaa)*

Wiremu's grandfather evidently did not explain why he called the centipede Tangaroa's grandchild. Years later, as an adult at teachers' college, Wiremu read *Nga Mahi a Nga Tupuna* and learned that Tangaroa's descendants had quarrelled and separated. Some chose to stay in the sea, while others settled on land where they became insects (Grey, 1928, pp.2–3; Grey, 1961, p.6). As Wiremu commented:

> The information came out in snippets in a variety of ways. You had to probe it, [then] you'd catch on. I think that was their method of teaching. Sometimes they would be hōhā and wouldn't tell us. Maybe because they were busy ekeing out a living.
> *(Wiremu Kaa)*

Sometimes dropping these snippets of information was deliberate, intended to stimulate children into asking questions.

> It would be a particularly rainy day and the mist would come over the valley where we lived. It was a very misty valley. The river that ran past our marae, our home and community was called Waikohu . . . Our particular mist, it was a kind of light, rainy mist. My dad used to point it out to us. Eventually I got to identifying it myself. The mist would hang over the valley with a kind of sunglow behind it. And when it misted in that fashion he would say in Māori, 'That is your ancestress!' – making herself known was understood. You didn't see a particular form but that was the physical manifestation of that ancestress. We learnt that her name was Hinepūkohurangi. *(George Parekowhai)*

In some communities there were agricultural activities from which the younger children were excluded. This too was a learning experience, raising questions that might not be fully answered until years later.

Before they plant the garden, they [the adults] go at night. Well, at the time we never asked them why they'd go. There is quite a few that go, the older people, go in the garden, and we [children] stay in the house. And they come back, and we are not allowed on the garden until about three days later. As we grew older, we have been taught by Dad and by the old people about Māoritanga. They talked Māori and I asked them why . . . Dad was saying they used to go and karakia on the gardens at night, at a certain time of the night, say like just before the moon hits a certain spot back home in Pawarenga there, and then they do their karakias. When they finish they come back, and the next day those same people would go and put the rows down, the second day. The third day they would go and plant from dawn and they could be planting practically all day in their garden – it was a big garden – and we didn't go with them . . . The two oldest brothers went on the planting but they didn't go on the night when everybody went to do the karakia on the garden.
(Nikora Atama)

For most of the kai-whakauru the marae had been the centre of community life and the most important site for learning mātauranga Māori. When members of the community gathered there (to work on buildings, discuss local issues, host visitors and relax with music), their children were usually there also, playing around the fringes with or without supervision, helping with essential tasks like peeling vegetables and washing dishes, seeing and hearing more than they were aware of at the time.

HAPI: We had a lot of freedom round the meeting-house and in this freedom you observed lots of things; you sort of couldn't help but learn what was going on. You saw the manuhiri being karanga'd on [see Glossary], especially at a place like Waiparapara, because they had a long way to walk, up that road, right to the meeting-house, and the person who did the karanga stood there and her voice went

right across. And as kids we ran around, we touched things that we weren't supposed to, and we were reprimanded . . . And although . . . the adults were involved in the in-thing, they were still concerned about you, and then they started to look around – 'Kei whea peā?' [Where are you?] – or they might call one child to tell you, 'Round everybody up.' They'd sort you out and different parents and grandparents would gather together their group of children and then bundle them off or even take them for kai. I can remember being taken and seated down and my grandmother providing some kai. But this wasn't very often. Most of the time she took us home.
HINEARI: And then once that actual pōwhiri [see Glossary] part is over, all the observations of what happens inside, the little rules and regulations that go on inside the meeting-house itself, inside the dining-room, even your sleeping arrangements.
(Hineari Babbington and Hapi Potae)

It was firmly impressed on all children from an early age that being allowed on the marae was a privilege and they must treat all its parts with respect, especially the marae ātea and meeting-house.

When you're a kid, you're playing around the marae during a tangi [mourning hui; see Glossary]. OK, that's alright, it's nice for the people sitting in the whare mate [house of mourning] to watch, they enjoy looking at the kids when there is no manuhiri around, but boy! did we ever get chased off when there were manuhiri approaching the marae, and if you didn't move fast enough you got whacked! *(Sonny Huia Wilson)*

Whether the children were admitted even to the dining-hall depended on the number and status of the visitors and the reason for the gathering. They were likely to be sent home if there were visitors from a distance or if there was a tūpāpaku (body) in the meeting-house or whare mate.

I found it was a matter of accommodation . . . If we could sit at a table with the visitors [i.e., if there was room in the dining-hall], then we were allowed in, but then you weren't allowed to talk. The admonition was, 'If you are going to talk, leave the table.' So therefore as children, you are there to eat, not to hold a conversation . . . I think that was one part of the learning. You sat there and you listened, and you learnt just by being there. *(August Tangaere)*

Where the meeting-house was concerned, the rules were particularly strict. Nikora Atama's father regularly took Nikora to hui with him, including tangihanga.

Dad's favourite saying was, 'When people come to the [meeting-]house, if you want to, come in, be there with us, but we don't want to hear you.' We used to go a lot with him and sit there with Dad and never say a word, but listen. Dad was very strict on us. He used to say, especially to me, 'Think big, say less.' *(Nikora Atama)*

The marae was a prime site for storytelling, whether or not a hui was in progress. Nikora recalled that the kaumātua who lived near or on the marae would sit together on the porch of the meeting-house when nothing else was happening and the children would join them.

There was a big group of us little kids. There's about three kaumātuas – and I'm talking about kaumātuas, real kaumātuas with their tokotokos [walking sticks], and old kuia, sitting around with us, and there's oodles of kids, and they're telling us different histories: stories about Tāne-mahuta . . . we started with Tāwhaki, Tāwhaki and Hema. I was only about seven and these old people were telling us . . . how people got to Pawarenga, the different names they gave for the [local] mountains, . . . how those mountains were named. And of course we are sitting on the marae and we are looking out at these different mountains. *(Nikora Atama)*

In those days it was a serious breach of tikanga to arrive at a marae after dark. At night, hosts and visitors settled down in the meeting-house to listen to the kōrero [see Glossary], which could range widely, encompassing debate about current issues and stories of both local and wider significance. Children were admitted as long as they kept quiet, as the Itinerant Teachers of Maori well remembered.

> **AUGUST:** You would never chip in. **HAPI:** You never joined in adult conversations. **JUNE:** Once you ate you were out. **AUGUST:** I think that was one part of the learning, Joan. You sat there and you listened and you learnt just by being there. Somebody mentioned the word osmosis. *(August Tangaere, Hapi Potae, June Tangaere)*

Some of the stories told in the meeting-house were directed at the young with specific educative intent. As Wiremu Kaa pointed out:

> Because of the informal, unstructured nature of learning in Māori society, quite often it is a catastrophe, a mate [a death], an error, that is time for instruction, the time for learning, the time for teaching . . . A drowning, for example. Someone drowns and all the stories about taniwha [supernatural water beings] or te awa [waterways] come out. All the talk about that awa, ngā tapu, ngā paenga [boundaries between worlds] comes out, and usually comes out at the tangi, in the whare nui at night, not on the marae [ātea] . . . And you were expected to learn from that, but sometimes you missed the cue; the younger generations particularly would miss it. *(Wiremu Kaa)*

The older children often missed these cues because they were not listening closely or had not yet acquired enough context to recognise them as such. The younger children missed the stories and their meanings because they had fallen asleep or been put to sleep too far away from the tellers. Joe Matete recalled that he got only 'wee bits' of the story his grandmother told about the naming of the lunar nights one night in the meeting-house.

> I don't know the story because I was way over there. They weren't told to me, they were told to the older ones. I was supposed to be asleep in the meeting-house – she was telling the older ones the story. *(Joe Matete)*

Joe regretted that he did not have the same opportunity for learning as his older siblings because he left home at fifteen to find a job.

Once visitors to a hui had departed and the hosts had finished cleaning up, they often sat down in the kitchen or outside to sing and swap stories; again the children were there.

> After a mate, when the funeral's over, that's when they sit and talk, after the manuhiris have gone. All the locals. And of course the kids run around. The old people lived on the marae. We'd go and sit with them and they sit there and tell us about these histories. *(Nikora Atama)*

CHAPTER THREE

Teaching and Learning

Teaching Roles

In the communities from which the kai-whakauru came, parents typically shared the responsibility for educating their children with other kin. In most cases parents concentrated on overseeing their children's acquisition of practical skills in house and house garden and on the farm, with help from grandparents, aunts and uncles when they were available. Where the transmission of mātauranga Māori was concerned, however, it was these older relatives who played the major role, with parents involved only if and when they had both the time and the requisite depth of knowledge. Siblings and cousins of the same generation also played a part in the learning process through the interaction of older children with the younger ones and in peer groups.

> It's not an abdication of responsibility, it's a sharing of responsibility, a preference for the third party. *(Wiremu Kaa)*

Before reading what the kai-whakauru said in this regard, it is important to recognise that they used both Māori and English kinship terms with a much wider range of reference than those understood by speakers of English. In their vocabulary, 'grandfather' and 'grandmother', 'pōua' and 'tāua' (the Ngāti Porou terms), 'granny', 'nanny' and 'tupu' (an abbreviation of 'tupuna') referred not only to a child's parents' parents but also to the latter's siblings and cousins of the same generation. While the terms 'grandfather' and 'grandmother', 'pōua' and 'tāua' indicate gender, the other three terms do not.* In talking about the parental generation, the kai-whakauru nearly always used the English terms 'father' and 'mother', 'mum' and 'dad', 'aunt' and 'uncle', but while they restricted use of the first four to their own parents, they used 'aunt' and 'uncle' to refer both to parents' siblings and to parents' cousins of the same generation.

In talking of members of their own generation they mostly used the English terms 'brother', 'sister' and 'cousin', but typically noted whether they were older or younger, reflecting the Māori distinction between 'tuakana' and 'teina' with respect to age and sometimes but not always with respect to seniority of descent. In the first descending generation, the kai-whakauru extended the terms 'tama' (son) and 'tamāhine' (daughter) from their own children to the children of the siblings and cousins of their own generation and recognised all the children of the latter as 'mokopuna'. Like its reciprocal 'tupuna', 'mokopuna' does not distinguish between the genders.

Grandparents
One thing that stands out in the kai-whakauru's accounts of their childhood is the important role that grandparents played in their education, imparting knowledge ranging from the practical to the metaphysical, teaching tikanga Māori (the right Māori way of doing things) and the underlying values both explicitly in words and indirectly through storytelling and their own example. While some grandparents were clearly more accessible and loving than others, in

---

* Ihimaera, 1972, pp.1–5. In Ihimaera's story 'A Game of Cards', the word 'Nanny' is used to address and describe both men and women ranked as 'grandparents'.

general they were remembered with gratitude for their teaching as well as affection for their love and care.

Some kai-whakauru highlighted the influence of one or two particular grandparents.

> As children we had so many homes to go to; we weren't always with Mum. Most times we were with our grandfather. He was widowed, and we used to spend a lot of time with our grandfather, and I am sure that is where we picked up a lot of the things that we still practise today. *(June Tangaere)*

> My grandmother, she had the biggest influence in my mind, she featured very greatly, because she was the one who everyone used to look to in the family. They lived with us, my uncle and his wife and my cousins, and there were other aunties, too. We were all living together, and yet she was the one who guided everyone, or if there was anything to learn about how you behaved, she was the one who actually taught us, the mokopuna, what to do. *(Liz Hunkin)*

> I was brought up by my father's sister and her husband. This couple had no children of their own. They brought up fourteen. I was one of the last three. We were all cousins; we called her Auntie. Her father lived with her too. He was a Ringatū minister . . . [If anyone had a strong influence on me] I'd say it was my grandfather. He never ever reprimanded us. If he did tell us off, he did it in a lovely, soft way. It made you feel bad and made you feel you wanted to cry . . . He's still alive, in his nineties. He's a beautiful old man, he hasn't changed from the day I was little, he's still the same . . . Even today, in this day and age, though he didn't go to the whare wānanga, he has so much to offer us . . . He never went to primary school or high school. His whare wānanga was his church, what he grew up in and what he did in his lifetime. *(Hone Pirihi)*

My nanny was a wonderful old lady. This is Mum's mum I'm talking about... Quite often my younger brother and I used to be left with my grandmother and that was a wonderful time in our lives. We got anything we wanted. She made sure we were tucked into bed and things like this, which made our lives at that time far more comfortable and made us feel more secure. With regard to kai, we got anything we wanted, within reason of course. Everything she had in the cupboard we could have... When I say that we were spoilt, I don't think it was spoilt, I think... we were being really loved and cherished by our Nanny. *(Sonny Huia Wilson)*

During his first nine years Haare Williams was nurtured by his paternal grandmother, who belonged to Whakatōhea and Tūhoe in the Bay of Plenty; in his teens he returned to the East Coast to live under the influence of his maternal grandmother who belonged to Te Aitanga-a-Māhaki. Both women were highly regarded by their people for their knowledge of whakapapa and tikanga but they differed markedly in personality and teaching methods.

My first grandmother: I think her greatest gift to me was her ability to talk to me all the time, either whispering or body language – with the eyes, the hand that comes around, the arm round my neck when I'd done something good or when I was crying. When I had experienced some mishap she would pick me up and really boost my spirit ... I cannot recall any form of formal teaching at all in the things I picked up from her... My second grandmother was very, very specific in what she wanted to see happen and talked about it often, that she wanted her grandchildren to succeed... This perpetuation of the culture and the values and the history and so on was very much part of Waioeka Brown's plan for us as her grandchildren, and she wanted us to succeed in the Pākehā world too: School Certificate and no less for her... The influence of both these women was very, very powerful indeed. *(Haare Williams)*

Wiremu Kaa had warm memories of one particular nanny and her indirect teaching.

> We always looked forward to seeing my mother's aunt. She was a widow. She was always giving us things, barley sugar or blackball lollies . . . And she played tricks on us. We'd go there and she'd be lying in the sun in her cane chair – she'd know we were there, she'd go 'Boo!' and we'd get a scare and she'd laugh her head off . . . She'd take us to her orchard, tell us not to eat those ones over there, 'Ānei ngā mea pai' [These are the good ones], and she'd point to ones that were good, make sure we weren't going to break the branches of her trees. She talked to her peach trees. Everything was alive [to her]. Her trees were alive – she talked to them, that was the fascinating thing about her. She talked to her cats and dogs, her trees and her apples and her lemons. I remember her picking some lemons one time and she was telling the lemons to make our coughs better . . . A real lovely lady . . . When we left we always had a kit full of something to take home. There was always caution and concern. Don't do this, don't do that. Don't gallop too fast on our horse, make sure we take it to our mother, and things like that. *(Wiremu Kaa)*

This nanny taught Wiremu things he didn't think his mother would have had the time or patience to do, such as how to light a fire.

> She'd tell us to go and light it, and we'd make a mess. We'd just burn all the brushwood and never have a fire. And she'd sit there and kōrero Māori to us, and she'd go 'Ārā ngā rārā!' [Then the twiggy brushwood!], and 'Ārā ngā tāwhaowhao!' [Then the bigger pieces of driftwood from the beach!], chanting, and we'd know which ones to put on top, the order of the wood, of the fire-building. And then the fire was burning and we'd be amazed. And so next time we'd say 'Ārā ngā rārā!' and 'Ārā ngā tāwhaowhao!', chanting what she chanted, and the fire lit, presto! *(Wiremu Kaa)*

TEACHING AND LEARNING

Wiremu's colleague Sonny Huia Wilson also remembered his mother's mother's effectiveness at teaching small children.

> One of the many things that our grandmother taught us was toilet training, Joan. She had this down to a fine art, and she'd do it through teasing and through a little chant that she taught us. Now, in those times going to the toilet was important, there were outhouses then, outside lavatories with a hole dug in the ground. But we kids didn't always go to the toilet, we were like little puppy dogs, made a mess all over the place, and it was too far away from the house anyway. When my cousins were growing up and there was quite a little family, she used to call us to sit around her and she taught us this little game. Now you know, mimi-tata [wet-your-pants] or tiko-tata [soiled-your-pants] is a very terrible thing to be called. In fact you knew you were doing it and your conscience got guilty when you were caught and you got pointed out. And she taught us this game. It was like one of those elimination games. You had to hold your fist out like this, and one person went round banging the fists as he passed the others, and everybody chanted, 'Nō wai e pōti* e rere waho? Nō Pere! Maumau te aweawe!' [Who owns the cat that rushes outside? Pere does! Waste of effort, you're out!] And if that person got labelled a tiko-tata, well, that was a big disgrace, and through this, being labelled as a tiko-tata or a mimi-tata, you learnt that you had to go to the toilet, and every time you went to the toilet and you decided you weren't going to get right to the toilet, you just remembered that little chant and that made you hold on. So that was one thing Nanny taught us, toilet training . . . [When we said that chant and someone got labelled tiko-tata] everybody would laugh like mad, and that embarrassed you

---

* 'Pōti' is a transliteration of 'pussy', and the line that accompanies the fist banging that counts someone 'Out!' refers to the fact that cats always go outside for toilet purposes, but children waste their effort when they don't make it to the privy, in these homes the 'little house out the back'.

enough to remember, go all the way to the toilet, not just halfway there. *(Sonny Huia Wilson)*

Other kai-whakauru were nurtured concurrently by several and even many 'grandparents'. They often referred to these collectively as 'the old people'.

They do play a major role in the whānau. Usually when there is a gathering, you'll find them all pitching in. If the mother and father are absent, they'll take their place. *(Lena Pirihi)*

Joe and Vi Matete, who grew up in different communities on the East Coast, capped each other's recollections.

JOE: It was always the grannies that did it [praised children] more than the parents. It's only spoken between the granny and the child. The granny would understand what the child was crying for. VI: The grandmother taught the little ones a lot. JOE: I look back and I can see so many little ones holding to her skirts. I used to do a lot of hunting and I could tell by the bark of my dogs what sort of pig it was. So the granny could tell by the cry, she knew and could interpret. VI: She was the one who sang all the lullabies . . . VI: It was not the parents, it was the grandparents, the old people [who taught us to get kaimoana]. Our father would have liked to teach us but he was always too busy . . . The old men were the experts. JOE: They knew where the places were. They'd say, 'You know where Auntie Lil's rock is? You go and get the parengo [edible seaweed], it should be right now.' They knew the time and the seasons . . . VI: It was old Tipere across the road who taught us how to make pāua hooks and the reti board [for catching kahawai]. Another old chap, an uncle of Dad's, taught us how to plant everything – kūmara, strawberries. He did it in the old way. He had a fenced-off plot with a mānuka fence round it and beds of everything. Not in big paddocks like today . . . Getting teaching from your grandparents – that's really true. **JOE:** Knowledge of these things was taught by the grandparents, Pōua and Tāua. *(Vi and Joe Matete)*

Like Vi and Joe, Hapi Potae learnt from several grandparents how to read the sea and gather kaimoana, but he remembers one in particular for sharing her expertise in finding crayfish.

I actually through my grandmother knew where the crayfish were and she actually taught me how to catch crayfish . . . I don't remember how she taught me or what instructions she gave me but just going with her all the time, it was sort of step by step by step . . . We went to certain areas, she'd take me and then she said, 'There's a rua down there', and you went down and you found there was a hole with an enormous crayfish in it. *(Hapi Potae)*

As a group, the kai-whakauru absorbed important lessons in values and right ways of doing things from what their grandparents said and did. The most basic of the values imparted was that of aroha (loving sympathy).

I was brought up by my grandparents. My grandmother used to say, 'That woman is unfortunate. Kei te mate pōrangi ia. Me aroha mātou ki a ia.' [She has the crazy sickness. Let us have compassion for her.] And she used to keep on repeating this every time it happened – it used to be at full moon actually – we'd all run away and put on the scared act, until gradually she conditioned us to accept this old lady. I'm sure that that experience of growing up sympathising with a person like that has given me an acceptance of people like that. I sympathise with those sorts of people now, and understand. I'm sure it is because of the way she constantly repeated and accepted. *(Hapi Potae)*

Hineari Babbington expanded on this theme.

> This brings to mind the other kinds of people who lived in our community. Like an effeminate person; a great big chap he was, but completely and utterly accepted. He was always the cook on one of our maraes. And a couple of women who set up house together . . . One of the women actually left her young family for this other person . . . They went away for a short time and came back again, and the people accepted it. It was, 'Hard luck, Uncle!' One of the aunties – one of his wife's sisters – took the children under her wing and they went about living. And a child who was a Mongol [Down's Syndrome], born to a young girl about fifteen or sixteen. My husband's aunt took this child. She had no children of her own but she had already adopted four or five kids and she took this child into her home. Her husband was on a pension. Everybody loved it. We were brought up among people like this. *(Hineari Babbington)*

Grandparents stressed the importance of the spiritual side of life, not least by the way in which they marked events with karakia.

> Grandmother, she always helped us out with the harvesting. I can remember asking why she always said prayers before the thing started and when they were all in and graded and everything was finished. I was told she was just giving thanks for the fact we had a good crop of kai, and I thought, 'Yes, that's right.' That's early teaching, early learning, learning to be thankful for what you've got. *(Hineari Babbington)*

George Parekowhai recalled his grandmother's role in the resolution of conflict in the family.

> My grandmother used to occasionally visit us [for several weeks at a time]. Some things I learnt from her: . . . if my generation got

into a quarrel she wouldn't take sides in the way my mother or my dad would. She'd let it occur but she would always protect the younger ones in the conflict and at some point she would make a stand and that would be the end of our conflict . . . When she chose to involve herself she would have the last say, and that was unanimously accepted. Whoever was in error, the dispute was over. [The same with my dad and uncles.] She would hear them out, sit in on the conflict, and at some point in the discussions, where it was summed up, she would have her say and that was the end of the matter for that generation . . . Another principle I learnt from my grandmother I have to admit is a generous kind of acceptance. It didn't matter what subject was raised, it didn't matter if she had detailed experience or little or none, you could always count on her according the subject the same space in her mind and in her attitudes [to both sides] . . . My grandmother was patient and you could take to her any subject . . . I never saw my grandmother get angry. I certainly saw my dad do so. I suppose I learnt [from her] that conflicts can be resolved without recourse to anger. I would never have learnt that from my father.
(George Parekowhai)

Parents

In our discussions, the kai-whakauru had relatively little to say about their parents as teachers and what they did say related mainly to the teaching of practical skills. With large families to provide and care for, parents were too busy to do much more. The role of fathers in teaching practical skills has already been explored in some detail, but some also left a lasting impression with regard to social behaviour.

> [Dad] had a lot of influence in our lives. And he was so blimmin' strict. My brother Hiwi is 53, he won't smoke in front of my father. That's from way back. *(August Tangaere)*

Our father wouldn't allow swearing around and all his friends knew that you must never swear in our house – that was one of the deadly sins. I had since learnt to swear – and I found myself curbing myself when Pine [Taiapa] came yesterday, curbing my language – and I've heard my younger brother swear and I've said to him, 'Watch your language, boy!' It is one of those early influences that certainly does stick. *(Hineari Babbington)*

The kai-whakauru provided even less information on the role of mothers as teachers. It would seem that learning household skills began so early and was so taken for granted that the details of the learning process were forgotten.

There are hints in the interviews that relations between parents and children were rather stiff and not openly affectionate, affected by the need of parents to maintain control and ensure compliant behaviour in the eyes of the community. Children hesitated to question or disobey parents. As Ani Pihema noted, when Māori children came home from school, their parents did not as a rule sit down and talk to them about their day at school.

They would say, 'Go and change your clothes, do this, do that.' It is all instructions and directions. *(Ani Pihema)*

However, the relationship changed as they grew up and as they learnt how to take advantage of differences in their parents' personalities and spheres of influence. Wiremu Kaa was brought up by an uncle and aunt who had already raised their own children to adulthood and thus were older than most parents.

It changes as you grow older. As you grow older, the generation gap between father and mother and son and daughter usually gets quite close. In my own case, when I became twenty-three or twenty-four, that's the time when I got close to the guy that brought

me up. I was able to ask him things directly and he was able to give me frank responses to any query I had. But prior to that, it was this fear or respect or whatever that precluded me from making direct advances. It was always through a third party. And the girls were like that; when they were young to get anything was always through Mother. Mother was usually the third party ... We used to want to go to the pictures and the only way we could ask for permission as teenagers was to ask the old lady. And she would go direct and talk it out with the old man. He'd make all sorts of excuses but in the end we knew she'd win so we'd go to the pictures. But we never asked him directly because we knew what the answer would be before we went to ask. It seems that fathers always have 'No!' imprinted on their minds and their tongues ... I am not suggesting that mothers are weak in allowing their children to go out, but I guess mothers are more tender and more approachable.
(Wiremu Kaa)

Several kai-whakauru noted with amusement (and a touch of envy) that their parents were much more relaxed with the younger children in the family, and even more so with their grandchildren.

Coming from a big family, I can remember, with my younger sisters and young Pat, Dad used to teach them counting games and those little nursery rhymes in the morning. It used to be the thing when they were little, they could go and hop into the parents' bed. So you hear this chanting in the morning. Pop would chant away and then you hear the little kids. *(August Tangaere)*

My father told his grandchildren stories. To my generation he concentrated on technical details but with the grandchildren he was much more expansive, he put humour into it.
(George Parekowhai)

> When we grew up and began having their grandchildren, my parents were completely different. And we used to say, 'Gosh, you treat them differently from the way you treated us.' Mum would get hold of her female mokopuna and talk about this and talk about that, not teaching them but talking about them, exposing them to different things. And Dad would get his male mokopuna and expose them to the things he was doing and actually teaching them and even helping them to read in their reading books. Now, never ever did they do that when we were kids, but I remember our nanny doing all those things. *(Sonny Huia Wilson)*

A teacher and social worker herself, Ani Pihema illustrated the difference between parents and grandparents as teachers from her own experience.

> In our household we'd come in after school and carry on to our mother about our lunches et cetera, give her all the complaints, and she'd knock us back. 'You are lucky to get lunches at all!' Then we'd go in and say, 'Kema', with a soft voice, 'can we have some bread and butter?' 'I thought you had your lunch to take to school?' 'Kino, didn't like it!' 'Heoi anō, he kai peā!' [But it's still food!] All this was teaching. Everything they said had a teaching point to it. She could have said, 'Hei aha! Never mind' and given us some. They always took the opportunity to get a point across. *(Ani Pihema)*

Aunts and Uncles

Aunts and uncles often filled the role of mediator between parents and children. Especially when they were tuākana (senior siblings and cousins) to the parents, they combined the authority of parents with the more loving style of grandparents. Noting that the issues of availability and authority made it difficult for parents to teach many things to their own children, Wiremu Kaa thought that it made sense to pass them over to relatives who were close but not so close.

What happened was, you paired them [your children] with someone older, someone other than yourself, and they did the teaching – older aunts and uncles or a cousin. We went out eeling and there were certain things about this river [my wife] Jossie didn't know about. I might tell her but probably she'd sit with my cousin Mereana or my mother and my mother will tell her. That will be her responsibility rather than mine. *(Wiremu Kaa)*

The best approvals came from outside the domestic unit. What came from uncles and aunts carried more weight in an individual's evaluation of himself. *(George Parekowhai)*

My aunties and uncles, the ones who hadn't been married [when we were born], really spoilt us, doted on us, and once they were married they used to take us away for weekends and things like that . . . Even when they had children of their own, . . . we used to get royal treatment from them, better than their own kids, and my brother and I looked forward to going to stay with them . . . The discipline certainly came from Mum and Dad but many of the other things were taught us by our uncles and aunts, through talking . . . Mum's eldest brother, he was always very formal when he discussed anything with us, with my brother and me. And we understood that, because we knew that he was the eldest one in the family, the rangatira of that family, the tohunga [see Glossary] of that family, . . . but all the other aunts and uncles, there used to be a lot of good humour coming through the discussion, good fun, so that you didn't feel as though you were inhibited at all and that you had to keep things back. We just completely opened up on all our little secrets and we knew many of theirs. *(Sonny Huia Wilson)*

The involvement of aunts and uncles in teaching practical skills in particular was taken for granted as a normal part of life by nearly all the kai-whakauru. Itinerant Teacher of Maori Liz Hunkin noted that as children they accepted both directives and requests from their uncles and aunts as a matter of course.

> I think we just grew up in it. It was part of life. Because it was the accepted thing, we just did that, without question . . . I presume we gave them credit for knowing that there was a reason why we didn't go to that part of Mahia to get kaimoana, and this was the part I just never questioned. Even to today, that's the way. If my aunts and uncles ask me to do something, there is just no question in my mind. I do it because they wouldn't ask me to do something I wouldn't be capable of. *(Liz Hunkin)*

> What my auntie and uncle said was as good as my mother and father telling me. *(Joe Matete)*

Inevitably, some of the kai-whakauru were more comfortable with some aunts and uncles than others.

> I've got favourite aunties. There's some aunties I can go and talk to more than I can to the others, and it's the ones who have actually had me for holidays when I was young, [the one] who brought me up when my own father died, and being named after her son who died. I feel I am closer [to her] than some of my other aunties. *(Jossie Kaa)*

Living with his paternal grandparents for his first nine years, Haare Williams named two paternal uncles who visited them from time to time as the other significant people in his early life.

> My grandparents, whom I called Mum and Dad, my two uncles, gave to me a very rounded Māori education . . . I suppose I still see the world through the eyes of my grandparents and uncles. *(Haare Williams)*

Returning to live with his parents after both his grandparents had died, Haare found his other, maternal uncles playing different roles in his life.

> In later life my mother's brothers and sisters took a firm grip on my life and with my mother's mother invested much of their own aspirations into me. My Uncle Pitau Brown had a passion for the Ringatū Church and the teachings of Te Kooti. My Uncle George Brown on the other hand was brought up mainly to pursue rigorously the ways of the Pākehā and how to succeed as a farmer, as a businessman and as an aspiring National Party candidate. My aunts were sort of spread out between these two . . . Uncle George Brown followed the doctrines of Sir Āpirana Ngata, especially on the farming side; that was for youngsters of the time to hasten after the symbols, the skills, the tools of the Pākehā and utilise the land . . . Whenever I stayed with Uncle George he would always emphasise getting on, getting on . . . To him work was important above everything . . . As I grew older George Brown and Pitau Brown became central figures who loomed large in my upbringing, culminating in my admission to Teachers' College at Ardmore . . . My parents had little to say in my development, in my adventures as a teenager. They were interested alright but left me largely to my own resources. [On the marae at Puha and Te Karaka] these uncles were naturally out front in the ranks in a practical way, showing the kids the right way, and when it was the wrong way, sanctions would be applied immediately. *(Haare Williams)*

Hapi Potae was aware of a difference in the way his uncles treated him.

> My brother and I were brought up by our grandparents. There was a little bit of envy and a bit of jealousy, I think, from my uncles, not all of them. There was one uncle in particular, and he would wait until I was out of sight of the old people, and then he'd grab

me by the ear, for no reason. When I thought about it afterwards I was quite amused by his attitude. Another uncle had a different attitude altogether. But now, looking back, and the way they were treated themselves by my grandparents – one was favoured more than the other. *(Hapi Potae)*

Sometimes an aunt or uncle had a special status in the whānau because they combined seniority of descent with special skills.

> **JOE:** I have one auntie that everyone looks to. She is the eldest. **VI:** And she's still teaching everybody to make kits and mats. She's eighty. She's willing to show how. When someone asks her how she says, 'Go and get the flax', and they all sit around.
> *(Joe and Vi Matete)*

In large families children often formed a special bond with one particular aunt or uncle and often this bonding, with the associated duties of care and teaching, was transferred to the next generation.

> The case of Hora having been nursemaid to you, your Auntie Hora, and then subsequently when you and I got married, we had some of Hora's children [to stay] on occasion. Even now one of them in Wellington here is very attached to us, has almost become our daughter rather than your cousin. Her children became almost our grandchildren instead of niece and nephew. *(Wiremu Kaa to Jossie)*

Siblings and Age-mates
Finally, the kai-whakauru also learnt important lessons about interacting with their natural and social environments from their age-mates and from the older siblings and cousins deputed to watch over them. Joe Matete spent most of his growing-up years in a community located on the landward side of a hill. In summertime everyone went 'over the hill' to camp at the seaside.

> When a group of children went off together, whoever was the eldest of the cousins was responsible – he was supposed to know what to do... *(Joe Matete)*

George Parekowhai's father would demonstrate technical skills and practices to his sons several times, then:

> At some stage we could expect that he'll say, 'Go ahead and do that bit!' and leave the three of us to work it out. If the three of us were in the learning process together, we'd pool what we'd been able to retain and get it done. It might take twice as long but we'd get it done. *(George Parekowhai)*

When their father told them stories including whakapapa, George recalled:

> My brothers would sit outwardly absorbed in the story: they were clearly interested and so was I. We didn't ask questions, we didn't try to direct the story into a particular line of development, even though I for one was interested in pursuing, say, a particular ancestress... Dad would just tell a sentence or a section until he felt he'd had enough... And later on, in discussing this with my brothers at another time,... they'd get things mixed up... I'd have to correct them. They soon learned I was the more accurate as far as remembering these things... This continued from the time when I would be about ten, my elder brother would be about twelve and we would be somewhere near the end of primary school going through to secondary school. *(George Parekowhai)*

Siblings and peers played an important part in filling in gaps in topics avoided by adults, for example, with regard to sex. The latter is a topic that will be dealt with later in its own section.

Learning at Different Ages

The kai-whakauru shared similar memories of being immersed in learning situations from a very young age and drawn into increasingly complex and challenging ones as they aged. The adults in their lives monitored their transition from stage to stage, placing as much emphasis on readiness and capability as on age in terms of years. While they were excluded from some tasks and some kinds of knowledge when very young, they were often given access to others at an unexpectedly young age by urban standards.

> They would teach us by doing things in stages . . . As we grew we were taught different things, coming up through the ages. We weren't taught things that an adult did until we got to the age when we were adult . . . For instance, when we were small – we had older brothers than us – we weren't allowed to go to the bush to chop trees, for the simple reason that we could hurt ourselves, it was a man's job, not a boy's job. When we got to their [our older brothers'] age we were sent in and they had to do some other chores, like looking after the gardens, doing the jobs the old people would think they were capable of doing, looking after things, more or less supervising us. *(Nikora Atama)*

For Wiremu Kaa, learning was very much a matter of context and a natural progression through time.

> It was really part of life and living. I knew how to do things like – put a pack saddle on a packhorse, strap it, how to pack posts – there's a special technique. How to pack timber, there's a special technique for that, too. You had to pack Number 8 wire with a different technique. In the beginning all I did was lead the packhorse, then eventually I had to put the gear on the back, then eventually I was part of the fencing bit. I did very little but still enough to know

the whole bit. My learning was a whole range of things over a long period of time. Similarly I guess with milking cows and planting kūmaras. All the things we did, they were to do with survival. When you think of your younger half-brothers, sisters, that you had to bring up, it was a big responsibility. *(Wiremu Kaa)*

Growing up together in an East Coast community, Hapi Potae and Hineari Babbington had complementary memories.

HAPI: The older you were, the more responsibility . . . I can remember at a certain age going through that apprenticeship of just pouring the water, and then the next stage of putting the tipus down, and putting the tipus down in a certain way. You had to place them towards the sun, because we planted our rows in an east-west direction and the kūmara plants lay facing the east. **HINEARI:** And as a small kid, once they were planted and they grew, then you had to help with the weeding, and then when the runners were long enough, they were tied in those topknots. It was our job as kids to turn them over each day. One day they were all flipped over on one side and then the next day you went along and flipped them over on the other side so that the sun would get at the roots. So that was our apprenticeship. *(Hapi Potae and Hineari Babbington)*

As Hapi and Hineari bear witness, many of the tasks given to the young at different ages were carried out in the context of group activity. Children contributed to the collective enterprise while learning at the same time.

Going to the beach: the first time we went to the beach, our first job was to pick the pūpūs [cat's eye mollusc], wasn't it? And then being taught how to behave on the beach: you didn't shout, you didn't yell, you didn't throw, and if you had occasion to open anything, you made sure the shells were way up the beach and nowhere near

the waterline. And then you sort of progressed to pāuas, then to diving for shellfish, which I didn't ever do: I had too many brothers and they did that. The conservation part was the most important, wasn't it? Just taking enough, enough for us and for Granny N, Granny W or Granny So-and-So. Well, there were no freezers in those days, so you just took enough so they didn't rot.
(Hineari Babbington)

We helped each other out, in the family. We did scrub-cutting, or when it comes to work like that, we weren't allowed to touch it because we were still young at the time, but the thing we had to do was to drag all the scrub they had cut away and heap it up, and things like that. Kids are kids, well, that's the type of job you do.
(Nikora Atama)

Where it was imperative that children learn certain kinds of knowledge, adults took steps to counter short attention spans and lack of interest.

I guess they realised your interest would be short-lived. Maybe, in a week's time they'd go through the same motions and maybe you'd go a step further in your exposure or your acquisition of skills.
(Wiremu Kaa)

I learnt to plait the plait four [out of four strips of flax] well before I went to secondary school because I used to have to help my grandmother when she was doing her mats and her kits. She'd cut the flax [blades], bundle them, strip them, and then she'd make me a whip. She started by making the whip herself... She made me this beautiful long stockwhip. And then after a while, with her showing me, I became very capable, making myself a nice long stockwhip with a lash. And that's how I learnt, sitting with her and talking with her and her showing me. *(Hapi Potae)*

However, age could be disregarded in the recruitment of a workforce when completion was urgent and time short.

> We'd go and manure the farm. We used to have all the kids down. No matter how young you are, put a sack over you, fill your sack up with lime, then you go up the hills and sow it by hand. The place is scattered with people, you know, with us kids, sowing the lime. *(Nikora Atama)*

The involvement of quite young children in certain tasks, especially as part of a large workforce, sometimes resulted in their learning things that did not figure in the school curriculum until much later. Hineari Babbington and Hapi Potae remembered learning to count at planting time by counting out 'tipu' (see Glossary).

> **HAPI:** The adults actually picked the plants, pulling them out of the sand. **HINEARI:** Then there was the counting of the tipu and the care that had to be taken over the picking and the binding and the placing in water ready for the morning. The counting was done by the women and children – we kids were all there, whether it was for the specific purpose of counting, I can't remember, but I can remember the counting part. I could count before I went to school, count to a hundred... **HAPI:** The mothers and the children sitting round, the tipu being pulled out of the sand and counted into bundles of a hundred, bound with flax and placed in tubs of water, old bath tubs when they got too rusty for bathing. We counted in English. They were placed carefully in the tub. It was important that the roots didn't get bruised or the stem broken. They were got ready the night before planting. *(Hineari Babbington and Hapi Potae)*

Hapi said that he learned to sort and grade things on the basis of selected features when the crops were lifted at harvest. As a teacher he later learned to call this process seriation.

You did that in the kūmara pits. You picked out all the tiny ones and the cut ones and you put them in a pot. Then you were shown the next size that was required, then that was sorted into another pot, then you would take lovely big kūmaras and that was all put in a sort of hollow . . . you had all the leaves round it, then you covered them and you left them there; and what you had would be the kūmaras, the tipus for the next year . . . Now, some of them were too small, but you didn't waste them, you kept them and you gave them to the pigs. The cut ones and the ones that were big enough to peel, you kept those for the table . . . Even with potatoes, we kept them separate, and the smaller ones we boiled, and boiled in their jackets . . . and the old ones and the firm ones you put aside and you 'dusted' them. *(Hapi Potae)*

Hineari observed that 'the expectancy of us was pretty high and that expectancy started early'.

We were expected to learn a lot sooner than our Pākehā counterparts in those days. My mother died when I was nine and so I virtually had the responsibility of seeing to everything for Sheba and me, and he was only six then. I bought his clothes, I saw that he was dressed in the morning. I was ten by the time we came back to Tokomaru and from there on I did all the shopping, always caring for him . . . Pop was pretty good as a cook, we never starved or anything like that; he was so particular about gardening, we were never without food. But all those little things that you'd expect a mother to do, well, I did it, because he would never let us go to the aunties, except for visits . . . They sort of kept an eye on things, but I was responsible for that and whatever cooking Dad didn't do, which wasn't terribly often . . . But if we went anywhere I had to look after him and that sort of thing and it is something I don't think is the norm for Pākehās. *(Hineari Babbington)*

> **HAPI:** I went with my grandmother to get the bark and the leaves off trees [for medicine] and I was expected to climb trees at a very, very early age. **HINEARI:** The youngest one nearly always had the job of chopping kindling, didn't they? **HAPI:** Yes, they used the axe just the same, and the knives were always razor sharp. I don't recollect anybody chopping their toes off. I think you just naturally learnt to be careful. One of the jobs I had to do was to take the animals to water ... When I took the horse down to give it a drink, I used to jump the fences, and quite often I used to fall because the horse would stumble over the fence, but I learnt how to ride over a jump. *(Hineari Babbington and Hapi Potae)*

From force of circumstances, such as the absence of adult men during the shearing season, boys especially acquired advanced skills and were given responsibility at a remarkably young age.

> Pre-secondary school we had the responsibility of looking after and milking our cows, my brother and my cousin and myself. We had a herd of thirty cows and we milked by hand. *(Hapi Potae)*

> My brother was ploughing at ten – this is my younger brother ... He was taught how to plough. He hung on to the handle and reins while Pop actually drove the thing, but within a couple of years after that he was doing it himself. *(Hineari Babbington)*

The eldest in his sibling set, Wiremu Kaa was drawn into many activities earlier than his younger brothers and sisters.

> I had lots of responsibility, like setting the kahawai net in the afternoon after milking or just before milking and then going to get it early in the morning before or after milking, and we had to use the sled to take the boat, to row out and come back. ... eight, nine, ten, when I was setting the nets, not by myself but helping set nets.

Six years old I think, swimming along the top of the net holding the floats and feeling if there was kahawai down below, and lifting it up and treading water and throwing it into the boat. About six or seven. At eleven I was packing, taking a team of twenty-five horses, my cousin and I – he was about fourteen. We would take it eight miles in over tracks. We were building a sheep dip. We did that every Saturday and Sunday for about nine months. I used to think it was fun, after milking. During the week our hired hand used to do it . . . I can shear sheep, I can shoe horses, I can put up fences, I can plumb with galvanised iron piping or copper piping. Most things of farms I am able to do because of the influence of the people of the past. *(Wiremu Kaa)*

When it came to tikanga attached to the marae, learning and teaching were graded very, very carefully. The route to the whare hui lay through the kitchens and dining-hall and took years to complete.

When you're a kid, you're playing around on the marae during a tangi, OK, that's alright, . . . but boy! did we ever get chased off when there were manuhiri approaching the marae . . . That was your first exposure. You knew there was a time to play on the marae and a time when you shouldn't be there . . . When you were a little older, you begin helping around the marae, . . . you're cleaning up and you're picking up rubbish, cut grass, and all that sort of thing, because everything ought to be nice by the time the manuhiri get there, and you're helping in all sorts of different ways like this. And then when you get older you begin setting tables and serving kai and taking empty plates away while people are still sitting there. *(Sonny Huia Wilson)*

[Children] from about seven to ten, they had just the plain ordinary day on the marae, looking at people, teaching them to meet people, to socialise with people. From ten upwards they were teaching them etiquette, marae etiquette, why people are doing this outside the marae, teaching cooking, why they are doing this: to keep the people going. People don't talk if they don't eat. As they get up to the teenagers, a bit older, they were beginning them . . . [in] the kitchen. They would say, 'You never start from the horse's head, you always start from the back. So you go in the back in the kitchen, and you work your way up.' I started off in the back. We were taught how to put the hāngīs down. We were taught how to cook for so many people. We were taught how to keep the fire going twenty-four hours a day, right through the night. We were taught how to schedule out cooking. We were scheduled to work in shifts, and when we knew how to do that, they would bring us out and bring another recruit in, take us in the whare kura [traditional school of learning specialising in benign knowledge]. Then they start. You are all ears. All ears and eyes: that's all you've got to do for a long time. You listen, you learn. You watch them move, everything. Then when they think you are ready, then they come and teach you, show you how to do it, why you do it. These are the things I went through. *(Nikora Atama)*

At the same time, questions of interest, aptitude and readiness were taken into account. Opportunities for learning were offered but were taken no further if there was no or inadequate response. Wiremu Kaa recalled:

We were never taught waiata. We used to hear it. I suppose it was up to us to learn if we wanted to. *(Wiremu Kaa)*

Wiremu's wife Jossie regretted occasions when they failed to appreciate the teaching that was on offer.

When I think back to Pine Taiapa [renowned carver and story-teller], he had such a lot to offer. When we were still at school, I can remember him taking us up to the church [in Tikitiki] and taking us in to [the meeting-house] Rongomai-āniwaniwa. But it didn't stick, it just went in one ear and out the other. Now I go back and look at those things and only wish I had taken notice. But we were young. We weren't ready to accept the commitment . . . When I was young we didn't have that feeling to want to know about those things, they were around us all the time. It is as you grow older that you feel 'I wish I had listened.' *(Jossie Kaa)*

Instead of writing off the children who were apparently uninterested in their teaching, the 'old people' sought the reasons why and, if necessary, were prepared to wait for greater maturity. Ani Pihema spoke from long experience:

When they found a child who didn't respond, they'd say, 'Tāna mahi, he mahi-ā-ringa.' [Manual work is the work for him.] There is always a job for everyone. In Māori eyes, everyone has a worth, a use . . . the old people would say, 'That person is not ready now, maybe in ten years' time.' *(Ani Pihema)*

On the other hand, children keen to learn were sometimes knocked back because they were considered too young or had tuākana whom they should not 'jump over'. Explaining why certain things should not be taught to children, Nikora Atama recalled his father saying:

Kids are kids, their brain is still only that small, they can only take so much. Their memory is good, very good. The things you want to teach them, is the things that they understand, in their grasp as kids. If you teach them man's work, part of their growing will be missed, and they would mature so quick that they would never last. *(Nikora Atama)*

Joe Matete, who was among the youngest in his sibling set, resented being shut out and told to wait.

I was well down. The older ones were the bosses . . . I stood at the back and listened. The older ones, our grandmother got them and they stayed with her. The great-uncles came and got the others and took them away . . . My grandmother used to tell a story of how these nights [of the full moon] got their names . . . This is only the wee bits I got, sleeping in the meeting-house when our grandmother told it to the older ones. I don't know the story because I was way over there . . . Whakapapa and whaikōrero, that was given to the older ones. I asked for that. They didn't say 'No', they said, 'Wait until your tuākanas have got it, then maybe you can get it.' The thing was, I wasn't to overstep my elders. 'Wait for your tuākanas', that was the words they used. They had it before me. There was no need for me to know it because they were the ones. Which naturally I didn't get, because I couldn't wait. In my own mind I said, 'Stick your Māori ideas!' *(Joe Matete)*

Knowledgeable kaumātua commonly refused to teach the more tapu forms of mātauranga Māori – whakapapa, whaikōrero, mōteatea [traditional poems or songs] and karanga – even to the older teenagers, on the grounds that they were not mature enough to handle such knowledge and could put themselves and others at risk by clumsy or improper use. Nikora Atama stressed the difference between the stories told to children on and off the marae and those told 'as the hui gets on'. The latter kind of stories were told by adults for adults and delved into the realms of mythology and the gods.

Whereas us kids, as children at the time, it wasn't for our ears, it was for the grown-ups, because it was too deep. We were told by the old kaumātuas that our brains weren't big enough to take those types of kōreros that they were having in the whare hui. The ones they were teaching us at the time were the history of our area and the history of the marae. *(Nikora Atama)*

Gender Differentiation

When it came to the allocation of tasks between the sexes, the kai-whakauru's experience as children produced two main patterns. In some households all the domestic chores – cleaning, washing, cooking and serving meals – were carried out by the girls in the household while the boys worked with the men on the farm. But in a significant number of households, at least up until puberty, boys and girls shared tasks inside and outside the house on the basis of need and/or physical capacity. This was certainly the case in the Atama household, as Nikora emphasised repeatedly.

> We were taught to do housework, every one of us. Scrub floors, wash clothes, cook breakfast, cook lunch, cook tea, bake bread. The only thing I never learnt to bake was cake, but all my brothers did. My sisters – we were brought up the same way as they were brought up in housework. Mum and Dad always used to say, 'It's good for you, when you get married, when your wife gets sick and your kids get sick, you know what to do in the house.' . . . The girls did the gardens the same with us, the only thing they weren't allowed to do was cut wood, bringing in heavy stuff. Going up [the hill] to catch horses, they'd do that, but breaking horses, the bigger brothers did it. Whatever we did, the girls would do . . . The girls did their fair share of work, the only things they weren't allowed to do was lift the heavy things. *(Nikora Atama)*

> [My sister], she used to help, . . . milking cows with me and then feeding the calves, carrying skim milk for the pigs, at a very early age, ten or twelve. *(Wiremu Kaa)*

> Back at Waikaremoana the boys and girls did the same chores. If we were putting crops down, we all did it. We played the same sports, there was no difference; we played rugby, hockey, whatever was

going, . . . certainly up until we went away from home. When I went off to boarding school we were told that there were games for girls. We knew we didn't go down the gardens or ride a horse [during our periods], but other than that we were involved in everything the boys were involved in. *(Rose Pere)*

When the girls reached puberty they were restricted from carrying out certain tasks or in the way they carried them out by the tapu associated with menstruation and the mana of the whare tangata (see Glossary). In the gardens, girls had to be careful not to step over growing plants. They could weed between corn and sugar cane, which grow straight and tall in their rows, but had to wait for the boys to clear the spaces between the rows of kūmara, potatoes and pumpkins, which send out sideways trailing tendrils.

[The girls] weren't allowed on there until we [boys] weed the bottom [of the trenches between rows] and weed the whole thing out and then clear the kūmara [tendrils] out, and then they would come after us . . . They are not allowed to step over any of our garden [plants]. You know where we have our rows of kūmaras, potatoes, pumpkins, corn and sugar cane? They can weed through the corn and sugar cane but where we have our rows of pumpkins and kūmaras and potatoes, [no]. They were long rows; if they have got to go into the next row, they have to go right down the track and come back the other way, then they haven't crossed over . . . There were certain times the girls were not allowed on the gardens [at all], must be [when they had their periods]. It never dawned on me then, I know now . . . And when we catch our horses, they weren't allowed to ride the horses when they had their period. They were not allowed near the water when they had their period.
(Nikora Atama)

In adulthood these restrictions continued to apply to women during menstruation and pregnancy, but otherwise the main difference between the work the men and women did was based on physical capacity and availability. In the course of our discussions, the kaiwhakauru made frequent reference to adult roles associated primarily with either men or women, but in most cases they did so indirectly. I identified only four direct references.

Joe Matete remembered men and women carrying out different tasks during the planting of crops but implied that the difference could be modified when circumstances required.

> The aunties and the uncles, when they planted, it was ten acres... The men did the ploughing and the discing and the women came along behind and did the planting... The harvest was awkward, usually it was shearing time. But there was always somebody there. The young boys drove the horses. The menfolk would be out shearing and it was left to the womenfolk. *(Joe Matete)*

Hone Pirihi and Wiremu Kaa reported local fishing practices that were associated with men only.

> We used to use hīnakis. It was always the men, the fathers and uncles, who made them. *(Hone Pirihi)*

> We were one of the few places on the Coast that had this method of fishing where you have got to be naked. There's only a few of us who do it now. I think it's been handed down as tradition, going naked. Women weren't allowed. *(Wiremu Kaa)*

While Hone did not explain the reason for restricting the making of hīnaki to men only, Wiremu made it clear that women were excluded from that particular form of fishing for reasons of tapu.

Hone Pirihi highlighted the provision of separate toilet facilities for men and women on the marae.

> When I was young all the maraes were very aware of sanitary conditions and toilet facilities. They always had a basin of water and soap, always a place for the men and the women. *(Hone Pirihi)*

While this separation was standard practice in the 1940s and 1950s as regards all public toilets, on the marae it was connected with the tapu nature of such facilities in Māori thinking.

From their many indirect references it is clear that the kai-whakauru accepted the association of certain roles with either men or women as tika, both right and just. As adults they recognised that other factors besides gender were involved and that the gendered roles of kai-kōrero (speechmaker) and kai-karanga (caller) were surrounded and supported by non-gendered roles filled on the basis of competence and availability. This issue will be discussed in Chapter 6.

Learning about Sex

The kai-whakauru did not spend much time discussing issues surrounding puberty, menstruation and sexual relations. As I recall, they did not deliberately avoid the subject but were simply more concerned with other issues. Nevertheless, several themes emerged clearly from what they said.

No one remembered any formal instruction on the subject; the transfer and discussion of information was carried out privately and informally between individuals. In most cases the kai-whakauru reported that their parents largely avoided the subject, imparting very little information about any of its aspects and conveying the clear impression that talk about it was tapu in the negative sense, 'dirty' and to be avoided.

> I don't remember sex ever being discussed, except that when sex was the subject, all that used to be said was 'He mahi kino, he mahi

kino' and that was all. It was 'a bad thing' to discuss, so you didn't discuss it. *(Sonny Huia Wilson)*

Keri Kaa's preparation for menstruation came from her older sisters. When she asked questions, they fobbed her off with 'explanations' that explained nothing.

When I asked why my sister wasn't weeding the kūmara I was told she had cut her foot on a bottle. You were not allowed to ride the horse, you might break its back. Not allowed in the cemetery. Not allowed in the garden to get vegetables. It was unclean, paruparu [dirty], mate wahine [women's sickness]. You didn't discuss it, you were really secretive about your body and its development. *(Keri Kaa)*

Even in adulthood this attitude was hard to shake off, as is illustrated by this conversation with two kuia from the Far North.

RAIHA: You never hear them mention that word. Never . . . **ANI:** True, true. It was like a crime, I think. **RAIHA:** Even the likes of us now, to talk about that sort of thing, I just can't, you know, Joan . . . It's jolly hard to talk about. **ANI:** It's not an easy question, but it's nice to talk about it when it is only us three women here. *(Raiha Paraone and Ani Maihi)*

Wiremu Kaa agreed that parental restrictions on discussion of sex amounted to a taboo.

That is very much so, even in Māori circles, that is still tapu. Mothers have great difficulty in talking – Jossie will tell you – about puberty to their children. Fathers have even greater difficulty, even with their sons. I don't think we had any direct guidance – not from the guy who brought me up. My education in terms of sex was through my peer group, through other friends and through animal behaviour and working closely on the farm. *(Wiremu Kaa)*

Given time, Ani and Raiha plucked up the courage to go into a little more detail, but they still spoke in general terms.

ANI: I can remember my own mother, that brought me up, saying to me that I will have that [monthly period], that will happen to me and – I can hear her saying it to me – that I've got to be very careful when I have it, and whatever I do, when you get that, if you are going with a boy, be careful you don't communicate with him. If you do, that's when you fall in and have a baby. Is that right, Raiha? RAIHA: That's what they always used to say. That's all they'll say. ANI: They always say to you, 'Now, don't you get in contact with a man, because if you do you'll have a baby, and who's going to look after your baby?' RAIHA: That's quite right. That's the only one I can remember them ever saying to us.
(Raiha Paraone and Ani Maihi)

A social worker familiar with the consequences of this parental avoidance, Priscilla Manukau, shared her personal experience:

I never knew, especially with my period. I thought I was dying. She never told me – I didn't know what was wrong. You hear your friends talking but it didn't sink in. I had gone swimming. I felt shy – I didn't know what to ask. I couldn't ask my mum because she never said a word to me about it. Do you know who I asked? My uncle – I went to tell him I was dying. He asked what was wrong, and when I told him he explained what it was . . . When I told my mum, she said, 'You don't talk about things like that.' We weren't allowed even to discuss sex. From my experiences I learnt that when my children were old enough they needed to be taught so they wouldn't feel that embarrassment. My uncle, he was the one who told me a little about sex, but not enough, even when I was married. I don't know – you just never talked about that kind of thing. Even so, they never got into trouble, perhaps because you felt it was a sin even to talk about it. *(Priscilla Manukau)*

Jossie Kaa's mother prepared her adequately for menstruation but stopped at that.

The menstruation part was alright but when it came down to sex, she shied away from that . . . I don't know if it was embarrassment to tell me about those things or what it was . . . I never asked anyway. I was shy to ask about those kind of things. It wasn't until I got to training college and actually saw a film – and I was embarrassed because there were males with us in our Section. To me it should have been only for girls and boys at a different time . . . I'd never seen anything like that before. I was quite embarrassed.
(Jossie Kaa)

Reflecting on this problem, Jossie's husband Wiremu Kaa hypothesised that

It was the influence of Christianity that helped develop this attitude in our parents – over-protection and even taboo towards the whole question. So it was a non-issue when Jossie and I were young. [When we had children] we were a little more enlightened, though still cautious about it. I guess our children will move a step further towards being very open about it. *(Wiremu Kaa)*

In those cases where parents did raise the subject, their main concern was to tell the girls what not to do, typically without going into explanatory detail. Hineari Babbington's widowed father emphasised the importance of keeping her menstruation from the males in the family.

My father, he said, 'You are reaching womanhood now and one day you will find you are bleeding. When this happens I don't want to know and you are never to let your brothers see anything from you. Then you'll be a woman and if you sleep with a man you'll have a baby.' That was it, my first sex lesson. And thereafter we never discussed it again . . . I just thought that was the right and proper thing. I've not decided yet why there had to be such secrecy. Nowadays there is no secrecy, brothers and sisters know everything about it. *(Hineari Babbington)*

From Whom Then?

If parents did not undertake the task of teaching their children about sex, how and from whom did they acquire the necessary information? The responsibility was typically picked up by an older relative. Ngaio Thompson recognised the debt she owed to her grandmother who prepared her and her sisters for 'becoming women' (that is, beginning menstruation) by talking about it from the time they were quite small. She told them to come to her when it happened and she would show them what to do. And when that time came she told them how babies were made and what to do to stop it. Ngaio commented that 'she had a beautiful way of putting it in Māori'. For Rose Pere, too, her grandmother was the primary source.

> There were times when I suppose it was the right sort of climate for it [the teaching] and it just happened. You know, there's no set time. And yet when I think of all the things she told me, they were enough to sustain me later on in life. But there was no set time. *(Rose Pere)*

Where an understanding grandmother was not available, aunts and uncles and older siblings filled the breach.

I think the third party played an important role for us. I guess even in my case the responsibility for transmission was still per the medium of the third person, in this case of an uncle. In the case of the girls, it was an older aunt in one case and in another it was the older sister who had got married and was a mother to the younger girls in terms of sex and sex attitudes . . . The boys just happened to know through the older boys, and through an uncle in my case. *(Wiremu Kaa)*

The peer group was generally an important source of information – and misinformation – for both sexes.

I suppose I am like any other adolescent coming through, learning about sexual relationships with others through groups of boys getting together. *(Haare Williams)*

While most kai-whakauru reported a general tendency for adults to avoid talking about sex with children, Rose Pere came from a community that was much more open.

All these things we'd discuss with the whole group, boys, men, the whole lot of us . . . We [girls] knew a great deal about the boys, they knew everything that there was to know about us, because it was discussed quite openly . . . And yet you had a feeling that you were talking about a serious, important part of your education. You know, it wasn't treated lightly, my feeling about it – it wasn't treated lightly. *(Rose Pere)*

Adults who were inhibited from discussing sex matters with children directly were quite direct among themselves. Sometimes they conveyed messages by allowing children to eavesdrop on such conversations.

Quite often there was discussion, maybe about us, for example, about me or about Mereana when she reached puberty. But it was about us over our heads (but we heard it all) amongst themselves. I don't think... Mereana was actually taught or asked once herself [about a proposed marriage], or her eldest sister who was just a year older. Never, never was the question addressed directly... When my cousin was courting with a guy, they [the adults of the whānau] discussed it, the probability of them getting married or her getting pregnant and not having married. They discussed it – she was there, embarrassed as anything: they told her she had to sit there anyway. You know, open discussion... [**JOAN:** Who did the talking?] Mainly the uncles, it was a male-dominant family. And the grandfather. The grandmother... she just sat there, providing the cup of tea... But when it came to the real issue, the nitty gritty for that cousin, Grandmother took over really. The men did all the loud talking, sounded off, but when it came to really giving her warmth and love if she actually became pregnant, Grandmother did all that, Grandmother picked up all the pieces. But as it turned out, there weren't any pieces. They had a baby out of wedlock, then they got married. I think it was through the grandmother.
(Wiremu Kaa)

In the case of both sexes but boys in particular, the whānau was concerned that young people should not get drawn into marriage arrangements considered inappropriate, with cousins too close on the whakapapa, with members of whānau with a history of hostility or with members of a particular church.

I don't recall any firm instructions from my paternal grandparents along these lines, but certainly between the ages of eighteen and twenty-one my grandmother on my mother's side had very direct views on relations with girls. When I was at Teachers' College she made it quite clear that I was to be very, very selective in terms of who I went with when I went back home to Gisborne. The whakapapa I think was the thing about her . . . She wanted to ensure that there was no way we were going to marry cousins. That was the only tapu sort of things that she talked about, . . . intermarrying with relations. *(Haare Williams)*

Correction

Correction was another subject the kai-whakauru did not talk about in any depth, but they touched on it briefly from time to time, clearly accepting it as a normal and inevitable part of everyday life. They used a variety of words to refer to the forms it took: a telling off, a reprimand, a growling, a whack, a clip round the ear, a kick up the backside, a hiding, a beating, a belting. Unfortunately, I did not ask for precise definitions of these terms. I was left with the impression that they were used quite loosely, without precision or consistency between speakers.

Two things stand out clearly: correction was not the prerogative of parents but was carried out by whichever adults were present at the time and physically closest to the offender; and the response to bad behaviour was typically immediate, not delayed.

When he was headmaster of a primary school in a community on the Whanganui River, George Parekowhai had ample opportunity to observe everyday interaction between children and adults.

> You had several families round the marae. The children would pass the marae and each other's homes [on their way to and from school]. The school pupils didn't have any chores and had an hour free after school when they wandered around. That was the time when they would report other relatives exerting pressure or disciplining them. For example, if someone knocked a peach from a tree on the way home, one of the aunts would lay into them for it, it

didn't matter which. An offence against one was an offence against all . . . It wasn't uncommon that Auntie Mary had chased someone else's child with a stick. It was threat more than punishment but a very important social control. A kid wouldn't hive off and plunder someone else's trees or eggs because he would get the same treatment from the nearest aunt. At the parent level of interaction, they had an understanding.
(George Parekowhai)

A Pākehā teacher present when the Itinerant Teachers of Maori discussed this issue recalled his own experience growing up in a small rural community.

In our community the disciplining was done in an unusual way. If it was physical disciplining, that went back [to our parents]. Our aunts – they used to stir us up but they would never touch us. But that age group of [Pākehā] parents, right through the community, if they ever saw us doing anything wrong, they'd never say anything but you'd cop it when you got home. They'd get on that telephone. A lot of the Māori kids that grew up with me – there seemed to be a slight difference there. If they were Māori parent peer group or elders, they'd turn round and clip their ears. They would threaten us [Pākehā children], but they wouldn't put a hand on us and they wouldn't ring home about us. Theirs was on the spot, we had to wait for ours. *(Anon.)*

As well as stressing the immediacy of correction, the kai-whakauru described it as being typically 'vocal' and 'physical'. The adjective 'vocal' implies that correction consisted of or was accompanied by loud criticism of the offender and the behaviour in question. The adjective 'physical' seems to have covered a range of meanings, everything from arm-waving and chasing-without-catching through a single slap or cuff to a 'beating'.

Respect and affection for older relatives was a strong sanction against seriously bad behaviour.

> This was something you grew up with, that everybody cared about you, therefore most of the time you tried not to offend any of your aunties. But if they were there, you'd get – it may not necessarily be a physical reprimand but you would get the reprimand.
> *(Liz Hunkin)*

Often, verbal reprimands were all that was needed to check misbehaviour. When delivered publicly, they induced whakamā (feelings of shame) and withdrawal behaviour.

> If we were at a marae for a Twelfth, if you did something wrong, they'd often call out quite loud and tell you off in front of everyone, sort of ridicule. You would wish the ground would open and swallow you up. It was a thing you would never ever do again. They didn't pull you aside and talk to you quietly; I think the whakamā came from everybody listening in. It was a big punishment for a child at that time. *(Hone Pirihi)*

Whakamā was an effective sanction in its own right because it diminished a child's self-image and mana. It could also be induced by expectation of a reprimand and by the child's own sense of responsibility to the whānau.

> Having been given these responsibilities at such an early age, to go out and bring the cow in and milk the cow: now, alright, the cow kicked the bucket and you made sure that you were very careful next time that you didn't do the same thing because . . . what happened was that it put its foot in the bucket because you hadn't tied the foot up properly. Then of course you just didn't have the milk, so you got home and of course you were reprimanded.

I think this is a whakamā thing, the idea of being reprimanded for doing something like that, for not being careful enough, that you felt you were being belittled, I suppose. Or you felt whakamā because you failed, you failed in a task. And talking about kūmara planting: you were conscious when you watered your kūmara and when you placed it down that that kūmara was going to grow and there's nothing worse than to see kūmara plants that wither up and be conscious that you were responsible for it . . . If it died and you were responsible for watering it, then the onus fell back on you.
(Hapi Potae)

Especially in domestic situations, verbal reprimands were often reinforced by quick physical contact: a slap, a whack, a cuff, a touch with a stick or twiggy mānuka broom.

The uncle who brought me up was immediate and sometimes physical, a quick kick in the behind or a cuff over the ear, it was immediate and over . . . He didn't bruise me or anything, never, never, but very vocal and quite physical . . . he never beat us, never belted us up to any degree . . . maybe 'Do that!' and that's it. Grandfather never hit us, but he threatened us, they both threatened us, as they all do, but it varied . . . [**JOAN**: What were the reasons for such punishment?] Not feeding the calves, letting the pigs out in the wrong paddock, spilling the cream when I was taking it to the cream truck on the horse . . . setting fire to the gorse by the cowshed not realising you were likely to burn the cowshed . . . boyish things, not serious crimes. Stealing watermelons from our own garden when we were supposed to wait for them to get ripe . . . leaving the gate open, the horse eating the corn in the paddock. Things like that. *(Wiremu Kaa)*

If there was anything to learn about how you behaved, my grandmother was the one who actually taught us the mokopuna what to

do, with a little willow stick that just touched you. It only had to touch you and you *knew*. I don't ever remember her giving me a hiding or anything like that, but it was just a gentle reminder. If she was doing her weaving and you came in and started to step on it, no matter how little, it just tapped your foot. Nothing else, no words. You just turned and went back. You *knew*. Or a look. She only had to look at you – say it was on the marae. If you got up to cross when somebody was speaking, she just looked at you, and you felt your knees going down and realised it wasn't time for you to move.
(Liz Hunkin)

We used to spend a lot of time with our grandfather . . . He was a lovely, gentle old man who used to have a tokotoko. He did the same thing, a tap on the shoulder or on the foot. *(June Tangaere)*

When Ngaio Thompson was young, her mother and grandparents would punish her with a swish round her legs with a mānuka broom. But they did not leave it there.

While you were crying they'd come and talk to you and tell you what you had done wrong and why it was wrong. You'd stop crying and they would wipe away your tears with the same hand that chastised you and give you a hug. After a beating there was always aroha. *(Ngaio Thompson)*

Once Ngaio got a 'beating' from her grandmother because she drowned some newly hatched ducklings. Her grandmother found out and 'swished' her repeatedly with the mānuka broom. Ngaio 'jumped and jumped' to avoid the broom. Then her grandmother sent her to bed without dinner. Ngaio thought her grandmother would probably have brought her something to eat later if she had not fallen asleep. In the middle of the night her grandfather woke her. She put her arms up round his neck and he lifted her. He told her he had heated up some hot food for her and took her to the table for 'a good feed'.

Priscilla Manukau also remembered the use of the mānuka broom but insisted that it never amounted to a 'beating'. Her parents punished her and her sisters by restricting their favourite activities.

> To clean the [earth] floor, you sprinkled water on the floor and swept it with a mānuka broom. The broom had two purposes, to sweep the floor and to hit our legs when we didn't listen . . . Eyes! If eyes could kill! Our mum and dad just looked at us, we knew what those eyes mean. I used to love singing and I used to sing at the wrong times, at the table for instance. I can remember I wasn't allowed to sing in the house for a month. I'd go to school and on the way home I'd sing as loud as anything – it's hard, the worst punishment I could have. [**JOAN:** The mānuka broom: just one quick swish?] Yes. I never got that severe kind of beating. You see mums screw their children's ears or drag them behind – I never got that. My sisters can't go to the pictures if they'd done something wrong. I used to go to dances a lot. I'd make sure that punishment wasn't put on me. *(Priscilla Manukau)*

Some of the kai-whakauru spoke of more sustained punishment, using words like 'hiding', 'beating' and 'belting', but the degree of severity involved was unclear. Usually such chastisement was administered by a parental authority figure for serious offences such as lying.

> In retrospect the person that has had the most influence on my life was my father, probably because he was the disciplinarian, and those were some of the things that were forbidden: for example, telling lies. If you told a lie and were caught you got a hiding. And he told you how many whacks you were going to get, too, and you had to whakamomore [keep quiet] till you got it all and then you'd duck away somewhere and let it go. *(August Tangaere)*

If we really did get into trouble, [my father] took the shaving strop to us. But I can only remember two of us ever getting a hiding, one of my brothers . . . and me. One of the deadliest sins as far as my father was concerned was telling lies, and stealing. I got caught out in a whopping lie . . . and I got this shaving strop on my bottom. My mother was never allowed to interfere in any of the chastisement. If my father growled, he did it all by himself . . . It wasn't until he went, then my mother took me and bathed my bottom. I never forgot that and by Jove I don't think I've told a lie since.
(Hineari Babbington)

Several kai-whakauru remarked that, while their grandparents disciplined them, they did it differently from their parents.

That was probably why we children enjoyed going to my grandfather's. He did discipline us, but he had a different way of disciplining us. It wasn't a physical one. With our mum, when she had occasion to punish us, she got out her stick and belted us. But our grandfather did it in a kind, gentle way without hurting us physically . . . My mum for a long time was widowed and I guess that is why she was such a disciplinarian with us. We lived with our grandfather but she did all the disciplining and we went to see Granddad for the loving and cuddling.
(June Tangaere)

George Parekowhai confirmed this difference between the generations.

The methods of teaching used by the elders? A twitch with a stick. My [widowed] grandmother never used a stick, but the next generation did. With my grandmother we had already accepted that what she said went. We knew that when she made a stand she had explored all the possibilities, whereas my aunts (my uncles never used the stick), maybe because of their place in domestic

functioning, they didn't have time to explore the options. They made hasty judgements that were often inaccurate. They often used the stick to get the action they wanted; it was pretty haphazard.
(George Parekowhai)

There were also differences between men and women. These could be a matter of personality rather than gender or busy-ness. Wiremu Kaa commented on the difference between the uncle and aunt who brought him up.

In the main, the immediate disciplining was done by the senior male in my particular experience, who was my uncle, the guy who brought me up. But when it came down to *real* disciplining, it was more his wife, my aunt. She had a different way. Sometimes it was a day, two days, weeks, before she would go back to the problem. She and I may be cleaning fish, for example, scaling fish and cutting, and she would talk to me about what had happened. I suppose it wasn't discipline but it was related to discipline, trying to get me to see that what I had done really was wrong, and talk me into thinking the whole problem through myself. Hers was a different way, the auntie, whereas the uncle was immediate and sometimes physical, a quick kick in the behind or a cuff over the ear. It was immediate and over and I guess purely male, whereas the auntie – sometimes the day after or week, the moment varied when she did the discipline . . . I found the grandfather was the same, too; his was immediate, his was loud, very vocal and quite often he'd talk amongst other men about it, and the uncle would do the same, whereas the auntie, never. She kept it to herself, it was between her and me. *(Wiremu Kaa)*

The situation became even more complicated when children brought up by grandparents in their early years later went to live with their parents.

My grandfather, no one was allowed to touch me, and my grandmother, she did tell me off, my grandmother did, but she never ever laid a hand on me. Now, the first person to hit me physically – you know, it almost killed me, I thought at the time – was my natural mother; and I was eight years old and that really broke my heart because no one had ever hit me at all physically. She did . . . Up to that point no one was allowed to hit me, even if I did something wrong. Well, if they said I had done something wrong, my grandfather would always say, 'But it was through you doing this or neglecting this that she did that.' I always seemed to have a way out . . . My grandmother was my mother, I really regarded her as my mother, and they had rows through me because of the other one disciplining me in the way she used to. My grandfather died when I was seven, but my grandmother she died when I was seventeen. She used to get very upset at the way my mother disciplined me, my natural mother . . . When I went back to my natural mother, she didn't like my attitude . . . I remember her getting terribly upset at times with some of my comments. *(Rose Pere)*

Haare Williams could not recall any physical punishment from the paternal grandparents who presided over his earliest years. Instead, they used positive reinforcement and reparation.

They would sit down and talk to me – 'Ka pai tēnā' [That is good] and so on. As we were planting the kūmara, 'This is the way to handle it', a very practical demonstration of the right way . . . I was absolutely spoilt of course, being brought up like that, and I was pretty cocky about myself whenever I met some of the other kids. I would be very much a whakahīhī [conceited or arrogant] sort of kid. When anyone came around I would go and hide all the eggs or I would really rumble if our best watermelon was given away. And afterwards my grandmother would take me aside and say, 'That's not a very nice way to be, that's whakahīhī, that's greedy,

te mea, te mea, te mea' [and so on] and she would make me go and get all the eggs and bring them out and I would have to take those eggs to the people involved or else I would have to catch the horse – and this is around six or seven – harness it up with the sledge and take a sack of kūmara to those people that I was being offensive to.
(Haare Williams)

When his kuia died and later his koroua, Haare went to live with his parents within the orbit of his maternal grandmother, Waioeka Brown.

I think of her in a different dimension. I looked up to that woman and her direct form of teaching and yet . . . very low key, very much behind the scenes. This non-verbal language . . . fortunately for me I was a bit older when I went back there, but I remember a couple of my cousins being marched round to the back of a meeting-house and getting a good hiding for laughing on the marae [at a speaker].
(Haare Williams)

Talking about punishment, especially corporal punishment, Sonny Huia Wilson said:

When I think back I can never ever remember the time when my nanny punished me, but I can remember her saying to others, 'Patua te tamaiti nā.'[*] [Smack your child!] But she would never do it herself. Now when I think back to my father who died just on ten years ago, *he* never punished his grandchildren, but he would say to *me*, 'Patua te tamaiti nā' . . . Most of the corporal punishment I and my brother ever got was from Mum. Boy, she could belt a lot harder than Dad. Whenever Dad punished us it was usually a

---

[*] 'Patua' is the passive form of 'patu', which is a word with a wide range of meaning: see Glossary. Nanny uses 'nā' (near you) to transfer responsibility for disciplining the child to someone else.

kick up the jack, but with Mum it was either with a stick or with her hand. But with Dad, to make an impression on him, when he kicked we used to take off, but it was really a jump on our part so we would land with a clatter on the floor and he used to think that was good. Punishment was really left to Mum and Dad. And there was a lot of it. When we were naughty we got it alright, and there was no two ways about it. And the thing was, if we ever got a hiding and we looked at Mum while she was talking, every time she would say, 'Kaua ō karu titiro mai ki au!', Don't your eyes look at me.* So you had to look at the floor, don't you dare look them in the face while they are telling you off or giving you a hiding, and don't you dare answer back . . . I didn't hate my mother for it either, not ever. Now what she used to do was belt us . . . and then she'd sit there and you'd have a little cry, and she'd wait until you finished, and you wouldn't dare move until she told you to move. Then after that, and this is what I liked best about being punished, she'd come and give you a little love and something to eat. And that way I think I learnt to respect my mother, though I got naughty again – you can't stop yourself from being naughty. But I never ever resented the fact that she punished me, never ever, because I think I liked the little cuddle and the little something to eat afterwards.
(Sonny Huia Wilson)

Later, Sonny explained that a 'beating' from his mother did not last very long.

> It was a quick bang with a stick, finish. And it was usually around the legs and around the bottom. But I don't remember getting whacked around the head. And there again, I think because we were taught later on that the head is tapu, and you never touch it, so it was never that. But she'd say, 'If you don't be quiet, I'll slap

---

* For a discussion of these issues, see Metge and Kinloch, 1978, p.13.

your mouth', but she never did, it was always round the bottom or the legs. *(Sonny Huia Wilson)*

Much of the physical chastisement that the kai-whakauru talked about was widely accepted practice in New Zealand at that time. They themselves seem to have been extremely fortunate in the attitudes and values prevailing in the families to which they belonged. Talking about their own community, Hapi Potae commented to Hineari:

> I can't recollect any family at all which showed any signs of violence, can you? You know, they were the most placid of elders back home, in the whole district. I can't remember anyone who came to school battered and bruised like you have today. There was concern for people in general. *(Hapi Potae)*

Several of the kai-whakauru reported being punished much more severely at school and their parents responding by removing them to another school or acting to have the offending teacher removed. Others reported parents taking the position that teachers were always right and punishing their children a second time whenever they got into trouble at school.

CHAPTER FOUR

Spirituality and Values

Te Taha Wairua

For the kai-whakauru, te taha wairua was, as the word taha implies, not just a part of community life but a pervasive *dimension*, the spiritual dimension. A matter of practice as much as doctrine, it was a taken-for-granted aspect of the social environment most of the time, punctuated by occasional dramatic events and surrounded by an aura of mystery, anxiety and restriction. In this context the words that cropped up most often in our discussions were karakia and tapu, both of which had their origin in pre-European times but were co-opted and re-defined by Christian missionaries. The words kai-tiaki, kēhua and mākutu (see following text and Glossary) were also used but less frequently.

Karakia

The kai-whakauru used this word, firstly, to refer to a form of words with religious content and purpose, equating it with the English word 'prayer', and, secondly, to refer to ritual events combining prayers with other religious acts such as the reading and exposition of religious texts. These events they described generically as 'services' and specifically as Holy Communion, Mass or the (Ringatū) Twelfth. Karakia with this meaning might be held in the home, in a church or on the marae. Buildings set aside for religious purposes were described as whare karakia.

Karakia in both senses were deeply embedded in the lives of all the kai-whakauru. Hapi Potae's experience of karakia in the home was typical.

> [It was] a practice that you very seldom see now, having to say your prayers before you go to bed at night, having to say grace for kai, all those faith cues you had to go through. For us it was more or less a Christian practice but in actual fact it came from further back than the advent of Christianity. But this tradition was still followed, along more Christian lines . . . It was the giving of thanks and also the prayers of protection; those were the two things that seemed to matter most. *(Hapi Potae)*

Productive activities outside the home were also framed with karakia.

> They had karakia every time they went out fishing, and before planting, asking for blessing before and afterwards. 'Thank you.' *(Joe Matete)*

When Nikora Atama asked his father why 'the old people' left the children behind when they went to the gardens the night before communal planting began, he was told:

> They used to go and karakia on the gardens at a certain time of the night, just before the moon hits a certain spot back home in Pawarenga. There and then they do their karakias. *(Nikora Atama)*

And Hapi Potae recalled:

> That same old lady, she always helped us out with the harvesting and I can remember asking why she always said prayers before the thing started and when they were all in and graded and everything was finished. I was told she was just giving thanks for the fact that

we had a good crop of kai, and I thought, 'Yes, that's right, that's early teaching, early learning, learning to be thankful for what you have got.' *(Hapi Potae)*

While karakia was a familiar part of life, the precise form it took varied considerably with the religious denominations and generations of those involved. Maori Marsden of Ngāi Takoto grew up in the Far North in the 1930s and 1940s as the son of a priest in the Anglican Church.

> The church was an important part of the tribal life and a lot of other activities revolved around our church . . . [On a Sunday] very few people stayed home; about 95 per cent were present at the church service from every community and village among those tribes [Te Aupōuri, Ngāi Takoto, Ngāti Kahu and Te Rarawa] . . . every home at seven o'clock you'd find them at their prayers. In the mornings before we went to school we sat around as a family and had our morning prayers. As for older Māoris, they normally had their prayers before sunrise. At first light the head of the family would get up, you'd hear a banging in the house and everybody was expected to get up. They didn't wait, just started off and people came in one by one, crept out of their beds. Some turned a deaf ear, the kids. In the smaller houses – they were poor in those days, some houses had a kitchen and dining-room combined, sometimes only one bedroom – everybody sat up in bed and had their prayers together. This was the norm . . . After dinner, prayers . . . Framed within these prayer times was the work during the day and going to school . . . Sundays, depending on where the [Communion] service was we went either to Awanui church or to Karepōnia church. On the other two Sundays we went to Maimaru Hall and there we had normal Morning Prayer. Here it was mostly lay people who took the services: the clergy were out on their rounds in different parts of the Pastorate. On the two Sundays when we didn't have

> Communion, 11 o'clock was the time everybody turned up. After church we had lunch together at the marae . . . In my childhood it was the accepted thing, when we went to Karepōnia church [on the hill], afterwards we came down to Karepōnia marae. On their way to church everybody dropped in a plate of meat or whatever as their contribution to the communal lunch. When we came down to the marae there would be the usual whaikōrero as lunch was prepared by the women. We'd all sit down to a meal. If there was any take [issue] that concerned the tribe, after lunch it was discussed and resolved. About milking time people began to disperse. *(Maori Marsden)*

Maori's father combined the roles of an ordained Anglican priest with those of farmer and rangatira of Ngāi Takoto. When he was old enough, Maori accompanied his father on his Sunday rounds, taking Communion services in different parts of his Pastorate.

> We'd set out early in the morning, about three o'clock and we'd go to Ōturu and take early morning Communion. From there we'd come back to Awanui church, take Communion there and from there we'd go to Sweetwater and all the people from the gumfields would gather at Sweetwater. We'd have lunch there and then we'd move on to Paparore and hold service there about three o'clock and after the service return home. That was just one of the rounds, all on foot. *(Maori Marsden)*

In crisis situations clergy often took the lead and karakia was an integral part of community action.

> One of the things my father did during the Depression was to plough up acres of land and prepare it for planting crops, mainly kūmara. When the planting time came we boys did most of the work preparing the kūmara gardens, discing, ploughing and so

on. Then he called the tribe in, normally at full moon, because immediately following the full moon were the main planting days. He would delegate certain ones to go fishing and bring back loads of fish, to go to Ninety Mile Beach to load up with toheroas, others to get tuatuas [varieties of shellfish], one or two to kill a beef, and he would have upwards of a hundred people gathered together. In the evening they would light a huge fire – it was normally in November – and after the evening meal together, all in together, then we would have karakia. After the church service (generally my father presided at the church service but every now and again he would ask one of the lay readers to bring us a word from Scripture), after the service, the elders got apart and they had whaikōrero richly interlaced with scriptural quotations . . . Most of the Māori adults were really knowledgeable regarding their Bibles. Many of the elders had phenomenal memories, they were almost like computers. Many could almost quote the total Bible from Genesis to Revelation. They used to try and top each other. They would quote some obscure text and ask the others where it was to be found. In those days I heard this quite often, and many preachers in those days were fond of doing this, quoting obscure texts and saying to the congregation, 'I am not going to tell you where this text is. Look it up for yourself.' And then he would expand on the whole thing. As far as the canticles were concerned, everybody knew them by heart. *(Maori Marsden)*

Nikora Atama, who grew up in a staunchly Roman Catholic community on the west coast of Te Rarawa territory, commented on the difference between his parents' church-oriented karakia and his grandmother's practice.

Mum's mum was a very strong old kuia, very strong . . . She died in her late nineties and her teaching was very, very old, very Māorified . . . When you had to sit down on the table and have a feed, you are not to talk, you are there to eat and when you have finished, you karakia. Her karakia was so different, like I said, it was Māori, very Māorified and whatever she did she would karakia and you could hear her mumbling, doing her thing. *(Nikora Atama)*

Brought up in the Ringatū Church, Haare Williams' experience was equally grounded in te taha wairua but differed in the details. Until he was nine years old he lived with his paternal grandparents in a raupō whare on the shores of Ōhiwa Harbour in the Bay of Plenty. Their nearest neighbours were about two miles away. In this secluded setting karakia was a key component of everyday life.

From time to time my grandfather went alone [into the bush]. He took me on only a few occasions but I believe that he went in there to karakia. There was a waterfall in there, in the bush . . . I knew when not to follow him because he was going in there for a special purpose . . . Whenever anything of a tapu nature occurred, my grandfather, my grandmother and myself, the three of us would sit, it wouldn't matter how cold it was, whether it was raining or whatever, we would sit by the creek, have a karakia there, and the sprinkling of water was very important. The water in my memory was never carried into the whare puni, our sleeping house. It was always out there [in the open]. But a lot of our karakia was done in the whare puni. A lot of karakia: a full Ringatū service right through every night and morning, and whenever my grandfather felt that someone had died, there would be another karakia then.
(Haare Williams)

Prominent among the purposes for which Haare's grandparents said karakia were dedication, blessing and protection.

I remember starting out at school, my koroua taking me to the side of the puna [spring], doing a karakia there; and some of the things

I can recollect in terms of that little service, that little blessing, was my koroua doing a karakia and the iriiri or sprinkling of water on my head, and sending this child to school, a sort of dedication for the purposes that he wanted me to have in life. And one of those was this idea of being a repository of information for the people; I recall that bit. I also recall: 'Give this child the wisdom and the ability to be able to understand the world he is going to go into, to bring peace to other people.' *(Haare Williams)*

Although they lived apart in their own whare puni, Haare's grandparents often travelled away from home to visit relatives and to attend Ringatū services and tangihanga. They always took Haare with them.

One of the things I do remember about my koroua and kuia also, whenever we went to a marae, any marae at all, there was always a karakia at a puna. Whenever a rainbow appeared, we'd sit down and karakia, pennies would be tossed over our heads. At night when we travelled there would be karakia. So there was very, very much this process of acknowledging the presence of the unknown, the kaitiaki, making sure that we were protected fully whenever we went to another kāinga [settlement] or to a marae. *(Haare Williams)*

In later years Haare was grateful for such experiences, drawing deeply on the things he had absorbed without being aware of it.

Tapu and Not-tapu
Whereas the kai-whakauru used the words 'karakia' and 'prayers' interchangeably, they consistently used 'tapu' on its own, never once replacing it with a English word. They could not remember when or where they first heard and learnt it: it had always been part of their vocabulary. It was associated in their minds with ideas of fear and negative consequences, and it evoked a largely automatic response of avoidance.

> That word tapu: then you just automatically retreated from whatever it was. You knew that you had to be very careful and avoid whatever, and that was it. The word tapu pressed a button in your mind somewhere and you just automatically reacted, or I did anyway. *(June Tangaere)*

The evidence of the kai-whakauru makes it clear that adults deliberately played upon the children's fear of tapu to make sure that they avoided behaviour that was socially inappropriate or physically or spiritually dangerous.

> They used the word tapu as a fear thing for children. Most of us loved listening to the ghost stories that our grannies used to tell us, 'If you don't wash your hands, So-and-So will come along at night and grab you!' A lot of our toilet training was based on this tapu thing . . . They used the word tapu like – detention. If you did something wrong, you'd be in trouble. It stops you from doing it. When Nanny was not around, this thing in your mind tells you, 'Don't go over there, don't touch that, don't do that!' You became self-disciplined. In that way I think tapu was very, very effective. Anything tapu to a Māori child at that age was a most frightening experience. We didn't want to have that frightening experience. It was laid on thick. When I was little they used that word a lot at the most appropriate times and appropriate places. *(Hone Pirihi)*

In Māori thinking the concept of tapu has both a generic reference (the state of being tapu) and a specific one (a particular prohibition) and is linked in a complementary relationship with noa (freedom from restriction and anxiety). Only one kai-whakauru actually used the word 'noa', but they all spoke of acting in ways that either showed respect for or fear of tapu or reduced or removed tapu, accepting the existence of noa without referring to it by name. On their own evidence it was plain that they had internalised at an extremely young age the knowledge that certain parts of the human body, certain actions and certain places were intrinsically tapu and must be kept separate from those that had a different kind of tapu or were not-tapu.

Of primary importance were the tapu associated with the human body. The kai-whakauru spoke with feeling of the deeply ingrained prohibitions against putting hats, brushes or combs on tables and sitting on tables and pillows, actions that bring tapu parts of the body – the head and genitalia – directly or indirectly into contact with food or each other.

> In those days you didn't put a comb or brush on the table or hair in the fire. Even today I hate to see them do that . . . You don't take your prayer book where you eat. It was really tapu. I don't like a hat on the table, anyone sitting on the table, even now. You never see old people those days having washing on the line on Sunday. *(Raiha Paraone)*

> You were taught, if you used pads, that you couldn't burn them [because] you burnt part of your body and knowingly destroyed it. You threw them in the long drop or buried them. Same thing with hair. I always had long hair. I cut it. When Father found out I was going to the hairdresser there was a lot of clucking because I didn't know what they did with the cut hair. For a long time I used to take a paper bag for my hair, then take it home and bury it. *(Keri Kaa)*

When talk turned to the tapu of the head, Sonny Huia Wilson illustrated this rule from his own experience as a teenager.

> [That's] one part of the body, especially of an older person, you never touch, because it is tapu. Now I wasn't told this formally but we learnt through this exposure thing I was telling you about . . . [In the dining-hall] it was part of normal procedure that, when you were putting food down on the table or when you were taking

plates with food scraps on them from the table, that you never lifted a plate over a person's head. Why? Because food should never be placed anywhere near a person's head. You took it from one side and you made sure of keeping it far enough away from the person's face or head, or when you were putting it on the table you did exactly the same thing.

Now here is a story. A cousin of mine, a female cousin, we were helping at the tables, and this old man came – we found out later on that he was a little mental, but he was old and he knew exactly the things young people shouldn't be doing. So he called out, 'Tamariki mā, he tī!' [Children, a cup of tea!] So my cousin was there, she was the teapot girl. She went up to him with the teapot and said, 'He tī māu, e koro?' [A cup of tea for you, Granddad?] and he said, 'Āe', and he got his cup and put it on his head. And she knew that she was not to put kai or drink anywhere near his head, and she just stood there. And he said, 'Kōtiro, homai he tī māku!' [Girl, bring me a cup of tea!] And she went and tried to take his hand down from his head but he kept it up and she burst into tears. And my dad who was the one in charge of the dining places saw this happening, and saw Maria crying like mad, and he came over and said, 'What's the matter, Maria?' And she said, 'That old man wants tea and he's putting his cup on top of his head.' So he turned round to this old man and he said, 'He aha tōu mahi i te kōtiro nei? Pōrangi!' [What are you doing to this girl? You're mad!] . . . and he turned and said to Maria, 'Kāore koutou e mōhio mai i tōu tupuna he pōrangi? Ka mahi pēnei, kaua e haria mai he tī.' [Don't you know your Nanny is mad? If he behaves like this, don't give him a cup of tea.] So he took the cup from the old man's hand and got my cousin to pour tea for him. She was still crying like mad, because she knew, had she done it, she would be doing something wrong. He put the cup of tea down and he turned round to this old man and he said, 'E koro, kaua e pēnā i ngā tamariki nei. I te pēnei koe i ngā tamariki nei, ka wehe tae mai te hari kai mō koe.' [Old man, don't behave like that to these young people. If you behave like that to these young people, they will stop bringing food here to you.] . . . That is where we learnt . . . through exposure. Through examples like that kids do learn at the marae what to do and what not to do. *(Sonny Huia Wilson)*

A number of kai-whakauru talked about the tapu practices associated with the kūmara crop. Reference has already been made to those that surrounded its planting but there were others as well. Wiremu Hohaia of Te Rarawa remembered what happened to the kūmara planted first when they were ready for harvesting.

They always went and dug the first one, the first kūmara. They always know which is the first one and the last one, and they always go to the first one first. And the first one, they give the first one away, that's what they do. That's the old people . . . They don't tell you why they do these things . . . they just go along and pick that first row, they pick up all that, and then they go and give it away . . . Although it was in me to ask why, I never did ask . . . they never said. But they always tell you that whatever first thing you have, you never want to have it yourself. *(Wiremu Hohaia)*

Joe and Vi Matete recalled that in Joe's home community on the East Coast, certain individuals and families had monopolies that were protected by tapu.

JOE: Some people that planted kūmaras, the kūmara was rough; some, the kūmaras were big; some, very smooth. They used to say that that was their speciality. They picked different people to do these things and that was all they did. The men did the heavy work like carrying the water, which they had to do all the time. **VI:** Auntie M said there was a patch of very big kūmara, she said none of the women were allowed to go into that kūmara patch till the harvest – men only, the men planted. She said that at Manutūkē women never ever planted these kūmara, they only harvested them. And the kūmara were huge. *(Joe and Vi Matete)*

As Wiremu Hohaia remembered it from his boyhood in Ahipara, the rule that 'the first thing' must be given away applied to fish as well as kūmara.

The idea of giving the first fish away – if you never caught a fish before, say, that's the first fish you ever caught, you always want to give that fish away. Now, if you didn't, you'd never catch another fish, and that's the idea of giving it away, so you'll catch more . . . When you eat your own fish that means you won't get any more. That's the tradition the Māoris have laid down. *(Wiremu Hohaia)*

Although he did not use the word tapu, Wiremu Kaa clearly indicated that the netting of kahawai at the mouth of the Waiapu River was a tapu activity when he identified it as 'a ritual' and reported that men shed their clothes before entering the water and women were excluded.

We had a ritual at the mouth of the Waiapu River there – it's peculiar to that area alone, no other area ever does it . . . They construct these oval nets, it's got a pole in the middle and a handle and a net. Only the men go there, and better when the weather is slightly dirty, with a bit of a flood, because the kahawai can't see the net or the poles. When the kahawai are chasing up the mouth of the Waiapu River, they get caught in these nets. We usually wait for an incoming tide . . . It was always quite a ritual – tying the net up on to the poles and round these supplejack frames, then taking off all our clothes (we had to do it naked) and then urinating on the net, then walking into the water holding it. When you catch a fish, you pull it out, then you take it out, never by the tail. As kids we knew that when our older cousin or brother got one, he'd bring it out into our hands, we'd dig a hole with our hands, put it in, put our stones there, we know that's our fish. Everyone's got little holes around in the sand with their fish in . . . and this particular place, Ngutuawa, women weren't allowed to go there. *(Wiremu Kaa)*

Wiremu went on to tell what happened when people stopped observing this tapu.

But that tapu was broken, and since it has been broken the catching of kahawai has declined from the time women went there till it's almost non-existent, because it meant that men had to dress up. It was a sign of manhood to be able to put that net into the water and catch some kahawai. It was a really neat feeling. Catching one kahawai was good enough but sometimes you'd catch two and that was a real beaut thing to do. *(Wiremu Kaa)*

In the kai-whakauru's communities the marae ātea and the meeting-house that fronted on to it were unequivocally regarded as tapu.

We were told not to run across here or not to sit over there, 'that place is tapu'. *(Haare Williams)*

In some places, however, the rule was applied strongly when visitors were present but relaxed at other times. The dining-hall and kitchen were not tapu but, as we have seen, children might be excluded on occasion for practical reasons, especially during hui. Attitudes to the toilet block, located separately whenever possible, were ambivalent: on the one hand its connection with human waste made it tapu, on the other it was the place where the tapu resulting from contact with a tūpāpaku on the marae ātea or inside the meeting-house could be removed by washing hands. Churches were also classified as tapu, as were wai tapu (sacred springs and pools) and wāhi tapu (places associated with death such as cemeteries and old

SPIRITUALITY AND VALUES

battlefields). Anything classed as food (including tobacco and alcohol) had to be left outside when entering such places, and people leaving places where the dead were lying had to cleanse themselves ritually with the water or bread provided.

> Going into the church and meeting-house was tapu, so you didn't take cigarettes, you didn't eat, you didn't smoke or swear in there ... Washing hands after going to the cemetery, that was a teaching practice. *(Hineari Babbington)*

> The majority of maraes, if they didn't have bathrooms, they had outside loos and washbasins left where it was convenient. That's where the tapu comes in. If you go to the toilet, when you come out, you've got to wash your hands in that basin. When I said, 'Why should I wash my hands? They're clean!', they'd say, 'If you don't wash your hands, that tapu will stay on your hands.' *(Lena Pirihi)*

> In digging the graves, an older person would come up with us, no smoking, no eating and no drinking. Afterwards they take us down to the river for a good wash and karakias. *(Joe Matete)*

Ephraim and Harriet Te Paa of Te Rarawa put together a range of tapu restrictions.

> **EPHRAIM:** It was pointed out to us where the major burial places were. They talked of the dead being secreted away in caves. Any holy place you are not to go near. They respected these places because of the sacredness of the area. Should you breach the tapu any misfortune that happened to you was interpreted as being due to your behaviour. **HARRIET:** They point out these places to the children: someone was killed or buried there – he tapu. Some things they don't allow people to desecrate, for example, where they bury the afterbirth, the places where corpses lay for days in

the past – that was always tapu. Our parents taught us, you don't put clothes or your feet on the table or sit on it. Women never walk over men. **EPHRAIM:** We heard that in a previous era some people, tohunga, had certain things reserved entirely to them, and certain vessels, such as a washbasin, were to be respected for their purpose and not used for any other. **HARRIET:** Not for baking.
(Ephraim and Harriet Te Paa)

Priscilla Manukau also emphasised the careful separation of fires and pots for preparing rongoā and craft materials from those used for other purposes, especially cooking.

The boiling of [plant materials for] rongoā was done outside, on a special fire, not where you cook your food. You prepare it outside – he took his own pot. My copper outside is just for [boiling] flax.
(Priscilla Manukau)

Often the children learnt to do the tika thing simply by following the patterns set by adults.

We picked up a lot of our learning about tapu. We lived just over the fence from the marae, and the old people didn't constantly say, 'Don't do this, don't do that, because of this, that and the other thing.' But we were there, on the marae, playing around, and we looked, and just did what other people did on the marae, without being told why. Now you take your children back to the marae, and you say, 'You mustn't do this, mustn't do that' and they ask you why. You know why because you've learnt from just observing the elders and following suit . . . We didn't ask. We weren't told why.
(June Tangaere)

Others drew their own conclusions from an instructive event.

I can remember going to a funeral. And my pockets were bulging. I was with my grandmother and just before we walked through the gate, she said, 'A-ha! Haere mai, haere mai. He aha kei roto i tōu paki?' [Come here, come here. What is in your pocket?] So I took it out and there were oranges and packets of lollies and she made me put them beside the gate. And I was really upset at having to do this. I was more concerned about somebody coming along and pinching my oranges – and then somebody else took their packet of tobacco out and put it beside my stuff. Then I realised, it's not just me, it's a practice. So after that I made sure I didn't have those things in my pockets. *(Hapi Potae)*

Children who asked for an explanation were given no more than was necessary to ensure compliance: tapu was part of a system of thought too complex for immature minds.

If you go into a cemetery, when you come out you have to wash yourself. I questioned it, 'Why do I have to wash myself?' 'So the tapu is washed off you.' I have carried that along ever since I was young. *(Lena Pirihi)*

I can remember back on our marae at Ōtoko, it was Ringatū, and down in the whare kai they had rafters like this, all round, and on top there would be all this money. It was put there by the elders. And as much as kids would have liked to have some of that money, we never did touch any of it . . . That was what the elders said, 'He tapu.' They didn't have to explain any more. That was enough for us . . . When the money accumulated, they would light the fire, in a special place down from the meeting-house, and we knew the money was being burnt. I can make some guesses [why] but I never asked. They burnt it and then they buried it.
(June Tangaere)

> Once I can remember we were fixing up a fenceline . . . I came to this corner post and lifted out the stay because it was all rotted. And just where this stay was in the ground there was a heap of these coins. My own feeling was one of recoil, like someone would recoil from a cobra or something like that. The old man picked them up and took them away. *(August Tangaere)*

Finally, the kai-whakauru also recognised certain kinds of knowledge as tapu, hedged with restrictions on when, where and by whom they might be held or imparted. These included the location of valuable natural resources such as fishing reefs, medicinal plants and springs; whakapapa (genealogies and ancestral histories), karakia and mōteatea; and the maramataka (lunar calendar) applicable in a particular territory.

> There's quite a few other things they do hold back and they hand it on from generation to generation, like herbal medicines and significant karakias, just for that family only. *(Lena Pirihi)*

Such knowledge was held in trust by pūkenga (repositories) qualified by descent and signs (tohu) of the requisite abilities. It was their responsibility to judge who was qualified to receive it and how much to release at any one time.*

Kai-tiaki

Only two of the kai-whakauru used the term kai-tiaki, although others spoke of situations which might warrant that interpretation. Several used the words 'taniwha' and 'guardian' as synonyms with the same meanings as kai-tiaki (Schwimmer, 1963).

Haare Williams used the term kai-tiaki to describe his grandfather's responsibility to care for places connected with Te Kooti,

---

* Refer Chapter 6, pp. 143–44.

the founder of the Ringatū Church, and also applied it to guardian animals associated with hapū and iwi.

> I was very much aware of the sacred nature of my koroua as a protector, a kai-tiaki of those places where Te Kooti put down his sacred footsteps and moved [around] and his death near Kutarere on the Ōhiwa Harbour. From time to time I recall my koroua and kuia talking about a tūī [honeyeater bird] that actually spoke, that was taught to speak. I neither saw nor heard a tūī during my time as a child but I do recall having some sense of awe, some sense of wehi, a feeling that this particular tūī was in fact there. For the Aitanga-a-Māhaki, there was talk of a white shark being our kai-tiaki. Some years ago while I was teaching at Matauri Bay, you know the first time I saw a shark, my first reaction was to have a karakia, and it was only a ground shark. Then my thoughts really shot back to this white shark as told in the stories of Te Aitanga-a-Māhaki.
> *(Haare Williams)*

Priscilla Manukau recalled a story her uncle told about a whale that was clearly a family guardian.

> I remember one story he used to tell us about Paneira the whale as it relates to our family. This lady, every time she's due to have a baby, she used to go on the whale and give birth at sea. One of them was my father, the youngest. I'm not sure if this was true but we were taught to believe that if we were ever out on the water, in the sea, and got into trouble, if we called, he would help us. I was brought up so much to believe it, I've passed it on to my children.
> *(Priscilla Manukau)*

Hapi Potae overheard adults talking about the ruru (morepork) in ways that associated it with death but did not understand its role as a guardian until a traumatic accident prompted an explanation.

You know how the ruru has a lot to do with death. Quite often I used to hear them talking: 'Matetanga o Mea, hou mai te ruru nei.' [Someone died, this owl appeared.] . . . For a long time I used to wonder why. Until one night – we were on the farm – my brother and I went out and we threw stones at this ruru and killed it and brought it home and put it on the tank. The next morning the old lady woke up and she was really ropeable, because she had had a nightmare. When she saw the owl she immediately connected the owl to her experience that night. Then she told us, 'Never do that, because that is a kai-tiaki.' It was just the experience of listening until something like that happened and she had to explain. It was just a lucky shot, picking up stones and throwing them, and one just connected. *(Hapi Potae)*

In George Parekowhai's family, tūpuna with particular gifts fulfilled the role of kai-tiaki to chosen descendants.

In every Māori kindred there is an exceptional carver or composer of songs or exponent of dancing or weaponry or whatever. According to the teachings, the explanation of that from the family is that it comes from the past, and it comes from the ancestress or ancestor who has been the top exponent in her family . . . As the youngsters come through you talk about a readiness or maturation. The way it was explained at home, the kid would express an interest in a particular skill, say carving, and the theory seems to be something like this, that surrounding a kindred are the spirits of these families' ancestors and they are observing the human beings acting out their daily lives, and the carver amongst them, who is the best carver, as the kid acquired the tools, the spirit carver says, 'That's the boy for me!', and from that point these kids pick up the tools and carve like they've been taught to carve . . . In the way we see it, all these family skills really have a spiritual entity involved in the present. *(George Parekowhai)*

Kēhua and Mākutu

While the kai-whakauru used the words 'kēhua' and 'mākutu' on a number of occasions, it was always with reference to stories they had been told as children, never from direct personal experience.

They used 'kēhua' interchangeably with the English word 'ghost' in the context of 'spooky' stories, which they often described as entertainment. Like the English 'bogey', kēhua were sometimes used as a mild threat to make children behave the way adults wanted them to.

> Uncle William was the storyteller in our family. He told us . . . a lot of kēhua stories. Kēhua was almost like *Star Wars* to us.
> (Fred Ellis)

> They talked quite openly about ghost stories . . . They knew so-and-so was dying because he had visited so-and-so last night . . . It was hard for us to tell whether it actually happened or whether it was just a fantasy, a legend or a myth . . . When you go back to bed you're frightened to sleep in the middle of the bed – you want to sleep on the outside part because they've just told you, 'The kēhuas will take you!', 'You better put the light out and if you make a noise after five minutes the kēhua will come and get you!'
> (Hone Pirihi)

Especially when associated with mākutu, kēhua stories could be genuinely frightening and were intended to be. They carried serious warnings against acting in ways that offended guardian and malignant spirits (see also Chapter 8).

As children the kai-whakauru had found the idea of mākutu much more disturbing than kēhua. They used the word without translating or explaining it, taking for granted that it was familiar to both Māori and non-Māori. It is in fact difficult to define in English: the terms 'witchcraft' and 'incantations' commonly used in dictionaries are totally inadequate. Basically, mākutu refers to a tohunga's use of mana and malign spirits to harm or punish others. Hineari Babbington remembered her grandmother repeatedly telling stories about relatives who had been 'mākutu'd'.

> **HINEARI:** All the kēhua stories my grandmother told, for instance about a relative who'd been mākutu'd and why . . . **HAPE:** In a lot of cases she was telling my grandfather about experiences she had had at Ringatū hui, stories of why people were afflicted with a hurt and how they had been treated . . . **HINEARI:** At that time they were believing in mākutu. **HAPI:** Very much so. **HINEARI:** A lot of their behaviour was governed by what they thought might happen if they stepped out of the bounds of some of the rules. Our church group went to a hui and Auntie T made us wait outside while she crossed the threshold and placed a penny under the doorstep first. We didn't know why. She explained later that that would stop any mākutu happening to us. She went inside and said her little prayers first and then we were allowed to go in.
> *(Hineari Babbington and Hapi Potae)*

As with kēhua, adults sometimes traded on the fear of mākutu to warn or correct children. Ani Pihema remembered a story an uncle told her about spending a holiday with his grandfather and a cousin as a boy.

> He said the old man was a cantankerous old man but good to the boys. The boys had their eye on a watermelon in his gardens. The old man had dug a hole and put the watermelon in. The boys dug it out at night, substituting another, and ate it on the beach. One night when they were sitting around, the old man said, 'I'd better go and look at my watermelon.' The two boys started to fidget. They asked, 'Will it be alright?' The old man said, 'Yes, I put a mākutu on it.' The boys went away and worried for days. That was all he said, letting the boys know that he knew, letting

their conscience deal with it. They had to go through the pain of it. *(Ani Pihema)*

Significantly, both 'kēhua' and 'mākutu' figure as entries in *The Dictionary of New Zealand English* (Orsman, 1997).

Values

Life in the communities where the kai-whakauru grew up was underpinned by a pervading set of values. Sometimes these were spelled out explicitly, sometimes they were encrypted in metaphors and proverbs, but most often they were so deeply embedded in practical action, ritual and storytelling that children absorbed them by osmosis and did not consciously articulate them until well into adulthood.

Sharing and Caring

Jossie Kaa spoke for all the kai-whakauru when she said:

> The biggest thing that was in my upbringing was the sharing. We didn't have a lot but what we had we shared and we never went without. Money didn't seem to feature. I saw it occasionally in my Nanny's tobacco tin: she'd take out a sixpence to take to the shop to buy blackballs. Usually I got blackballs because she liked them too. But money just wasn't around. But we were never ever hungry. There was always something there. Because if they knew our rua [storage pit] was empty, well, 'Haere mai, kohia i tētahi kai, ētahi anō nei; he kai anō, kohia mai.' [Welcome! Come and get something to eat, then more; take still more.] *(Jossie Kaa)*

Others said the same thing in a variety of ways.

> There was a lot of sharing and caring. There was no family that went without bread. If a family was a bit low on groceries, there was

always someone to help them. There was never anyone starving. *(Lena Pirihi)*

My dad, if he went eeling and caught a lot, by the time he got to our place, there was none left. *(Priscilla Manukau)*

HINEARI: That was quite a fantastic thing, that sort of sharing around. Horses were a sort of communal thing, the time when there were no tractors. Everybody knew who was going to have a horse next and who was going to help whom to plant, who was going to get more plants from whomever. **HAPI:** My grandmother used to prepare the kūmara beds so she could grow tipu, and when that was ready she supplied a lot of people. In [a named place] where it is nice and sandy she would have several plots and people just went along there [and took what they needed]. Or she even picked tipu for different people, to make sure I suppose that it was picked gradually. She bundled them up and we'd have to go and take them to certain people around the district. *(Hineari Babbington and Hapi Potae)*

Occasionally my grandmother would take me to Rūātoki to meet my great-grandfather and my great-grandmother . . . This old man going out to plant a big field, planting all this kai. There was just the two of them living there. From the outside people would probably wonder why two old people should have these huge gardens. We all know the reason for it. I suppose these things come quietly, sort of slip into your whole lifestyle, your whole outlook on life, your whole philosophy. The giving idea: the planting, the big garden, is part of that concept of giving, of sharing, the aroha concept. They don't just talk about it, they understand the true spirit of it. They give in the feeling of the wideness, the immensity of the meaning of that word aroha . . . The other thing that taught me a great deal about the giving idea was my grandmother having a big bundle of money, and she used to have these long bloomers on under her black dress and she'd tuck it in underneath. She kept that specifically for playing cards and for giving koha [reciprocal gift] to the marae when there was a tangi or a hui at the local marae. Firewood – giving firewood: if anyone didn't have any money, they either helped in the kitchen or did the work around the marae – everyone did that anyway – or brought the firewood or brought kai, watermelon, or went out and got some kaimoana. *(Haare Williams)*

While the kai-whakauru mostly used English words like sharing and caring, it is clear that the values at work were those of aroha, whanaungatanga and manaakitanga, three words that are closely linked in meaning and action. Aroha, which is usually translated as 'love', embraces not only the many meanings of that word but also ideas of compassion, yearning, gratitude and approval. Whanaungatanga, formed by adding the noun ending '-tanga' to the word for relative, is literally 'kin-ship'; it refers to the feelings and actions appropriate among kinsfolk and may be applied metaphorically to non-kin. Manaakitanga is similarly formed from the verb 'manaaki', which means 'to show respect or kindness to someone' and is aptly translated as generosity and/or hospitality. These three words, which have always been central to Māori discourse, have also become part of the vocabulary of New Zealand English in recent years.*

Significantly, the kai-whakauru spoke most often about sharing food. In the limited-income communities in which they grew up, food was a key symbol of the three values just mentioned, the main way of both expressing and maintaining loving relations with kin on the one hand and manuhiri on the other.

Food was very important in our lives. It was more important than money. You had to have plenty to feed the people at hui.
(Hone Pirihi)

---

* See Glossary; and Orsman, 1997.

Those who went to the coast for kaimoana delivered some of their take at the houses they passed on the way home.

One thing I really used to like was when they went out to koko [net] kahawai. And always we knew if anyone had caught kahawai, we'd be sure to get some. *(Jossie Kaa)*

On occasion we'd catch a cartload [of kahawai] and take it round to the neighbours and everybody gets fish. We learnt how to fillet them, steep them in salt water and hang them out to dry. We kept preserved kahawai like that. Every house had them – some had only kahawai because meat tended to be wasted, because of the heat and no refrigeration. If anyone killed a mutton, they shared it out as quickly as possible. So we just lived on kahawai . . . Another thing we used to do was set a net in the estuary and that net caught mullet and kahawai. It was always a habit of the guy that brought us up to send some of the mullet, particularly mullet, to the older people, such as old Jazz and the guy across the road; the vicar always used to get some. It was always our job to go around and distribute fish to these people. It was good for us: we used to hop on our horse and it would be in a bag and we'd go up to the station and drop them some fish. They'd know who it was from by who brought it. *(Wiremu Kaa)*

Families routinely planted more than they required for themselves, in order to have enough to share with relatives in need and with visitors to their homes and marae.

If you ran out of vegetables that you had had stored for a season, you just automatically went over to auntie's, because auntie had helped you to dig your crops anyhow [and been given some of the harvest in recognition]. Nobody ever went without.
(Hineari Babbington)

During the war years there were a lot of people living in Widows' Lane. My dad used to plant potatoes and there were so many [rows] for this widow and so many for that widow and so on. We had to dig it up, and plant it. It was only when we got older you knew what he was doing – teaching us a sense of charity and sharing.
(August Tangaere)

Another thing that happened at home too in those days . . . When they would plant, they would say, 'Aa, this is for us, this is for the marae.' My mother's uncle would say, 'Aa, mō ngā mea pani', for the orphans. So there would be main crops for the family, some for the marae and some for the orphans. *(Wiremu Kaa)*

When we planted kūmara, my father put aside about fifty lines, between fifty and a hundred metres. Special pits were made for those and they were earmarked for marae use only. When there was a tangi or other function on the marae, people went and got enough kūmara from those pits. The same thing applied during harvest. Mum always put aside so many hundred bottles [of preserves] for the maraes. *(Maori Marsden)*

They tell you as you plant, that's the old people, they tell you, they say as they go along, memorising is a good thing, don't forget. It is far better to forget anything else, but the main thing is, anything to do with eating, you never want to forget that . . . They don't handle money. They don't know what money is. Actually money was no object to them. The biggest thing was that there was food, such as kūmaras, potatoes, corn . . . and what they call decayed corn, put in water, kānga kōpūwai [custard made from corn fermented in running water] . . . and dried kūmara. *(Wiremu Hohaia)*

Kūmara, potatoes and corn were staple foods grown for both home and marae. Kānga kōpūwai and dried kūmara (kao) were specialty dishes, served on special occasions to guests. The provision of foods of both kinds to visitors was a matter of pride. Visitors must always come first.

> One thing I was taught as a child was never to leave visitors at the door – bring them in. *(Lena Pirihi)*

> I suppose, all of us were taught that if you are having visitors in the home, you stand back and let the visitors eat first, and if there is nothing left at the end, well, that's too bad for the family. We were taught that visitors must have the best things first, and if anything was left over at the end, you were lucky . . . And very often there was very little left when the manuhiri had gone. And that's the way they taught us . . . Sometimes we were told, 'You wait till the visitors are gone', but mostly they would say, 'You go and play', or 'You go and do that job that hasn't been done yet', and in the meantime the visitors are being looked after. And when they have gone, the children come and are fed. *(June Tangaere)*

Reciprocity

Sharing was not a one-way affair but part of a wider pattern of reciprocity within and between communities. Although none of the kai-whakauru actually used the word 'utu', the idea was implicit in much of what they said. Giving back was an integral part of both intra- and inter-community relations. Recipients on one occasion became givers on another.

> In some way it would come back. None of them ever accepted all that giving and never gave anything back. He parāoa [home-baked bread], kete would come, or whatever . . . This is why I feel our growing up was something very special, precious. There were times when I know we were being ripped off but on the whole it had this feeling of giving. *(Liz Hunkin)*

SPIRITUALITY AND VALUES

When Hineari Babbington won a scholarship to Hukarere Maori Girls' College, the list of clothes she was required to take presented a problem.

> It didn't occur to me to wonder where my clothes were coming from. You should have seen the motley assortment when I did get to go. The aunties all gave something – my mother died when I was nine, there was only Dad and the relations that brought my young brother and I up. Pop got the list of things, he showed his cousins and sisters, and I went with all my gear, though as I say, what a motley assortment. Pants that were too big, a raincoat rather than an overcoat, which I rolled up and left in the train, so that Pop had to buy me a new one, somebody's cast-off shoes. I had some new things but they never thought it was necessary to have all new things. I didn't like them but I thought how marvellous really that they should have all cared enough to do it. It is an everlasting lesson. *(Hineari Babbington)*

Once learned, this value-based pattern of 'giving it back' was carried on into adulthood.

> So when my great-nephews and nieces are going off now, I have always bought them something, whichever ones I have heard about. Three went last Christmas, so that cost me three pairs of shoes. *(Hineari Babbington)*

> Even today my cousins and I who live here in Wellington do exactly the same still. If one of our kids is getting married, we are all in, there is no question about it. We just do it. *(Liz Hunkin)*

Reciprocity also worked to bind communities together, notably through the exchange of hospitality during hui. Home folks feeding visitors on the marae prided themselves on providing local specialties to which their visitors did not have easy access.

To us it was a kind of deprivation to stand aside and watch all those lovely goodies being eaten up. You never ever appreciated it till later on, that by making your manuhiri feel content, you were pleased that they did go away content, because when the occasion was reversed, the same thing happened to you. So there was this kind of sharing out. *(Hineari Babbington)*

Hone and Lena Pirihi both grew up in the Bay of Plenty, Hone in an inland community, Lena on the coast.

HONE: One thing we didn't eat was kōuka – we didn't have cabbage trees growing. And we didn't eat pikopiko because we didn't have any bush. It's a question of what you have in your environment.
LENA: We were known for having round taros, the old Māori taro.
HONE: Even though you lived only nineteen miles away, your food was different. We were five miles in from the sea. Only the kaumātuas had fish at our place. My uncles weren't adept at fishing, like Lena's family. Our specialty was eels. When an important visitor came we'd give them a big box of dried eels and we'd exchange eels for fish from the coastal maraes. **LENA:** Taro – that was our gift for giving to other people. Te Rere had eels, dried eels. **HONE:** For swapping, you'd pawhera [split] it, open it out and salt it and put it in the sun. **LENA:** Tūhoe had pikopiko and wild kiore: bushrats and pikopiko were their exchange gifts. So, many tribes, they've got their own gifts of exchange but they always give food. *(Hone and Lena Pirihi)*

Whakapapa

Whakapapa was one of the Māori words that the kai-whakauru nearly always used in preference to its usual English equivalent, 'genealogy'. Sometimes they used whakapapa with a limited meaning, to refer to the lines of descent linking ancestors and their descendants, which take the form of sequences of names chanted on appropriate occasions and recorded in 'whakapapa books'. But the most important reference of the word was to a much larger body of knowledge that included all the kōrero, waiata and whakataukī for which these names served as mnemonics. This body of knowledge was at the heart of mātauranga Māori and was held in its fullness by some but not all the kaumātua of whānau, hapū and iwi. The kai-whakauru held these experts and their knowledge in high regard but varied widely in the extent to which they themselves sought or were given access to such knowledge as children. Only four of the kai-whakauru spoke about whakapapa and their interest in it at length, and even within that small group there were marked differences in experience and attitudes, reflecting differences in personality and in iwi and church affiliations.

Maori Marsden was born into a leading family in a senior descent-line in Ngāi Takoto, a small iwi located on the shores of Rangaunu Harbour in the Far North, closely connected with neighbouring iwi by whakapapa and history and with the Anglican Church since the establishment of the Church Missionary Society's Mission Station in Kaitāia in 1833. Because of his enquiring mind and near pōtiki [youngest child] status, Maori's father and uncles allowed him unrestricted access to tribal and inter-tribal discussions in which whakapapa was interwoven with biblically based theology.

> From an early age I exhibited interest in these sorts of subjects ... At that time every marae [in the Far North] had several elders – kaumātua – and the majority of them were steeped in their culture ... [In my whānau] when I was a child there were at least a dozen outstanding orators ... My father, being an Anglican priest, ministered all round the area and I used to accompany him as a youngster on weekends, going to churches, to huis and so on, and so it wasn't long before I came to know many of the elders and they came to know me ... These elders were expert genealogists: they knew exactly how they were related, their kinship ties, their whakapapa, their social status, the pecking order among

themselves and their wider relationships . . . Their various positions in terms of tuakana–teina were clearly demarcated in their own minds . . . After evensong during planting they would have a fair discussion about the service, criticise the preacher. Someone would pop a question: who was so-and-so's father? And that was the signal for them to move into recalling their past. This is where I heard the experts giving the genealogies of the various families, their relationships and their history. I was one of those who sat at their feet. The elders were fascinating storytellers . . . Here was one of the main ways in which we learnt, the children, as far as the lore and history of our tribe was concerned. We heard about the battles, we heard about the warriors, we heard about the successes, the defeats, more success than defeats naturally. We heard the boasting. *(Maori Marsden)*

Because of his interest in and capacity for learning, Maori's uncles obtained permission for him to attend meetings of the Tai Tokerau whare wānanga while he was a teenager.

During his teenage years, Haare Williams moved from one learning situation to another. Recalling his early years living with his paternal grandparents on the shores of Ōhiwa Harbour in the Bay of Plenty, Haare did not actually use the word 'whakapapa' in connection with these grandparents but had warm memories of their continuous storytelling. This was related mainly to particular places and activities and to the name and history of the prophet Te Kooti.

I remember . . . reading in Māori in the Bible, the passages that were favourites to me, that my koroua would read, and he would tell me the stories of Māui from time to time, the story of Rangi and Papa, but mainly the stories of Te Kooti were the stories I heard, in our whare raupō, in the dark with a little fire in the middle, just the ashes of the fire . . . I learnt quite a lot about the history of that harbour during the times we were out there fishing or gathering kai or cooking it in a hāngī or shelling the shellfish for preservation . . . My first grandmother, I think her greatest gift to me was her ability to talk to me all the time . . . I cannot remember any formal teaching at all in the things I picked up from her. It was always the talking, the talking, the talking, the talking . . . My second grandmother Waioeka Brown was regarded as the repository of whakapapa, of genealogical history for Te Aitanga-a-Māhaki people. [Prominent elders] round the East Coast consulted her vast grip of knowledge . . . I remember a long time ago Waioeka singing 'Pō! Pō!', ngā waiata a Te Kooti, 'Pinepine te kura', all of those [song-poems of genealogical and historical import]. I used to think it boring, hell of a boring, listening to that sort of thing. *(Haare Williams)*

As an adult with a mature appreciation of whakapapa, Haare had these insights to share:

One of the things that intrigues me about whakapapa is that they become oral tablets of the transmission of very, very fine details of history. You come down a line, then branch off laterally, then you look at another person's name, then you tell a little story about that person, and then you come back to the main descent-line, then you come down about two or three generations, then you move off on another lateral line, then you tell a little story there. I find that whole notion of remembering whakapapa is reinforced by these little anecdotal things that personalise a character on the whakapapa. Just to pick one that comes to mind, Tahupōtiki, my grandmother talking about his personality, what a good-looking man he is and his ability with the people, his caring, and how he was really in love with his brother Porourangi's wife. Waioeka suggests that Tahupōtiki was the senior of the two brothers but in other areas Porourangi is certainly the tuakana. It is only when we write it down in books, put it into the Pākehā genre of writing these things, that we can notice the inconsistencies, but in whaikōrero

out on the marae, in the oral situation, these inconsistencies are very much part of that presentation. I find it very, very fascinating now to look at my grandmother's whakapapa which I have written – I realised halfway through that was the wrong way to treat whakapapa. Whakapapa is not a written thing, it's a spoken thing. It is all these little stories that are associated with each key figure as you come down the line. Waioeka Brown was very much of that key era and so was my first grandmother.
(Haare Williams)

When George Parekowhai was growing up on a farm near Te Karaka on the East Coast, his father took advantage of family gatherings after the evening meal to tell stories about their ancestors and the land along with the whakapapa connecting them with the living.

From an idle remark he may give a proverb and the proverb would reflect on a family incident. By our response – and I was always interested – he would start off and he'd tell a story, and it would relate to this proverb and it would relate to historical facts. And he would also connect that incident with himself by line of descent. And these sorts of stories would vary in length of names in the descent-line from about ten names in a descent-line, sometimes fifteen. Much more than that was taxing even myself . . . I do remember my dad saying . . . as far as whakapapa was concerned . . . it was a gift that would go down to one of the descendants. In his case he was the only one in his generation who was interested or certainly who could remember accurately the order of names and the associated historical data that went with it . . . I am very keen, too. I don't know why but I have found it easy. I would support the traditional belief that some people have the gift and I happen to be one of the lucky ones, with regard to the family whakapapa anyway . . . I don't ascribe my skill in it to any kind of intellectual supremacy I have over my brothers. It is simply that the whakapapa

expert in my family is looking over my shoulders and suddenly decided that's the one who would do the whakapapa.
(George Parekowhai)

Nikora Atama grew up in the Far North in a Roman Catholic community where the older generations were (as he put it) 'steeped in Māoritanga'. Nikora was exposed to endless stories about local history when staying in the homes of whanaunga (relatives), hanging round the marae and attending hui with his father, but was excluded from the deep discussions held in the meeting-house at night. For long enough Nikora simply absorbed the stories he heard, but as he grew older he began to question the contradictions between the teachings of the kaumātua and those of the Church and to seek deeper understanding of the former. His father advised him to respect and conform to the Church's teaching and refused to go more deeply into mātauranga Māori until Nikora had become fully adult.

> It's mainly storytelling that they tell us . . . after mates [mourning the dead at the marae] . . . We used to sit and listen to them in the meeting-house, we were hōhā and ran away outside. Of course, we know that when we come back home, that's when they start telling us different things, the history again. Again, they've got to be in the mood and you've got to really catch them on the hop. If they don't tell you, they are just not going to tell you. We've been lucky that they were there when we needed them. *(Nikora Atama)*

Mana, Tika and Tikanga
While the kai-whakauru used the words 'mana', 'tika' and 'tikanga' comparatively rarely in our discussions, they clearly recognised their importance. It was as if the concepts were always there in the background, not needing to be spelled out. The word 'mana' they used always in relation to people, although I know from other conversations that some also attributed mana to places and actions. When they

attributed mana to particular persons, the word might be interpreted with its old primary meaning of power derived from the supernatural realm or with the meaning of high social standing, authority and prestige, the meaning usually attributed to it in modern dictionaries and glossaries. They used the words 'tika' and 'tikanga' mostly with reference to the importance of doing things the right (Māori) way on the marae and with reference to people of high mana such as kaumātua, rangatira and manuhiri.

> The ritual of marae protocol is absolutely astounding when you think about the things that come from it. There is self control, there is respect one for the other, there's observation for the dignity of the situation, there's aroha for the bereaved, and there is a remembering of people who have gone on, and there's total respect for the occasion. You have to observe all these things before you can go and enjoy yourself again. *(Hineari Babbington)*

> As far as the marae was concerned, it seems to me that you had to be fully clothed from top to bottom, that was the feeling I got, and that also goes back to the past, in that the people who spoke on the marae were fully clad; even the chief speakers wore their cloaks, the whole bit . . . I'm very conscious of it today when I go on to the marae; that's why I wear the long dress, because it not only works well for my own old people but also for the Pacific Islanders.
> *(Rose Pere)*

Called upon unexpectedly to act as kai-karanga at a hui when she was wearing a trouser suit, Rose wrapped a blanket around herself before responding.

If not consciously then unconsciously, the kai-whakauru learned as children that the way they behaved – the things they did and did not do, and the ways they did them – reflected on the mana of their own whānau vis-à-vis other whānau and on that of their community vis-à-vis manuhiri. When he acted under the direction of his matua whāngai (adopted father; see Glossary), Wiremu Kaa knew that the community at large regarded him as the latter's representative.

> He had this older batch [of offspring] and then the next batch with me. I was the oldest except for one girl and then he relied on me to be the tonotono [dogsbody] for all sorts of things. I got sent to Tikitiki marae on a cart to take three muttons for a tangihanga and people knew that I came from Uncle Henare, and I got sent to someone else because an old kuia up the road wanted some kai. I was always the figurehead for him and his activities... I went [to the marae] with him. He went to the paepae [speakers' bench]; me and my younger cousin, the girl, we were on the cart, we always went round the back (we never went to the front, we went around the back) and unloaded the meat and kūmara, then we went straight home... If the tangi was for someone else's whānau and if we came after [Uncle Henare] had already been there, it was always just to bring kai. If it was something to do with close relatives of ours, very, very close, we were there the day before. All our involvement was to do the work, to cart or sledge loads of wood, to take the meat and hang them up underneath the pine trees. Maybe we had to peel the potatoes, for the first meal only. We did the menial things and then our next involvement would be at the end: take all the rubbish away, clean the marae. We were working for the uncle, representing him at that kind of thing. We were always involved like that, never to the paepae. *(Wiremu Kaa)*

Because young people represented not just themselves but also their whānau, stress was laid on being whakaiti (humble), and any tendency towards conceit or arrogance was squashed, especially by their parents. In discussion with the other Itinerant Teachers of Maori, June Tangaere remembered:

I used to have to wear all my brothers' small clothes even down to their shorts and boots to school. I didn't mind while I was little but as I grew older I did. And I rebelled against it and I used to get hidings because of it I felt. I used to be told I was whakahīhī and all that. *(June Tangaere)*

Hapi Potae commented that 'this was a training in humility'; Hineari Babbington added that it was also a training in frugality.

I know now that that kind of early training has made me economise a great deal. I never throw things out. Once when my aunt came to stay, she found these particular things among my ironing. I said, 'I can cut them down later for the kids.' And I still do this. Some of my skirts I have saved for my daughters to cut up for pants for their kids. This is my very early training.
(Hineari Babbington)

Modesty (whakamōwai) and how to protect it was another value that was learnt at an early age by a combination of imitation and eavesdropping. Sleeping in the meeting-house or crowded bedrooms, children became adept at dressing and undressing under the protection of blankets. In carved meeting-houses, they learnt to face the centre with their backs to the poupou (carvings of ancestors lining the walls) when changing, and similar tikanga governed behaviour getting in and out of the water. When Rose Pere and Wiremu Kaa were children, bathing suits were unknown in their communities. Adults and children alike swam 'in the raw'. However, children learnt that there were right ways of handling their bodies in public, for example, by turning side on to others and by the proper disposition of hands and arms.

ROSE: We certainly didn't have anything on and that included the whole lot of us, old people and all. **WIREMU:** The kids were swimming around and the adults would come in and have a wash, right at the end of the pool or river. **ROSE:** Although we swam or bathed together without clothing we remained covered by the water. One did not expose herself openly. You were very careful how you went into the river or wherever you were going. I kore koe e whakaatu ō karihi, you didn't expose your genital region, because that is an insult. I remember learning at an early age that you didn't expose your posterior to anyone, so therefore you had to be careful about the way you got undressed to get into the water in any case. [**JOAN:** Did anyone show you how?] **WIREMU:** No, you saw the others doing it. **ROSE:** Then you would hear them in discussion talking about it. *(Rose Pere and Wiremu Kaa)*

Care of Land and Sea

The kai-whakauru all stressed the value and sacredness of both land (whenua) and sea (moana) and the imperative of care for their community's natural resources, although they did not actually use the word kai-tiakitanga. Participating in productive activities from an early age, they encountered the many tikanga that governed interaction with the natural environment. Prominent among these tikanga were: the use of karakia to ask for spiritual protection before and during such activities and to give thanks at their conclusion; the use of the lunar calendar based on experiential knowledge of the local environment; the careful disposal of waste material to fertilise and/or prevent pollution of local resources; the use of rāhui to allow resources to build up for hui, to recover from depletion after harvest or damage, and to respect the tapu associated with death; and giving away the first fruits of crops, seafood and craftwork. Frequent reference to these tikanga are to be found in most chapters, but especially under the headings 'Learning Mātauranga Māori' in Chapter 2, and 'Karakia' and 'Tapu and Not-tapu' in this chapter.

The extent to which particular tikanga related to particular territories and their resources was illustrated by Hone Pirihi who had to learn a whole new set when he visited his wife's coastal community after they were married.

> When we went to the beach her father said, 'Whatever you do, put your footprints into my footprints, so you don't walk all over the beach . . . And also, when you go to collect mussels, don't crack a mussel on a rock and eat on a rock.' I asked him why and he said, 'Because the other mussels will smell it.' If a mussel got smashed on a rock and fell into the water the other mussels will see it and move away. Conservation comes into it again. The food will move somewhere else and we will have no food in our area. *(Hone Pirihi)*

The most highly valued of the food crops and the most vulnerable to pests and disease, the kūmara was closely governed by the maramataka and tapu restrictions placed on its planting, weeding, harvesting and storage.

> When the planting came it was really important. The beds of kūmaras were prepared first in a special place, specially set in sand. The right size kūmara had been predetermined and set aside. The tipu came at precisely the right time. The calendar was watched, everyone discussed the planting time. *(Hineari Babbington)*

The Tūhoe pūkenga Ereatara emphasised the importance of respectful behaviour in the bush, working with instead of against the natural order and avoiding waste and pollution. For example, he taught his pupils to take leaves and berries for rongoā from the side where growth was most vigorous.

> You don't go to a tree and pluck leaves from the north, south or west side, you take it only from the eastern side. Why? Kei te hāri koe ki te rākau rongoā, tangohia mai i te taha rāwhiti, kei te ekenga ake o te rā, kua hoatu te mana ki te tuawhenua. [When you gather

medicinal plants in the bush, take them from the eastern side. Mana is given to the earth at the rising of the sun.] The sun gives mana to the whole earth. *(Tawhao Tioke)*

None of the kai-whakauru mentioned the placing of rāhui on a stretch of sea coast where someone had drowned, although they were undoubtedly familiar with the custom, but several mentioned the use of rāhui to preserve food stocks. Hone Pirihi (for example) recalled how the Ringatū Church used a rāhui to prevent crops being lifted too early.

The Ringatū Church believes that you shouldn't lift the vegetables you planted until the first of January. There was conservation again. You left the vegetables to mature and on the First you had a harvest celebration. *(Hone Pirihi)*

Growing up in Tolaga Bay on the East Coast, Joe Matete recalled how the practice of rāhui was used to shut up food stocks of kaimoana before a hui.

They had the rāhui as well; for three or four months we would go to the other side of the beach. If they had a big hui coming up they wouldn't go to a section of the beach till the hui was near, and everyone, fifty to a hundred people, would go down and get it all in one day. *(Joe Matete)*

Rāhui were imposed by community leaders to meet community needs. Everyone shared in the sacrifices involved while rāhui were in place and rejoiced together when they were lifted. When a rāhui was lifted from a stretch of coast in Tokomaru Bay, Jossie (Oho) Kaa celebrated the event with a song of joy naming the activities and resources now free to be enjoyed.

Kua hīkina te rāhui, kua wātea te tāhuna.
Kua wātea mō te kohi pūpūrangi, mō te rapa ngākihi, mō te tākirikiri kuku.
Kua wātea mō te kimi pāpaka, mō te huhuti parengo, mō te māngoingoi.
Kua wātea mō te ruku pāua, mō te tiki kina, mō te hopuhopu kōura.
Kua wātea mō te hī ika, mō te tō kaharoa, mō te koko kahawai.
Kua wātea te tāhuna mō te hararei, mō te tākaro, me te kaukau hoki.
Kua hīkina te rāhui, kua wātea. Auē, te ora e!

Jossie's poem has a musical dimension difficult to replicate in English. The following translation concentrates on the literal meaning of the words, adding explanatory detail where helpful.*

The rāhui has been lifted, the beach has been cleared of tapu. Cleared for collecting shellfish, looking for limpets, prising mussels off the rocks. Cleared for hunting crabs, pulling seaweed off the rocks, line-fishing from the shore. Cleared for diving for pāua, getting sea-eggs, diving and catching crayfish one after the other. Cleared for fishing with hook and line, hauling drag-nets, catching kahawai in scoop nets. The beach is cleared for holidaying, for sport and for swimming too. The rāhui is lifted, the beach is open for use. Auē! All is well!

---

* See Glossary for individual words.

CHAPTER FIVE

Learning in Maturity as Part of Living

Although by the time they entered their teens the kai-whakauru were almost precociously competent in practical matters, they still had much to learn about the deeper aspects of mātauranga Māori, including the reasons behind traditional ways of doing things learnt in childhood but not fully understood.

By their mid- or late teens nearly all had moved out of their home communities into the wider world. In most cases this move was generated by parents and kaumātua who saw formal education in state or church schools as *the* way to improve both individual and community fortunes, and/or by school teachers who helped secure places and financial backing for the kai-whakauru. Thus supported, they attended Māori boarding schools, state schools in main centres, teachers' colleges and, in a few cases, university. Some migrated to the city with their parents or left home on their own initiative in search of employment.

Wherever they went after leaving home, the kai-whakauru were exposed to new ideas and influences from members of other iwi, from Pākehā institutions, friends and work-mates, and from academic writings and debates on Māori language and culture. For a decade or more after that, travelling, courting and probationary employment kept them fully occupied. However, once they had matured and settled down with permanent jobs and families of their own, they began to seek and/or take advantage of opportunities to learn more about mātauranga Māori from kaumātua in their own and other communities.

> Every time I go back, there is something I am learning all the time from the old people. It didn't just finish when I was little, it's an on-going thing... I believe you never stop learning till the day you close your eyes. *(Hone Pirihi)*

Several kai-whakauru reported that previously reticent elders had started to 'open up' when they came home after some years away. Hapi Potae's grandmother taught him how and where to catch crayfish when he was quite young, but:

> For a long time no one else in the district actually told me [any more]. It wasn't till I was much older, I think I might have been teaching then, when George Ngawai (this is Ngoi Pewhairangi's father), one day he came down to the beach when I was there and he sat with me, and he was starting to tell me what they used to do when they used to go among the rocks, and then he started to point out the different rua kōura [crayfish holes] to me, and he was saying, 'By that rock over there, if you went down that channel, you'll find there used to be a nice rua.' He actually was one of the few who told me about this... Old Potene Awatere, I remember him, and it was again at a very formal occasion where he came to the school (we used to have these night gatherings when I was teaching there) and talked to us about the streams there... the names of all the streams in the bay and how they came to get these names, the legends that went with them. *(Hapi Potae)*

Hineari Babbington confessed to feeling 'slightly cheated' that they had to find out about these things as adults; she wondered why the elders had not talked about them when they were children. Hapi suggested that passing on the knowledge was not a matter of urgency in their day 'because there were so many people'.

> There were busloads: when you went to a tangi there were buses and buses. I can remember anything up to a dozen buses lined up along the road to a tangi, so it wasn't necessary then [to teach these things to everyone]. So the teaching actually was quite different. It wasn't till I went back [as a trained teacher] that people like Potene Awatere and George Ngawai came along, even College Collier, . . . and spoke openly to our group of people.* Ngaropi White was another person who felt that we were old enough or mature enough for her to talk about lots of her experiences. So you can just about term it a wānanga.† This was how these pakeke [elders] were actually imparting their knowledge. *(Hapi Potae)*

Kai-whakauru who took up teaching positions or visited their spouse's whānau in a community other than their own learnt about resources and tikanga different from those they were used to. Hone Pirihi, who grew up in an inland community, had new tikanga to learn when he married Lena, who came from a coastal one.

> When I went to Tōrere after we got married I found a lot of things different to our marae. For example, before they went diving, their father told me to go behind a bush and urinate on to my hand before going into the water. I said, 'What a dirty lot of people!' And he said, 'Don't laugh! I'll tell you why.' And he gave me reasons why. This tapu thing, this sacredness came into it. *(Hone Pirihi)*

Sometimes the kai-whakauru did not recognise the depth and importance of what they had learnt to know as children until they were alerted by other people's reactions. Hineari Babbington said that she did not appreciate the importance of the marae as the focus of

---

* College Collier was on the school committee, and Potene Awatere was one of the elders. 'Our group of people' met at the school at night on a regular basis.
† See Glossary; and also last section of Chapter 7.

community life and learning until she took a group of city children on a visit to her home community.

> This realisation came to me through the parents of the children saying, 'It's marvellous, we didn't think children could be involved in anything as moving as this'... When you are part of it you don't think of what's actually going on. I suppose because we've been immersed in it for so long. *(Hineari Babbington)*

Many kai-whakauru reported making sense of information and experiences they had ignored or been puzzled by as children after they had been exposed to the wider world, including other iwi and books. Thinking back to his childhood, Haare Williams reflected that:

> There was mention of the stars, but at that time I really didn't take much notice of those things. In later life, and especially when I was teaching in Matauri Bay in the Far North, as I listened to people like Broughton Pere, Martha Broughton and others – when we went out fishing, we would start talking about the stars and the seasons and the planting, and some of those ideas crystallised and came back to me, about the approach my koroua and my kuia had, very much associated with the Ringatū calendar, for the planting and for harvesting, and the appearance – I think on reflection now it must have been the star Rehua, Antares – telling me little stories about the stars, actually pointing those stars out to me when we went out at night... As I moved up through university and started to look back again on these things, you know, those principles were well established there in story form, in waiata... You know, all of that teaching was there, all of it informal I think, and it is just tremendous to be able to relate the two, the fusion of my education in a university... to the things they were talking about.
> *(Haare Williams)*

Wiremu Kaa remembered watching his grandmother gathering flax for weaving.

> She'd go and cut flax, she'd sit there and get it all ready [a lengthy process involving stripping the spine and edges from each blade] and she was methodical. She put the waste round the bush. I always wondered why she did that. She always said, 'Na, he kai matū.' We didn't know what she meant. [It was] only in after years that we realised what she was saying, that the waste was food for the flax. We didn't realise this – it was just part of her upbringing, whereas we'd go running around through the flax and be growled at by her. *(Wiremu Kaa)*

Recalling how his father made them plant and harvest rows of potatoes for 'the people living in Widows' Lane' during the war, August Tangaere commented:

> It was only when we got older you knew what he was doing – teaching us a sense of charity and sharing. *(August Tangaere)*

Practices acquired mainly as a matter of habit in childhood could be embraced in adulthood once their meaning and purpose were fully understood. Living with his paternal grandparents for his first nine years, Haare Williams was accustomed to the everyday use of water and karakia to bless and protect everything they did. As a mature adult he continued to find the practice helpful in the context of a spiritual understanding of the world.

> I find myself now, when I go to a strange marae, if I forget to do a karakia outside the gate, I do it when I sit down and prepare myself for the whaikōrero. I close my eyes and just think for a while. I find myself whenever I sit down for a meal, I pick up a bit of bread or get some water and sprinkle it on myself, either in the toilet or from a

tap outside . . . or sometimes I get a bit of bread and just rub it in my hands, because that's the way they taught me to look after myself, to protect myself. But it wasn't really hammered into me. I just picked it up by observing these practices. When it was relevant to them it was certainly relevant to me. And so there I was being imbued with that spiritual thing, soaking it up and becoming very much an important part of my life . . . In more recent years I am going back to the Ringatū Church and listening to what the people are saying, listening to the words of the hīmene, the karakia and songs. I am astounded at how much of that I do remember. I can get up and karakia – I can't lead it on my own but I can certainly follow the group. *(Haare Williams)*

CHAPTER SIX

Storehouses of Knowledge

As well as learning experientially through their involvement in family and community as children, a number of the kai-whakauru reported being singled out by relatives to receive personal instruction in specialised and often restricted forms of knowledge. The teacher–learner relationships thus established were distinguished by elements of conscious choice and the excluding of other learners. The kai-whakauru identified the teachers in these relationships as belonging mostly to the older, grandparental generations in their communities but a few were parents and parents' siblings approaching kaumātua status. Some of them had taken a child or children at birth and brought them up as their own; others had established the teaching relationship when the child had shown aptitude for their special field. In these cases the teaching itself might take place in the child's home or the teacher's, at the marae, in the bush or beside the sea; and it might be embedded in everyday interaction or involve occasional periods of concentrated instruction. Sometimes, especially where tapu knowledge was concerned, teaching was delayed until the learner was fully adult.

In talking about teacher–learner relationships of this kind, the kai-whakauru laid stress on the kinship status of the parties, used the Māori terms in general use for teachers and learners (tauira, kai-ako, ākonga) and often identified the teachers as pūkenga. The dictionaries translate this term into English as 'repository' (Williams, 1975, p.307) and 'storehouse of knowledge' (Ryan, 1995, p.200).

In the minds of the kai-whakauru, the word 'pūkenga' was associated in the first place with mātauranga Māori 'tuku iho nō ngā tūpuna' (handed down from the ancestors) such as whakapapa, whaikōrero, and the visual and performing arts, but it could also be applied to experts in practical fields such as building, farming and marae management. Pūkenga were expected not only to preserve received knowledge but also to enrich it with their own learning and to pass it on to a trustworthy successor.

Chosen as Children

Although they had no direct personal experience themselves, Hone and Lena Pirihi commented in general terms on the frequency with which grandparents took a grandchild to live with them and the reasons why.

> HONE: It was usually the grandchild they took with them. And that's a lucky child because all the grandmother's taonga or gifts will be handed on; spiritually or whatever, the child will get them later on. LENA: It's usually the firstborn. HONE: The first mokopuna, yes. And that's why it's a privilege if anyone takes your first child, especially grandparents, because he or she will get all the heirlooms, all their worldly goods as well as all the spiritual things that they have got and which made them what they are. LENA: It's not so much the material things, it is the spiritual things that they get from the older people. They are exposed to what they do. HONE: And later on, it's like a computer, you feed them in the data and you press the button and out comes what you want. So it's input, what they are doing, isn't it? *(Hone and Lena Pirihi)*

Chosen at Birth
Haare William's early childhood was a particularly intimate example

of the relationship between grandparents and a grandchild chosen at birth. Haare's paternal grandparents took him as a baby to live with them in an isolated spot on the shores of Ōhiwa Harbour in the Ringatū heartland and he lived with them until his grandmother died when he was nine. Much of his learning in those years has been presented in earlier chapters as embedded in daily living, but it was experienced in a close and mostly exclusive relationship with a couple steeped in traditional and Ringatū knowledge and included numerous experiences not known to his siblings and cousins or not experienced in so continuous a form.

> My father came from the Waikaremoana–Rūātoki area, so he was Tūhoe, but from the age of about fourteen he went shearing on the East Coast area and married my mother, one of the Browns of Te Aitanga-a-Māhaki, so those are my two tribal designations . . . I was born in Te Karaka, a little place out of Gisborne. As far as I know, before I was born my paternal grandparents wanted to adopt me, and I think their idea was that one child of the family was to be imbued, to be fed, with the tikanga, with the history of the tribe . . . I was the only grandchild brought up by them . . . Of my six brothers I was the only one brought up in that fashion. . . .
>
> I was brought up in a little place out of Ōpōtiki, Karaka* on Ōhiwa Harbour . . . a little valley where later in my life I found out that Te Kooti actually died . . . My koroua was a Ringatū tohunga. He felt it was important for him to live there to keep warm the memory of Te Kooti . . . Very early in my memory I remember going round to this little place with them. The place was covered in blackberry and bracken fern . . . we went round there by boat. He built a kaponga house for us, just as a temporary dwelling, with thatching, with

---

* It is coincidental that the two places where Haare lived as a child and a teenager were both named Karaka. The one on the East Coast is Te Karaka.

raupō and a wee bit of nīkau . . . Once we settled down, [there was] the clearing of the land to plant kai and of course the kaimoana was right there at our doorstep . . . There was a little bush at the back, and [then came] hauling out some timber, cutting down timber to build a whare, cutting the raupō and bundling it up and digging it into the ground, bending it over to thatch it, about a foot thick, and then when it was completed covering it with dirt, so that part of the house, on the outside anyway, was submerged. . . .

Our nearest neighbours over the hill were about two miles away and the other neighbours on the other side, around the bay, were about two miles away also . . . Around the bay we would go each Saturday night, my grandfather, my grandmother, they would either carry me on their back or on a horse or on a sledge; by however means, we went to listen to the radio. I remember hearing Big Ben, all the family and all the neighbours, sitting around the only wireless in the whole area, and listening to Bill Parker reading the news in Māori on the activities on the war front. Very much an isolated, secluded sort of upbringing in my early childhood. *(Haare Williams)*

During Haare's first six years, before he went to school, learning practical skills and mātauranga Māori went hand in hand. He went everywhere with one or both grandparents: he was with them preparing the soil for planting and growing crops, gathering the products of bush and swamp, collecting and preserving kaimoana; he slept with them at night, listening to their recital of karakia, whakapapa and stories; and he attended Ringatū hui with them.

It was very informal . . . there was no real teaching. For the first six years of my life I internalised very, very deeply those Māori things; culturally I was very much a Māori, in the language, in the way I felt about things, the cooking of the kai and sleeping with my grandparents . . . Being present at the birth and death of some of my relatives. My koroua being a tohunga, he was required to go there and exorcise the spirit out of the people. I must have been about six at the time when I remember him chasing the wairua of another person in one of my relatives. That was quite a frightening experience. When someone had died, my kuia would sit there and clean the person and put a shirt on. [We had] a very close association with birth and death. . . .

The other thing I remember in early childhood was the karakia, the very intense moments when my grandfather had a feeling that someone has died. I would know someone had died because of the very nature of the karakia or the prayers that were delivered in the middle of the night or early in the morning. And in the morning he would say, 'He aituā', someone had died. He would talk about it and I would ask how did he know – I knew how he knew, because that person had visited us that night. . . .

Then reading in Māori in the Bible, the passages that were favourites to me, that my koroua would read. And he would tell me the stories of Māui from time to time, the story of Rangi and Papa, but mainly the stories of Te Kooti were the stories I heard, in our whare raupō, in the dark with a little fire in the middle, just the ashes of the fire. That was another wonderful thing I recall vividly . . . We used to go out for a whole day and light a big fire, cut down all this big stand of mānuka and get this heap of ashes and put it into a big tin, a twelve-gallon tin, might be bigger than that. We'd put all the ashes in and take it into the whare puni and pour it out in the middle. I don't know how it wasn't burned down, being a small house with a low door. Talk about warm! That would go for about a month and all we'd need to do to get the warmth coming through was to scrape the side away, the dead embers, and the smouldering ashes would come through in the middle. . . .

As a young child I remember fencing – I used to be able to put up a fence myself. My grandfather used to let me do those sorts of things, put a strainer post in with a foot on the bottom and ram it down with a rammer. Collecting kōuka [cabbage tree leaves], collecting food from the bush, collecting eels, drying them, getting the worms to go out to a certain place at the creek and sitting down all night, and waking up in the morning with all this mass of eels lying around, and we'd take them home and pawhera [split open] the tuna. Collecting the pipi [bivalve shellfish] and drying them, putting them through a certain sort of rushes: you'd pull out the strands and thread all these things and hang them up in the sun to dry. Cutting up the strips of fish like herring and flounder and hanging them in the same way, and they'd turn round and round in the sun as they dried. Tremendous cultural information . . . I remember the story of the island that stands in Ōhiwa Harbour, Hokianga Island. It is an urupā [burial ground]. He used to tell me about the social activities that went on there when he was a young man. We would go out and collect kaimoana from a certain place, the tuangi [cockles] especially. The tuangi seemed to be one of our staple diets . . . we'd go in a little boat, we'd get a big pile of pipi or tuangi and bring it back and dump it in the little bay where we lived. Whenever we wanted some I would go out and fill up a kit and take it home. That is something I haven't seen since. They would keep there for about a month or so. They didn't grow, they didn't produce their own little tuangi or pipis . . . I would go out with a kit and fill it up and take it home. The fishing places where we got the tāmure [snapper] from, the flounders, the stingray, the sharks, different parts of the harbour were well known to them. The mussels – we didn't get many mussels but we knew where we could get them. Tuangi was certainly our staple diet whenever there was a hui . . . I guess I learnt a lot about the history of that harbour during the time we were out there fishing or shelling the shellfish for preservation. *(Haare Williams)*

Living alone with his grandparents Haare had not one but two full-time teachers who shared a close affinity with nature, with the seasons, with the trees, with birds and insects and kaimoana, but also had their own special styles and fields of action.

> I think of the times my grandmother spent in talking, in telling stories, in explaining things or giving a lot of love and patience, that kind of thing was really done at night or whenever we worked in the garden. She got up very early and spent a lot of time in the garden . . . My grandfather wasn't so much into the talking, into the explanation of things, but rather working in a very, very practical way in the things we did together. And, of course, there was very, very much the use of language coming through all the time whatever activity we shared . . . I think the bush and the land and the very practical sort of work that my grandfather did is balanced up with the things my grandmother did. They seemed very complementary, one did one thing and the other did the other.
> *(Haare Williams)*

Even while he described his grandfather as more practical and less talkative, Haare recalled the explanations and stories his grandfather imparted as they worked together and his frequent use of karakia. Practical skills and cultural information were not and could not be separated. In the years he lived with his grandparents, Haare was involved in learning experiences that were rare in Māoridom even at that time.

> The informal instruction, in things like sorting out kūmara, for example: the sizes, the way to handle it, putting these things into the rua with my grandfather, carrying it up a steep hill and why the kūmara had to be treated so gently, in a certain way. So I was one of those kids who actually saw a pit on the side of a hill and the way it was dug, the way it was shaped on the top and the lid on the top

to avoid water getting down into it. I remember handling kūmara individually and putting it down into a kūmara pit like that, with bracken fern to line the bottom and the sides of the pit.
(Haare Williams)

A firstborn grandchild, Rose Pere lived with her grandparents in a large farm household that included a lot of adult uncles and aunts until her grandfather died when she was seven. Her parents lived thirty-five miles away by road; during those first seven years she saw her mother only as an occasional visitor.

I was the only child [in the household] really, the only one from my age group. We used to have a lot of relatives from Ruatāhuna who would come through on horseback going to Gisborne or Te Rēinga and places like that. My grandfather had a long-house with a fireplace at one end: he built that himself [for these visitors]. [A sheepfarmer] he was one of those people who worked from dawn to dusk . . . his pātaka [storehouse] was always full, he always had a lot of kai for people. He never bothered standing around to entertain relations: he would always be out working, but that place had plenty of kai . . . He was the only Māori farmer in this whole district; we were surrounded by what you would call white settlers, I suppose. And they had a high regard for him because none of them could work the way he could, and he knew the land and the history of the block. It was Kahungunu land, not Tūhoe land; it belonged to his father's people, between Waikaremoana and Te Wairoa. He was half Kahungunu and half Tūhoe . . . The aunts and uncles living in the household were from the generations before me . . . They were related, cousins, second, third, fourth or whatever in English but to us they were all mothers and fathers, whaea and mātua.
(Rose Pere)

Like Haare, Rose was constantly in her grandparents' company and received special teaching from them both. While generally in agreement with each other, they sometimes favoured different topics and different tribal sources.

> I always slept with one of my grandparents or with both of them when they were both still alive . . . My grandfather had a peculiar sense of humour . . . My grandmother tried to teach me the English alphabet, she was half English and half Tūhoe, and then my grandfather would come in and do things like putting a cross across the 's', changing it into 'f'. He did a lot of those things when she was out of the room and we would have a chuckle to ourselves. But most times she fell in line with my grandfather in terms of me, but sometimes she would try and bring in part of her English side. She would concentrate on the Tūhoe side after my grandfather died . . . We [my grandmother and I] used to always sit with my grandfather. It could have been on the verandah or he could have been [elsewhere] on the marae. He was the oldest but he actually had his younger brother do all the speaking on the marae: he was a far better orator. But wherever my grandfather was, I was there.
> *(Rose Pere)*

Sometimes Rose's grandfather dropped Rose and her grandmother at the marae with a load of food and went straight back to work, but whenever he did go to hui, on their own marae or elsewhere, he took Rose with him.

> When I think back, what he was doing was introducing me to his relations. And at the same time he was telling me who our relations were, because it was such a big family. He had a lot of first cousins, people at Rūātoki, people in Ruatāhuna . . . Whakapapa was important in our family . . . My grandfather died when I was seven. A lot of my teaching came from my grandmother after that.

> There were just so many things that she told me, about the people and the community, their history and how far back these traits went because their ancestors did such and such. She took time out to do that, and although I thought that I hardly listened to her I must have alright, because those things came back all the time.
> *(Rose Pere)*

As a teenager Rose lost interest in the marae, especially what happened 'out the front', but years later she remembered the whakapapa her grandparents and mother had shared with her and treasured them as a legacy to be passed on to a worthy recipient. Her grandmother was also an expert weaver but Rose was not interested in learning that skill from her. Instead she received encouragement from an uncle who was a renowned carver.

> When my [grand]mother tried to teach me I had no ears. I never paid any attention because I've never been interested in weaving; for myself I've always been interested in carving. And I have done carving. One of my uncles was a carver in Tūhoe. And I remember asking him if I could carve. And he said, 'If you want to carve, you carve!' And I've always carved [representations of] my own tūpuna and when people made any comment I said, 'They are not your people, they're mine!' They say, 'Women don't do this and do that.' But my uncle was recognised as a carver in Tūhoe and he had been involved with a lot of the carvings in the [meeting-]houses. He was special to me and I was his special niece. *(Rose Pere)*

Chosen Pre-schoolers

Even if they did not choose a child at birth and take them into their own household, grandparents might still engage in close companionship with a chosen grandchild. This was most likely to happen with widowed grandmothers and children not yet at school.

One of the basic patterns that was clear to me, not only in my own family but when we taught in the fifties and sixties on the Whanganui River, is that children and the grandparents, mainly female, had a special kind of role. Granny would go and stay with one particular family and sometimes she formed a particular attachment to one particular mokopuna and that mokopuna in her pre-school days accompanied Granny on her visits to other homes and to Māori institutional things like tangihanga and church services... When we were teaching on the Whanganui River we saw the same thing happening... where this pre-school kid was almost the grandmother's indulgence, and even her own generation saw her as being spoiled and indulged. I don't think there was any clear animosity; they used to tease her but she wasn't isolated, she was still very much part of that kin structure. When this grandmother arrived in a particular household, she would serve the needs of this one as well as the others but the interesting thing extra that I noted was that she would take the kid to Rātana huis and things and that kid... could chant the Rātana liturgy, long passages of karakia, very accurately. I wouldn't go so far as to say she knew the meaning but she would chant it off in chunks that would take as long as 'Pō! Pō!' to be sung... We also saw the change as this mokopuna came to school. She was a devil of a child to manage at first – very articulate. She would have spent most of her pre-school days being exposed to Māori language yet she was one of the most articulate in English in her family. We can't say this skill came from her grandmother, because the grandmother spoke mainly Māori... She came to school and had an enforced separation from her grandmother. And the grandmother took another one, another pre-schooler, and carted that one around in much the same way. *(George Parekowhai)*

Chosen for Learning Capacity
When Priscilla Manukau was growing up in the King Country, she received special teaching from three different members of the

household. Most of her education, she said, came from the 'uncle' who lived with them. He was the main orator on the marae in Mangapēhi. As well as telling stories and teaching mōteatea to all the children with whom he shared a bedroom, this uncle singled Priscilla out for special teaching when she was about twelve.

> Most of my education came from my uncle. He taught me to karanga, not my mum . . . He'd just say, 'Say what comes out of your heart for the occasion.' He'd get me to do it and say, 'Not high enough.' He was the one who got me going . . . [he taught me to choose the words appropriate] for different occasions and the feeling you have for the person who died or how close that person is. When you are taught in a culture, if you know what you are talking about, it just automatically comes . . . I even learnt medicine from my uncle – like flax for different things, mingimingi [a divaricating native shrub] to clear a woman out after birth. He taught me how to collect and boil them. We used to go with him to collect it and he used to talk about it. Boiling was my job, anything to do with boiling water. I was to prepare hot water and to prepare the medicine, put it in jars. He'd tell us why he was doing it, why you picked the young branches instead of the old ones, why you used this instead of that. Explanation is important where medicine is concerned because it's other people's lives . . . He always said, [take leaves and bark from] 'tēnā taha' [that side], always the north side [of the tree], . . . perhaps because of the sun. When we picked the mingimingi, he always said that and he said it was because of the sun. The boiling was done outside, [on] a special fire, not where you cook your food. You prepare it outside: he took his own pot.
> *(Priscilla Manukau)*

While they were living in Mangapēhi, Priscilla's father delivered babies for his relatives.

Someone would run and get my father when a woman was about to give birth. He used to take me to keep the water boiling. I was always thankful – through it I learnt to deliver babies. I delivered my two sisters' babies. It was a learning thing. Because I used to go with him a lot, you just automatically picked it up, especially seeing it happen. My father delivered babies for aunties because he was an older person, in his sixties. Māoris had different methods of delivering babies to white people. There's no embarrassment. The woman is kneeling and you kneel in front of her. You count the pains, you time them so you would know when to apply your knee. You put your arms round the woman and bring her forward against your knee at the same time . . . I think you've got to earn respect for women to trust you . . . My father always thought women ought to learn and young girls ought to go to births . . . He'd never say anything there. If the birth was close by we'd walk and on the way home I'd ask questions. He'd get me to tie up the cord and later I'd ask, 'Why didn't you just cut it?' *(Priscilla Manukau)*

Valued as a weaving tutor in adulthood, Priscilla learnt to weave flax from her mother.

I used to hang around when my mum was weaving a kit at night . . . My sisters, they were allowed to go and do something else . . . I was the nosey one looking at her, she made me sit down and learn. I learnt from her. I'm glad now. It's terrific too – when I take a class, I set rules down, how I was taught. With any flax work I make sure there is respect. I make sure where we work there is another table where we eat. There's sense in it, so food won't get caught up in the flax [and attract mice]. I learnt piupiu, tāniko, kete, whāriki, all that from my mum, and korowai. A lot for someone who would prefer to look for a boyfriend . . . All the weaving I learnt was done in flax, including tāniko. I have a flax bush out the back from the old homestead. I wanted something of my mum's. *(Priscilla Manukau)*

Far from being the firstborn, Nikora Atama was the second youngest in a family of nine. According to his mother, his father identified him while a child as the one who would take over his knowledge and role as family head, in spite of the fact that he was a harum-scarum child. His father steadfastly refused to tutor Nikora in whakapapa and whaikōrero until he was fully adult, but he prepared the ground for later learning by taking Nikora with him when he visited the sick and dying and when he attended tangihanga, on condition that Nick kept absolutely silent. As a result Nick saw and heard much that was unusual for children of his age. On one occasion he was present at a deathbed.

> Dad was a very social man, he helped everybody in Pawarenga . . . He was a Maori Warden and he had to go out a lot. When the old people died, all they asked for was Dad and a lot of these times I used to go with Dad. And we would get to the house . . . he would go into this room and do whatever he does. One particular night [an old woman] was dying, on her last breath, and she called for Dad. It was raining, thunder and lightning. This man came down and asked for Dad. I was about twelve . . . he took me, he wanted me to go with him. So I went into the room with him and it was the most frightening experience I have ever had. *(Nikora Atama)*

Chosen as Kai-tiaki

The kai-whakauru also reported cases in which kaumātua selected young relatives when they showed the signs of special ability and/or readiness to be the recipients of the special knowledge the pūkenga held in trust for the family.

> VI: My uncle Pat, my father's uncle, chose the ones he wanted and tutored them. He took my dad. He had three boys and one girl, which I thought was odd but no one ever told me why . . . He took the girl from one family and the boys from three other families.

He took them and taught them. They went and lived with him in Pōrangahau. JOE: I can only remember my grandmother; she nursed most of us. We lived with her or she lived with us. She never stayed in one place. She lived in Gisborne but did the rounds . . . VI: Our grandmother did the same . . . JOE: The older brother – he was the one she took, the one who had more to do with her. I was never taken, never went with her, I was way down the ladder, I was too young to go . . . It [grandparents taking their eldest grandchild] wasn't a rule as such, but it was accepted – trying to bind the parents back into their parents so they will keep coming back, giving such a link that it doesn't break. *(Joe and Vi Matete)*

In these cases aptitude and thirst for learning were even more important than direct descent.

My grandfather's brother was a great fisherman. He had a whaleboat that he used to row out almost out of sight of land. He knew all the grounds but he didn't impart his knowledge on to his son for some reason or other. He wouldn't, and not many people knew exactly where these grounds were. But my Uncle Jack, he often went with him and he was shown or told about some of these fishing grounds. There is a case of a guy who wouldn't show just anyone, yet he was the most knowledgeable person of the area as far as fishing grounds go. *(Hapi Potae)*

In George Parekowhai's family it was believed that ancestors with specialist knowledge and skills played a part in choosing descendants to inherit their gifts.

In Māori belief in some parts of education – whakapapa is one and art is another (that is, carving and weaving and tukutuku and waiata) – some of these formal skills, they come largely from a particular spiritual attitude with the past. Certain skills, one can only achieve that by a particular attitude of mind. This argues against

Piaget's theory of learning. Nevertheless, the old people would say, if you are the right person and if you have the right frame of mind, you'll be gifted with that information. As far as art is concerned, unless you were chosen to be that craftsman, if you don't acquire that particular frame of mind, the skills will pass you by. That's an attitude to learning that wasn't taught to me specifically but it was certainly extracted out of the input of learning from home.
(George Parekowhai)

Teaching Adult Learners

Pūkenga recognised as repositories of special knowledge might in certain circumstances share aspects of that knowledge with chosen children but they often held aspiring learners at bay for years until they were fully adult. A pūkenga's decision to accept a particular individual as a student was based in the first place on their descent from key ancestors but also on evidence of maturity, mental capacity and humility (whakaiti).

In most of the iwi to which the kai-whakauru belonged, tikanga decreed that preference be given to the eldest in a sibling set and that, even when they had mastered the required skills, young men and women should not display them in public as long as their parents and older relatives were alive to represent the whānau. These tikanga were however sometimes set aside in particular cases, for example, if the eldest in the family was unwilling or incompetent, if a younger sibling was more gifted or more determined in pursuing instruction, or if the teacher himself directed the learner to perform in carefully chosen situations as part of their training. Significantly, a number of the kai-whakauru who had been chosen for special teaching were not mātāmua (firstborn) in their family. Nikora Atama (for example) was nearly the youngest in his sibling set.

The men, you weren't allowed to mihi [make a formal speech of greeting] if your father's alive, your uncle's alive, your older brother's alive. Say I'm the youngest in my family, if you were to go through tradition I would never get up. When I first started, that is what they said to me, that rule was lifted in Kaikohe. I'm not sure whether it was the 1930s or the 1940s, but it had been lifted . . . by the tribes like Ngāti Kahu, Ngāpuhi, Te Aupōuri and Te Rarawa, the old people when they were alive. *(Nikora Atama)*

Nikora commented that he didn't think his generation would have gone on with their learning if that rule had not been lifted (hīkina), but he continued to adhere to current teaching that a man should not stand up to speak on the marae until his father told him to.

Karanga
As a noun, 'karanga' (call; see Glossary) has a special application in the distinctive chanted speech that women use when fulfilling certain ceremonial functions. Best known as the call of welcome with which women representing the hosts invite visitors to enter the marae, it is also used for other purposes: by visiting women in reply, to acknowledge the presentation of koha, to honour achievement and to speed departing guests. The kai-whakauru remembered that in their growing years this ceremonial call was reserved not only to women but also to older women, especially those of kuia status.

> When I was taught they told me that it was tradition, classic, a woman never karanga'd until their mother, aunties or aunties' cousins or mother's cousins, until they die. So, in other words, it's just impossible for a young woman to karanga.
> *(Nikora Atama)*

The karanga must only be done by an elderly woman. She's unique because she's the wahine karanga . . . Even people like Lena, her age group, tremble a bit when asked to karanga. It seems to me that karanga should be given not just to anybody but to somebody who is trained that way. *(Hone Pirihi)*

Ideally, a community had several kai-karanga who worked together as a team. It was the responsibilty of current kai-karanga to choose and train younger women to succeed them. They quietly observed a likely candidate over a period of time, then they invited her to stand with them on actual occasions and learn by listening to what they were saying and how they said it. In the course of a long apprenticeship, they moved her on in stages, beginning by directing her to call basic phrases in unison with them, then to call on her own when only family were present, until they literally 'gave her the nod' to call with them in unison and on her own, as part of the team.

Although the proper approach to the role of kai-karanga was through this formal training, women sometimes found themselves thrust into the role by circumstances, in which case years of listening unexpectedly came to their aid.

The kai-whakauru insisted that the karanga was the women's form of speechmaking. Rose Pere told me: 'I can say anything on the marae that a man can say – I just have to remember to hold my notes'. Like whaikōrero, karanga required a deep and sophisticated knowledge of te reo Māori, tikanga and inter-group dynamics. In their karanga of welcome, the kai-karanga did not simply invite visitors to enter the marae, they also supplied them with vital information: the names of the local hapū, its leaders, landmarks, marae and whare hui, and the purpose of the hui. According to Rose Pere, who travelled widely and often acted as kai-karanga for visiting groups, the karanga made in reply to the hosts' invitation should include greetings to the mountains and the marae, a poroporoaki (see Glossary) to the dead, and information about the identity and membership of the visiting group. The exact wording depended on the occasion.

It depends on how I am feeling, how I'm related to the people and the marae. I always prepare myself beforehand kia mau tonu te mauri me te mana, to ensure those things that are important are protected [from harm]. *(Rose Pere)*

Talking about what was currently happening in kura kaupapa Māori schools and bilingual whānau units, several kai-whakauru expressed reservations about the practice of teaching children to karanga.

I'm against children doing the karanga and the pōwhiri like now, which seems to be a common practice. Looking back on what we did [as children], we didn't handle the karanga but we were taught a waiata [to use instead]. When we had a visiting rugby team or whatever, we still stood and gave them a little bit of a mihi.
(Hapi Potae)

However, they accepted that teaching children to karanga was perhaps necessary when the language was under threat. Hineari Babbington was confronted with this problem when she was appointed as an Itinerant Teacher of Maori in a circuit of Wairarapa schools.

When I came into this job I was a bit concerned about some things being taught, in particular about the karanga. So I consulted with Ngoi Pewhairangi and with one of our kaumātua, and they both said the same thing: out of desperation we've got to start training our children now. The onus is on us to make children realise that it isn't just a thing we do any old time, they are privileged people who do it. *(Hineari Babbington)*

At a wānanga weekend for Taranaki people living in Auckland, Sonny Waru was teaching young girls, high school age and some who had just left, the art of karanga. They practised out in the paddock and they practised when they came in to us. That was very, very good. I thought it was wānanga at its best. *(Hone Pirihi)*

Tangi

The kai-whakauru used the noun 'tangi' to refer to the keening cry with which the women of their communities mourned the dead during tangihanga and on ceremonial occasions. The tangi might or might not include words. Like the karanga, the tangi was reserved to women and appropriate occasions. It was neither taught nor practised. Women familiar with the sound of the tangi in childhood simply found it welling up within them in a time of loss.

Whakapapa, Whaikōrero and Associated Arts

The kai-whakauru who had sought tutoring in whakapapa, whaikōrero and the associated arts of mōteatea and whakataukī reported that it took years to attain competence, let alone excellence. Nikora Atama and New Amsterdam Reedy, both of whom had reputations as effective exponents and teachers of these arts, spoke about their own learning at length and with passion. Their accounts reveal not only the difficulties and rewards of such learning but also the differences between their circumstances and experiences.

Growing up in Pawarenga, Nikora Atama was exposed, along with the other children of the community, to endless storytelling focused on key ancestors and the local environment. He picked up a lot about the tikanga of the marae by being involved there during and between hui, but his father, Topia Atama, resisted Nikora's requests to teach him whakapapa and whaikōrero for many years. By the time Nikora had sowed his wild oats, served a stint in the army, married and settled down in employment as a family man, he was into his thirties. Then and then only did his father agree to teach him whakapapa.

To begin with, Nikora said, his father gave him only five names ending with his own (Topia) as the fifth. When Nikora had learnt those five by heart, his father gave him another five, including the wives.

Then he added a few more, going further back, and so built the genealogy up until Nikora could go back to Nukutawhiti and beyond. When his father had taught Nikora all the whakapapa he knew, he sent him to his uncle. Nikora and his wife Moana took a week off and went and stayed with this uncle. Nikora and his uncle stopped only for meals and slept only four hours or so the whole time. The old man was so exhausted he ended up in hospital – or perhaps, Nikora thought, he knew he was getting sick and wanted to pass on his knowledge while he could.*

Nikora also recalled pestering his father to teach him how to mihi for about ten years. When his father finally agreed,

> Moana and I used to come to his place, . . . Mum and Moana used to go to housie, . . . Dad and I would be in here, the lights are off, the TV's off, put the kids down first and we'd sit in the sitting-room, and he would get up and mihi. We would talk about different subjects, like a mate [death] or an unveiling. He would get up and he'd mihi to whatever subject we're on, then he sat down. Then he'd say, 'This is how you do it.' Then I would get up and mihi. I'd practise with him . . . He would stop, he would go out and growl somebody and come back and he'll carry on. He'd never go off his subject that he was doing. Whatever he taught in all that, I never wrote it down. It was 'whakaako te māngai' [the mouth teaches] . . . When you are mihi'ing he says to be precise, come to the point and never beat around the bush. That's how he first taught me, for a long time, like years. And then he turned round and he says I'm being too abrupt; make it smooth and nice so you don't hurt people. So again we practised that one. . . .
>
> As soon as I get it, then we go on to tauparaparas. Once he'd taught me tauparaparas – he taught me a heck of a lot – and then from

---

* The information in this paragraph was conveyed in conversation and recorded later.

there, he used to stand up and mihi, and he uses the tauparaparas and he connects [the tauparapara with the occasion]. He says to me, 'The mihi will be on – a birthday.' I say, 'OK.' He says, 'You've got to use a specific tauparapara for a specific date. Is that OK?' At the time I didn't know what the heck he was talking about. So he would get up and use a tauparapara but he would connect different tauparaparas to suit the purpose. And it used to be blinkin' hard. It's hard to rip one up and connect it to suit the purpose... I found it was very, very hard until he said to me, 'Just go to the maraes and listen.' I picked up a few things from how he used to carry himself; he was a great orator as far as I was concerned....

At the time he wouldn't let me stand on the marae. Till the day he said to me, 'Well, the next hui we go to, you are going to get up.' 'Oh!' and I was panicked: 'I'll show you, you old brute, what I can do!' ... When he said I was ready, I was thirty-six ... He said, 'Never ever stand in Auckland. You go home and start from home.' So I went on the marae at home, we had a mate [death] there. I sat beside him. Then he nudged me: 'You get up.' I got up and I only said three words, he told me to shut up and sit down. My goodness, I felt a big joe. I sat down. You think he's asleep but he's not. He's got his head down and his eyes closed and he's talking. He says, 'You don't say this, and you don't say that.' I say, 'OK.' So he gets up and he corrects it, corrects my mistake. Halfway through the night he says to me, 'OK. Start to mihi.' Up I got. When I was halfway through my mihi he told me to sit down before he kicked my backside in; so I sat down. And my second time I said, 'I'll never stand up again.' I said, 'You go to hell! A man's just getting up!' He said, 'If you don't do this, the next time I'm not going to tell you, I'm going to kick you!' So, about two o'clock in the morning, the mihis are still going, people are still mihi'ing, and he gives us a nudge. I got up again. This time I thought I was home and hosed; just about finished and pow! he kicked my backside, told me to sit down. So I sat down and that was it. When I sat down, during the day when he told me to stand up, I walked out. I went outside, I sat outside, I thought, 'That's not how he taught me!', so I went back in the hall again, sat with him. He nudged me again so I get up. This time he never stopped me; a fourth time, he never stopped me. We came home, and he blew me up. He said he didn't stop me because of what I did, I walked out. He said, 'You never made a mistake. But had you made a mistake I would have kicked your heart out.' I said, 'All right.' From then on he made me get up and just say little things, short mihis but different all the time. I progressed along like that and I got to know how to mihi. He said to me, 'Don't get a big head, your head will always be the same size, but never get it big. Now stop your mihis and go and find something else from other people.'...

When he was bedridden I was the only one that could understand him because he was speaking in classic Māori. Very, very classic Māori. When he was bedridden, he said to me, 'You take my place while I am in bed. I'll never be the same.' That's how I really got into mihi, oratory, and into my Māori. I knew my dad was going. I had to learn while he was alive, and I had to learn while he gave me his blessing. This is why now, when I get up on a marae, I am very confident of myself, because of what he said, because I know that he is always with me when I am mihi'ing. Sometimes I just don't know what I have said. People will say, 'Hey, beautiful!' and I just don't know what I have said. I always believe that he is always behind me, and that gives me a lot of encouragement on mihi. *(Nikora Atama)*

After his father told him to go to other experts, Nikora approached Haimona Puhiriri for further teaching. Haimona was an old man, a great-great-grand-uncle to Nikora; he died in his nineties. Haimona began by telling stories, short stories with a mystical element, for example, about the ancestress of Ngāti Hine giving birth through her armpit. When Nikora asked why certain things in these stories happened, he explained that they were the result of tohunga punishing insults or offences against the people.

> Then I said to him, 'Why are you telling me these things?' He said, 'Because when your father sent you to me, it's deeper than mihis that you want. I am telling you these things to see how you take it and how you believe in it . . . I know that you have it, that you want it.' So he taught me, taught me, as I say, going into tapu things, teaching [the same way] as Dad. I never was taught by just sitting down and saying it but I was taken through the procedures: 'This is how you do it, that's how you do it, you walk this way.' He and I are walking together, he's holding my hand. Tokotoko [walking stick] in mihi – he would take a tokotoko and he would hold it. He says, 'This is the type of mihi you would mihi when you are holding a tokotoko that way' . . . When I grab a tokotoko and I hold a tokotoko like that [demonstrating], that's exactly how he put my hands there . . . That's a different type of mihi, this way a different type . . . This way is peace; both your hands are locked, you are holding your mana and you are holding your people up, that's peace. That way [demonstrating], you are trying to taunt people. This way, from your right, you are telling them where to go, you are the chief. By pointing to the top, you are whakaiti'ing yourself. When you come down, you never come from the front [because] people are sitting there. And you never point your tokotoko at a person, because you are belittling them. So when you come down you always come pointing to where they go and then down to the ground. You must end up there. And the way they taught me, exactly how you hold it, they show, show you how to use it . . . Any time that you are mihi'ing, your tokotoko must not get away from you, because [they said] once that points to the cloud, you'll drop it. And ten times out of a hundred, you will. I wouldn't know how, but it does. *(Nikora Atama)*

When it came to learning tauparapara and apakura to introduce and complement speeches on the marae, Nikora explained:

> Everything I was taught, Joan, it was never written down. It was from māngai to māngai. They go through the thing once, then they would explain it to me, what it's all about . . . It would take them about half an hour or an hour to explain the meaning of the whole thing and why they are to do for a certain occasion and for what occasion they are to do. Half an hour to an hour. When they finish, [they] go through it again and then they say, 'That's for your ears.' When they are finished, they go through the rangi [tune]. They would say the rangi so we could catch it, the note, the tune of it. And once we catch it with our ear, then they would say it, probably say it about four times: the fourth time is for your ears. When they finish, they would say, 'Na, ki a koe' [Now, over to you] . . . If you say two, three lines, or four lines, they would say, 'You've got it.' They leave you alone. I used to sit there and tremble, because I know within myself I haven't got it. But you'd be surprised. By the time you get up in the morning, you've got it alright . . . When I get up in the morning and I know I've got it, I'll write it straight in my book. I knew after that, whatever they teach me, I wouldn't forget, but I wanted to write it down for my children, my nieces and nephews, for whoever would be interested in these things when they get old.
> *(Nikora Atama)*

When I asked Nikora whether his old people taught him on his own or with others, he explained:

> At one stage there was about five of us. Sometimes I would go to Puhiriri's place, there's some other people there and they included us in. Sometimes Dad, he'd have somebody else here and we'd all go through with him. Not many people can stick to it, they get lost. At one stage there was five of us, and if one would make a mistake,

they would just take time. If you were a quick learner, which I was, ... I would just have to sit there and come up with the rest. There was no such thing as you keep going ahead while the rest come up.... When it comes to apakura, you would notice a lot of women, old kuias, they would come in and teach apakura, more than the old men did. *(Nikora Atama)*

New Amsterdam Reedy came from a prominent Ngāti Porou family, trained as a school teacher and in the early 1980s was a lecturer on the staff of Wellington Teachers' College. Early in 1982 I sat in on a two-hour session he conducted teaching the long and difficult Ngāti Porou mōteatea 'Pō! Pō!' to students in the Māori Studies stream. When I spoke to him afterwards, he confirmed my intuition that he modelled his practice in teaching mōteatea on his own experience of learning under Ngāti Porou mentors like Pine Taiapa and his uncle Wi Pewhairangi. Reflecting on this experience, he insisted on the importance of the personalities of teachers and students and the quality of the personal engagement and communication established between them. He had vivid memories of his own teachers.

Pine the carver, while we had sessions with him, again it wasn't so much the voice, though I can still hear him, it was his personality and how he put things across that was important and which helped me to retain things in my mind. Pine, of course, was a great orator, a great speaker; he also used to be regarded as an eccentric. You never forgot anything he taught you. You never doubted the value of things Māori, just by his very attitude. My uncle Wi, Wi Pewhairangi, his specialty was in mōteatea, waiata tangi [laments]. His knowledge of waiata tangi was unsurpassed in my hapū and possibly in the whole of Ngāti Porou. To hear him sing mōteatea as well as to talk about mōteatea was a real experience because he's only one step away from the greats of our sub-tribe Te Aitanga-a-Māhaki. Again his approach was direct, oral. Pine would be very instructional, dramatic, forceful, whereas my uncle Wi would be very, very analytical... In a teaching situation, where we would talk about mōteatea, whakapapa, Māori tradition, you not only saw them at close quarters in a kitchen or study but you also had the experience of seeing these men orate on the marae... Indirectly they were teaching me when they were on the marae, though they were talking at huge gatherings like a tangi or a hui. I'd follow them through both kinds of situation. Again the personality is the important thing that seems to stick out, because they affected not only me but so many people; these [two] could move audiences. They were teaching, and everybody learnt from them. Their reputations live on because of what they were like. Uncle Wi – his method of reciting whakapapa varied from taotahi ['single spear'] to whakanohonoho [naming spouses]. He'd pick an ancestor like Kahungunu – Ngāti Porou have seven or so lines that they trace from Kahungunu – and he'd say to me, 'You go away and learn these', like that, and he'd give me some time, and I'd come back and I'd always have learnt the lines. He was astounded. Here was this inspirational [encouragement] from my own uncle. Without any doubt I saw that he treasured the whakapapa and when it came to learning whakapapa and even waiata, I would do it in half the time that he asked of me. I think that is important for a teacher, when he inspires, if he can inspire and gain the confidence of his pupils... it seems to open a whole lot more of the senses that are involved in learning. I feel that you learn by touch, by feel, by sight. When I think of Pine Taiapa, I could just about draw every line on his face, I was ever so close to him. And the same with my uncle Wi. Everything about them, not only their personality but their physical make-up, I can still see them. This is the closeness, the intensity that the relationship developed as the time went on....

My Uncle Wi, Uncle Wi Pewhairangi, the learning of mōteatea, that was his specialty. He knew that I was keen to learn. He would take me into the sitting-room, make sure there was no one, no traffic around. We would sit there, I would sit beside him rather than facing him and he would sing a waiata, and then he would talk about it . . . in general terms, explaining the composition. He'd make a very important point, who taught him also. He would recite certain phrases in the waiata, anything of historical interest. This is on the basis that I knew Māori of course, and that he knew I wanted to learn. He would talk about various facets of the waiata that belonged to the family, any genealogies, any whakapapa, any related information to the whole of the waiata. And then I'd listen to him [sing it] again. He gave me instructions to learn the text. The simple method was this, to go away and learn that waiata. I wouldn't see him for a week, two weeks, sometimes a month, depending on when I could get back from working in Whakatāne to the East Coast. The message was, learn the waiata. And the technique of course – he actually told me that 'This is how you learn. A waiata is written [i.e., composed] in how we speak Māori. Learn them in sentences: Pō! Pō! E tangi ana tama ki te kai māna!' He would never say, 'Pō! Pō! E tangi.' This is the important thing in mechanical learning, learn them in [meaningful] phrases. Of course he would speak in Māori: 'Me pēnei te whakaako i te waiata, i te rārangi kōrero: Pō! Pō! E tangi ana tama ki te kai māna! Kua mōhio koe ki tēnā rārangi, ka heke mai ki te rārangi tuarua.' He said, 'Once you have learnt one line, go on to the next line. When you've learnt the next line, always go back to the first line, ka whakaheke [carry on] right through, the whole way.' And the test was that he would ask me, 'Kua akona koe i te waiata rā? Have you learnt that waiata?' I'd say, 'Yes' and he said, 'Waiata mai!' He'd listen, listen as I waiata'd. If he disapproved, he would screw up his face. If he approved, he would nod his head and grunt with satisfaction. . . .

Now the test was not only the sitting-room but there came a time when I had to do this on a marae. By then I hadn't graduated to speaking on our own marae at the front. But in the case of my own father, when he died, I had to sit through and listen to all the whaikōrero, and I'll never forget him saying to me, 'I want you here tonight. This is your father's death, this is the last night, and all the mihi will be directed at you.' And all he taught me, he wanted to see – you know, it was prophetic in a way that I should be put on my mettle that night because of my father. Here I was, I had to show to his people and my people, my uncles and aunts and cousins, what he had done to me as a pupil. In one waiata there I stuck. He had put me up to sing a waiata for him. He had given the speech and then he said, 'E puta mai ki taku waiata!' [Start my waiata!] Of course, he was putting me through the paces then. I sang one waiata there. There was a slight bit of gamesmanship because I knew – he'd taught me so long – he actually forgot a line, he missed out a line in the waiata. And this particular waiata, it's got two lines there, if you don't watch out you can miss them out easily and carry on with the waiata and not know you've left them out. And he sang this waiata one night and I stumbled and he made me stand up later on and I sang it the same way. And [at my father's tangi] I could see him listening to me like this and . . . I could see he was all ready to go on, to miss those two lines out if I did, and when I sang those two lines he gave a smile of satisfaction and said, 'Ka tika tāua' [We two are correct]. I suppose he was building himself up to [impress] these old people with what a good job he'd made of me, but this was the test, on the marae. And what paid off is that now when I sing waiata they say, 'That's Uncle Wi singing.' So I've probably inherited his style, the way he sings. If I've got any mana from singing waiata, it's from him. People have said to me that that is Uncle Wi, 'Ko Wī terā!', that he lives because of me. . . .

Ngata's philosophy was, master the text, and that goes for waiata, for haka, whakapapa is straight out recitation. He could hold you up. He'd say, 'Taihoa! Me pēnei. Wait! Like this.' While you were reciting it to him, he wouldn't growl you then, he'll growl you afterwards. Ngata had no hesitation in growling you if you mispronounced Māori words or Māori place names. If he was leading a waiata, Uncle Wi would have no hesitation in stopping. But he knew, he knew, he had seen it within me that I was going to learn come hell or high water anyway, and he could do anything he liked. He knew that the drive was there, the need, the want to learn was there. But he never stopped learning. His praise wasn't extroverted. I wished he'd pat me on the back. Uncle Wi was always amazed that I could learn things so fast and he didn't realise that he was the one inspiring me to learn. I'd learn a waiata probably within a couple of days when he asked me to go away and learn it, I was that motivated to learn. *(New Amsterdam Reedy)*

Refuting criticism of the repetition and memorisation involved in this method of teaching, Amster said:

I am making the comparison with a great piano recitalist or a great opera singer – the performance depends totally on memory and the interpretation comes from their knowing their subject matter thoroughly. You could use Kiri Te Kanawa as the modern opera singer. First of all, the mechanics of the thing is that she knows the subject matter of the thing thoroughly, and then on the night comes the performance, when after hours and hours of practice and repetition you get a grand performance. It is exactly the same with mōteatea, because no performance of mōteatea is ever exactly the same. Depending on the circumstance, whether it's a tangi, whether it's a hui, a wānanga, or just an ordinary get-together session, that will determine the type of performance . . . Every time we'd have a hui tōpū we'd have these old people there too and they'd teach us a specific waiata. We'd just get stuck in, no discussion, no nothing. They'd introduce the waiata and the emphasis would be on group performance. The same waiata sung at a tangihanga takes on a different aspect – it's not the same. When you sing it as a group performance you are singing it with no [feeling]. I suppose, us being young too, we had some idea of the language but we were conscious that we were performing for the sake of performing. But I know, if you hear a hui tōpū performance and you hear the same waiata sung at a tangi, you notice the change straight away... The learning of things Māori, there probably is a formula, just like there is in the composition of Māori waiata, where you have a basic formula. If you were writing waiata tangi, the metaphors and figures of speech are there for your use, but it's how you use them, in the end, how you are able to create, using those images and metaphors. *(New Amsterdam Reedy)*

Over many years Amster had adapted his own teacher's teaching methods and style to changing circumstances and ultimately to the challenge of teaching students from disparate backgrounds in a state teachers' college. He liked to call it 'the wānanga method'.

I use the term 'wānanga' because it seems to imply the whole gamut of what's involved in learning rather than teaching. To me the word 'teaching' implies, you talk, you instruct, the pupils do what you tell them to do and so on. When I say 'wānanga', I'm talking in a personal sense, where the pupil and the teacher are fairly involved in communicating with one another, not so much through just the medium of instruction, but personalities are involved. We are trying to evoke response between one another. They react not only to my voice but they react also to the personality.
(New Amsterdam Reedy)

In contrast to Nikora Atama and New Amsterdam Reedy, Tawhao Tioke did not himself seek instruction but was sought out for it by his grandfather. Preferring physical pursuits as a young man, Tawhao left home to apprentice himself to a Scottish shepherd on the East Coast. After he and Hurihia married in Gisborne, he took her home to Waimana to live. It was then that his grandfather invited himself to stay with them, as Tawhao said, 'to complete me.'

Granddad was a Mihaia, with Rua Kēnana. He wanted to spend time with Hurihia and me. We had three months together. Every night when his fingers went up, I knew it was whakapapa. I got hōhā. He brought in my elder sister and my mother's sister. They were going faster than me. Granddad was a bit disappointed in me; he brought them in to boost me. I took my time. They got hōhā and faded out. He included Hurihia, he didn't bar her . . . During the three months I spent with Granddad on whakapapa and Māori philosophy, he told me, when speaking on the marae, te kawa o te kōrero is, first you speak to the meeting-house, 'Tāne-whakapiripiri, tēnā koe.' Then you look to the grounds, 'Tūmatauenga, e te umu pokapoka e hora nei, tēnā koe.' [Tūmatauenga, the steam-pit oven lying here before me, greetings.] Then he said, 'E toru ngā umu kei a koe e tuwhera ana. Te umu tuatahi, ko te tutūanga o te puehu. Te umu tuarua, ko te kotinga o te tangata. Te umu tuatoru, ko te kotinga o te kupu kōrero, ka ruia ki te marae. Ka whakakīia ki roto i a Tāne-whakapiripiri, ko tōna kōrero he kupu kōrero kua whakairia ki te pakitara whare.' [There are three umu for you to open on the marae ātea. The first umu is the stirring up of the dust by the feet of the challengers. The second umu is the dividing of the people in two, that is, into tangata whenua and manuhiri. The third umu is the dividing into two of the speeches made on the marae; they are broadcast over the marae ātea. The speeches made inside Tāne-whakapiripiri fill the house and the words of those speeches are hung up on the walls of the house (as a lasting adornment).] He explained 'te umu pokapoka' by saying that 'the marae ātea is like a steam-pit oven; it is no-man's land, a hot seat for both manuhiri and tangata whenua'. That's why Tūhoe never

do certain things [e.g., fighting with words] indoors. They must be done outside, to establish that you come in peace, then you go inside the meeting-house. The second round of speaking [the peacemaking] is conducted inside, bringing warmth to what has been said outside, something personal. I said, 'Why don't we hear this anymore?' He said, 'People are much closer today, so people use Papatūānuku [instead of Tūmatauenga for the marae ātea]. That's why we have a marae ātea, so we can separate from our manuhiris and throw words at each other.*
(Tawhao Tioke)

Tawhao loved and respected his grandfather. In spite of his initial reluctance, he worked hard to learn what his grandfather wanted him to know, keeping a record of their sessions in fourteen exercise books. In later years relatives came to him in search of knowledge, although they were older than he was. In particular, Tawhao remembered and lived by his grandfather's moral beliefs and his example of humility.

He said, the first rule of whakapapa, never call the next person he teina. When I am sitting with high-ranking Tūhoe I never like to open my mouth because of what he said to me, even when they say to me to get up . . . My grandfather used to say, 'In the presence of every generation stand the baskets of their forefathers and they contain much that is good and much that is evil. When you reach for the basket, reach for the good things and leave the bad. The bad

---

* Tūmatauenga, Tū, was the Māori god of war. Using his name to address the marae ātea highlights its function as the place for expressing hostility, fighting with words. Tāne-whakapiripiri is also Tāne-mahuta, the god of the forest. The name Tāne-whakapiripiri describes the way the meeting-house was traditionally constructed using valuable woods, kiekie and harakeke from the forest, bound together by flax cords. Using Tāne's name to address the meeting-house highlights its function as the place for peace-making and binding together the groups who have been fighting on the marae ātea.

things are mākutu and despising people for no reason. The good things are aroha and manaakitanga.' *(Tawhao Tioke)*

These three accounts of learning whakapapa and whaikōrero as adults were amplified by interviews with respected orators Wi Tarei and Cambridge Pani. A minister (tohunga) in the Ringatū Church, Wi Tarei was sought after by young men eager to learn to speak on the marae (Tarei, 1978). The second son in a family of fourteen, Wi had been accepted by his brothers as kai-kōrero for the family. On the subject of teaching whaikōrero, Wi said:

When the old folk taught oratory to young people, they taught it in an atmosphere of sanctity. They weren't allowed to be distracted. My father said the best place [for teaching] was out in the scrub . . . A Māori does not think of these things till about forty, then, when he is neither Māori nor Pākehā, he begins to look back at his identity as a Māori, recognises he has lost something . . . About six I've taught protocol and the fundamentals of speechmaking. I encouraged them, sat alongside them during their maiden speech. I said, 'If there is any criticism, I'll bear the brunt.' They've gone from strength to strength. I give them the word when they are ready. After that they can find themselves . . . Some of the reasons why the elders screen the young people for learning speechmaking and genealogies – they are looking for humbleness in them. I didn't know my father was a good genealogist till I heard him in Wanganui. I asked him to teach me. Father shook his head. He told me it could lead to all sorts of things and worst cause me to be whakahīhī 'because you'll be looking through genealogies where you are the elder.'...

The younger generation come to me to learn oratory. I say, 'No one can teach you the words, only the basic principles. The language is different to everyday Māori' . . . When I started speaking on the marae, I was eighteen. My father was always there. No one ever told me to sit down. But he taught me I was not ready to speak on someone else's marae, only on my own. Only when I was in my thirties was I able to speak elsewhere. My father said, 'Speak! I'm behind you.' If anyone had knocked me back he would have defended me. If you are attacked, sit down and keep cool while others fight it out . . . In Māori families, it is usually the eldest child that gets the brunt of everything. My father was terrible on my eldest brother. I was privileged [that] he took a liking to me, why I don't know. His last words were, 'Never desert the pā and never desert the church. Without you those two things will die.' I rather regret that I left home at sixteen and didn't come home till my thirties. I had a good memory, regained all I had learnt as a child . . . When I was talking to my two uncles they said, 'Leave it to us, we'll support you. We see if a child is whakahīhī or koretake [useless], pick out the ones that are going to be active on the marae.' Not only my father but my uncles took to me. This fear that a child will become whakahīhī is quite real. So they are very hesitant about imparting too much knowledge to a child and so contributing to the child losing confidence. If their parents don't have confidence in them, how can they have confidence in themselves? Perhaps I was lucky getting away. I had to assert my own identity. If I'd stayed at home I would have been under the shadow of the identity of my father and his domination. *(Wi Tarei)*

In 1979 when we spoke together, Cambridge Pani was a leading kai-kōrero for Ngāti Rākaipaka, a northern hapū of Ngāti Kahungunu. A widower, he lived in Nūhaka with a granddaughter of school age. Like previous speakers, Cambridge stressed the importance of humility as a primary qualification for being taught whaikōrero.

Never praise yourself, let other people praise you. Never whaka-papa right down to yourself, only whakapapa to a certain ancestor:

you bring every one else in that way . . . I say to the young ones, praise your friend, not yourself. However, to me, you shouldn't whakaiti [belittle] yourself as far as [public] education is concerned. I'm concerned to teach the moko I have here that it doesn't apply at school. Kaua e whakatoi i a ia. [Don't criticise him/her.]* If he's bright he should carry on whatever his friends say.

I used to sit around with the old people. I sat and listened at tangi. They noticed and asked me, 'Are you listening to what we are saying?' My uncle started teaching me. Those days it was, children should be seen and not heard; you daren't open your mouth. My uncle told me to stand up and talk, because I was interested. They also liked me because I questioned them. I found if you didn't question them they wouldn't tell you anything. Everything I wanted to know I asked and they answered. That's how I got whakapapa and became one to whaikōrero, because the old men taught me and they answered my questions. When I started to stand up all the things they had told me started to come. My cousin Hemi and I are the only ones in the family to speak . . . I was only about sixteen, out working, when they started teaching me. I was eighteen when I first stood up to speak and by twenty I was standing on the marae, though I hadn't got a grasp, but they were happy I was standing up. The first time he said to me, 'Stand up!', I said, 'I don't know how', and he said, 'After a while, all the kōrero will come, it's in the air. It's in the starting, that's the hardest.' Uncle taught me to whakapapa in the house back of the marae. They used it as a wānanga. Early in the morning he'd light a candle. He would quote and I had to follow. I have never forgotten whakapapa taught that way at that time. He told me far more, to look at the book; again, the starting is the thing. The only thing I didn't take much to was the singing. I have never showed my books to anyone but Hemi. We were taught

---

* In Māori, 'ia' covers both 'he' and 'she'.

that way, that the books are tapu to you. I quote whakapapa to my mokopuna, though she is a girl, without restrictions, so she'll know who she is, not to go speaking on the marae. . . .

Whakapapa – I always know the occasions when to bring it to myself and when to stop. It depends on the occasion . . . Another thing my pakeke told me – when you go into a marae, in the South Island or the North and you see the name on the meeting-house, know it and see the connection, and when you stand up you quote whakapapa connecting you with them. Or if they name their tribe and tūpuna, you quote whakapapa to connect. Then the tangata whenua will know who you are. Then the tangata whenua on the paepae will make a gesture, a cupped hand away from the head like a wave, meaning 'I understand' . . . When their speaker stands up afterwards, they recognise you all the time, talk a lot about the fact that you are a descendant of those tūpunas, find a lot of things to talk about. *(Cambridge Pani)*

Cambridge quoted the following saying of his old people: 'Kaua koe hei noho, e tū, kia tau tangata. Ka kore koe e tū, ka pēnei koe i te pikao moko nei.' [Don't just sit there, stand tall like a proud man. If you don't stand up, you will be just like a speckled hen.]

Handing Knowledge On

From the preceding accounts of learning as adults, it is clear that the pūkenga took their time about passing on the knowledge they held in trust, including what they had learnt from their own experience. The whole process lasted for years and often resulted in a special life-long relationship between teacher and learner.

Several of the kai-whakauru referred to a traditional belief that pūkenga should not teach everything they knew but 'always keep something back'. If they did not, it was said that they would lose all or part of their knowledge store.

> Old Man Tio, he had a family tree, and he didn't want to give the family tree out, because the knowledge he had, if he had given it out to anybody, he would have lost all the knowledge he had.
> *(Wiremu Hohaia)*

> I was always told that by teaching everything they are taking everything out of you. One day you look at them and you see yourself – all your skill has gone to that person and you have nothing left. In piupiu dyeing I always use commercial dye when teaching and yet when I'm doing it myself, not teaching, I still use tea-tree and paru [the traditional mordant and black dye].
> *(Priscilla Manukau)*

While they suspected that some kaumātua hugged their knowledge to themselves for reasons of mana and status, the kaiwhakauru with personal experience recognised that there were good reasons why pūkenga placed limits on what they taught, when and to whom. In the first place, pūkenga were trustees with a responsibility to protect the knowledge they held from dilution, misuse and misappropriation.

> The old folks had a tradition to believe that so the medicine will cure, it's best not to give it out. That's their tradition, that's their belief. I did ask them once, the old people, and I didn't ask them again. But this is what I asked them: 'If you knew these things and we don't know, how are we to know?' And this is what they say, that 'We can't pass too many things on because we will lose the power of that medicine.' *(Wiremu Hohaia)*

Learners' accounts of the process of adult learning establish that pūkenga routinely paused in their teaching from time to time to test their students and make sure they understood and properly valued what they had learnt. Nikora Atama recognised that withholding the most tapu items of knowledge was designed to protect students from the dangers attendant on mistakes and misuse.

> One thing I wanted them to teach me and they never did, I got left behind, was Hinenuitepō's whakapapa. I went as far as Kupe down to me and that's all. As far as Hinenuitepō was concerned, they said I was too young to learn – and I was in my thirties! I said, 'How old do you have to be before you learn that?' 'Oh', they say, 'when you hit sixty, seventy!' I said to them, 'It's no good to you, you are half dead already!' They said, 'No. That's because the brain doesn't take it in.' *(Nikora Atama)*

George Parekowhai suggested that it was those pūkenga who failed to keep learning themselves who exhausted their knowledge if they gave it away.

> In traditional times when the kids were all in the community, they'd return to the fountains of knowledge, the punawai kōrero, and the fountain would keep displaying and playing. At some time the fountains were unable to provide anything more. I've seen old people in the community, some kaumātua who have exhausted their learning, and of course the learners have gone elsewhere to get progress and get newer insights and more information, and the discarded elder just shrivels up and dies, having no further contribution to make. *(George Parekowhai)*

Much in demand as a weaving tutor in South Auckland, Priscilla Manukau emphasised the importance of not being too responsive to student demands.

That is how I teach. I demonstrate. At every [Maori Women's Welfare] League meeting we have some Māori art. I demonstrate enough for learners to get it and really work on it. They are at the stage where they go home and think about it, try it, then they get stuck and ring me. When they ring I know they are really trying. They say, 'Why don't you take longer [and teach us everything]?' I say, 'If I did you'd think you know it and go home and forget it.'
(Priscilla Manukau)

A leading weaver and teacher of Te Rarawa cast further light on the subject when she said that she taught the learners in her weaving class all the basic techniques and patterns, but at some point she stopped answering their questions and insisted that they work out for themselves how to handle the difficulties they encountered. However much she taught, there was one thing she would not and could not pass on and that was her own creative spark. The best thing she could do as a teacher was to encourage her students to develop their own.*

Whatever their reasons, wise pūkenga always kept something in reserve until the last moment. When the time came they passed it on in an ōhākī or oral will.

GEORGE: My dad was pretty crafty, you would never have time to learn everything he knew . . . The last time we saw him alive was in the August holidays. **ROSE:** We went to Gisborne to see him. We hardly got back from Gisborne than bingo! we found he was shouting for us from Wellington . . . I hadn't even unpacked the bags and we were on our way to Wellington because he wanted to see us all together. **GEORGE:** You know how the history books say that the old people have a premonition or whatever that that's their last appearance. Whether he arranged it for the holidays I'm not

---

* This is a paraphrase of a conversation with a woman who is not referred to elsewhere here, or included in the Biographies.

sure, but it happened that way and he did call us and we did sit around and he did make the traditional ōhākī. It is clear in my mind that that was the last time we would see him alive and he knew it in his mind too, and he told us at that point certain things he'd never divulged before . . . Much of what he said in the ōhākī was in Māori and at one point he said (in which I was quite surprised), he said, 'He matakite tērā o koutou', which is literally, 'That one of you who is not present is a matakite' [a seer] . . . I can appreciate my father having gifts [I did not know about], but I didn't realise that there was in my generation a member who would inherit that gift . . . And, of course, the implication was that despite my better education I would need to consider his point of view and see him as a repository of family tradition as well.
(George and Rose Parekowhai)

Marae Ātea and Meeting-house

As already indicated, it was an almost universal rule when the kai-whakauru were growing up that formal speechmaking on the marae ātea was the prerogative of men, not all men but older men qualified as kai-kōrero by their whakapapa, oratorical ability and inheritance of specialised knowledge. Some iwi widened this tikanga to include similarly qualified women, while others limited the role even further to the oldest male in a whānau. This tikanga was often expressed in English in the formula 'Women are not allowed to speak on the marae' and interpreted by non-Māori as relegating women to second-class status. None of the kai-whakauru mentioned this criticism or its interpretation. When I asked Nikora Atama how his kaumātua had explained restricting women in this way, he replied:

The old people, the kaumātuas said why they let their women sit and not get up and speak – when people get up and mihi on the

marae ātea, there is always somebody rubbishing him or her. If she was a good speaker, there is always somebody to pull her down. So the old kaumātuas said, 'The woman carries two; we don't carry anybody. If they mākutu, there's only one of you gone, but if they mākutu a woman, that's your woman and your child going with her.' That's why they didn't allow women to stand. To counter those mākutus, that's where the tokotoko came in. If you ever see old kaumātuas stand and mihi on the marae, they would stand with their tokotokos, especially a marae they are very new on. There is a reason for that tokotoko. It's not just for showmanship but it is just to safeguard them from tohungas, mākutus, things like that. They say if they do mākutu you, it bounces off the stick or it clings to the stick, it doesn't come to you . . . The stick has mana. A tokotoko has always got a name, a name is what gives it mana. So that is why a woman is not allowed to get up on maraes and mihi. They say, 'Te wahine e rua, ko ia me te pēpē. Kei te mākutungia a ia, ka mate te pēpē. Mehe ko koe i whakamākutu, koe i whakamate. Ko te tāne, kaha tū te mahi o te tāne, te wahine, e rua tana mahi.' A woman is two, her and her baby. If she is mākutu'd, her baby dies. But if you are mākutu'd, only you are killed. It is man's work to stand strong, woman's work is to make two. I think it's common sense.
(Nikora Atama)

While they knew there were other explanations as well, none of the kai-whakauru spelt them out. Those who tackled the general issue of women's status emphasised that most of the older women in their communities were as knowledgeable as the male kai-kōrero despite not having had any special teaching. Discussing how that came about, Hineari Babbington and Hapi Potae remembered the way their grandparents talked together in bed in the early hours of the morning.

HAPI: Because the conversation went on all the time, about different things. They talked about their waiatas, and their waiatas

were involved in love stories [and thus whakapapa]. **HINEARI:** It was not only husbands and wives. My father and his cousins and his sisters, they talked about anything and everything that was going on. I'm sure this was how the women had their knowledge. **HAPI:** You have to bear in mind, too, that older women were on the marae ātea, they were out front. Although they were not directly on the paepae, they were near to it [in the rows immediately behind]. They were there when whakapapa was quoted – people identify themselves through their whakapapa – so they were exposed to all that as much as the men. Although the men went to all these wānangas, the women were the power behind the throne. **HINEARI:** You see women prompting the men when the men are up speaking.
(Hineari Babbington and Hapi Potae)

Nikora Atama pointed out that although Tai Tokerau women did not speak formally on the marae, they knew the songs, stories or whakapapa on which the kai-kōrero drew for their speeches.

You know, a woman is more knowledgeable than a man. They pick up more than men. I hate to say this, but they do. I am only speaking of my grand-auntie and my grand-uncle. Whatever this old man knew my grand-auntie knew, and I'm sure that is where they pick it up, through their ears . . . I am sure that in the old days it was through their husbands that the women got to know it. And women are the ones that's very clear-minded, much longer than the men; well, I've found that. When I was under the tutorship of my uncle in his eighties, his wife was propping her husband. He would go, 'Ko Mea, ko Mea, ko Mea,' and the wife goes, 'Hey! You've missed somebody out, you come back here.' 'Oh, āe, āe', and he goes back. She's listening, she never chips in, but only if he goes off, then she comes in. I think a woman has more part in it than many people would know. A lot of people have pride and they don't like to let on that women in their area do this, they like to say that they do it themselves. Even in Tūhoe there, some of the old kuias know better than some of the men. Up my way, definitely, old kuias know more than these old men. All they do all day is sit there and absorb everything, where men like to get up and blow themselves up and skite 'I'm the big rangatira and that is it!' and they don't listen to nobody. These women sit there and size up everything. Mind you, that is from my own beliefs. When I was learning, like I said, I was all ears. I listened to a lot of these things. I can weigh them up, and sometimes the men are making fools of themselves trying to tell everybody that they know a heck of a lot where some of these women know more than them. *(Nikora Atama)*

Women of kuia status had their own roles on the marae ātea, roles which complemented that of the kai-kōrero. They were good at multi-tasking. Some were kai-karanga. Many had built up a large repertoire of mōteatea and were expert at choosing and starting one which did not merely embellish but added to the message contained in a speech. According to Nikora Atama, 'the majority of the time that I've seen back home, women are the ones teaching apakuras'. They came into the men's sessions on whaikōrero specifically for that purpose. Knowledgeable kuia provided their menfolk with advice and criticism before, after and sometimes during their speeches. Cambridge Pani told me that he sometimes envied women not having to speak on the marae because they saw the whole picture. While he had to concentrate on listening to the previous speakers in order to work out how to respond, his wife heard the kōrero as a whole. When she was alive he always consulted her when he was preparing a speech and she always accompanied him when he travelled to other marae as a kai-kōrero.

Hapi Potae commented that the men of certain iwi were well-known for always travelling with 'a lot of beauties' – kuia with moko (chin tattoos) – to watch over and protect them.

> Waikato do that a lot but I have seen Ngāti Porou do it too. Certain groups of women were renowned for supporting their men. They turned up, they had all the songs, the waiata, to support the men.
> *(Hapi Potae)*

Speaking from wide experience as teacher and observer, Keri Kaa observed:

> We are not just bugles for the karanga. I believe women see themselves in the role of educators about protocol. I learnt this watching my mother on the marae. Like the young man who was so thrilled to be home, he stood up and said he was happy to be home on *his* marae. She stopped him and told him, 'Never say, "My marae". It is always the marae of the iwi.' *(Keri Kaa)*

Keri recalled a friend rebuking a male speaker privately after he breached protocol at a meeting.

> She told him, 'You've got to know what you are doing. I'm telling you because I care.' It's the role of women to fix things up.
> *(Keri Kaa)*

Far from being excluded from discussion and decision-making, older, knowledgable women played an important and often key role in those activities. In most iwi their exclusion from speechmaking applied primarily on the marae ātea. Once speakers and listeners moved inside the meeting-house, older women assumed another of their roles as mediators and peacemakers. They did not necessarily speak formally as often as the men, they often waited till the men had had their say before rising to their feet, and they used humour to make their points and defuse tension and conflict. Even on the marae ātea, they deflated male pretensions with *sotto voce* interjections and ruri, improvised and chanted comments on current events and personalities, and they could force a speaker to cut his speech short by starting a waiata.

As an observer in a community far removed from his own, George Parekowhai summed up the relationship between the senior men and women in words that applied to his own and many other communities.

> In Parekino the kai-kōrero would pursue a line of whaikōrero, and what they were saying depended on the assent of the women there. If the women formed gossip circles, the men backed up. I am sure the women knew as much and were as influential in public gatherings in a way that you would miss unless you kept your eyes open. At Parekino, nothing got done if only the men said it was a good idea. If the women did, it got done. *(George Parekowhai)*

CHAPTER SEVEN

Wānanga

In the late 1940s and 1950s, when I was a university student and the kai-whakauru were growing up, the term wānanga was used almost exclusively in the phrase 'te whare wānanga' to refer to the 'school(s) of learning' reputed to have existed in pre-European times to preserve and transmit sacred knowledge passed down from the ancestors. It was also sometimes used as an unofficial, descriptive name for New Zealand's Western-style universities.

The Traditional Whare Wānanga

The main source of information about the traditional whare wānanga was *The Maori School of Learning: Its Objects, Methods and Ceremonial* by Elsdon Best, a Dominion Museum Monograph published in 1923. In this monograph Best drew largely on the handwritten record of the teachings of Te Mātorohanga and Nēpia Pōhūhū at hui held in Hawke's Bay in the 1860s, endorsed with the seal of the Tane-nui-a-Rangi Committee of Ngāti Kahungunu and held in the museum archives, with supplementary comments by Pākehā writers. On this basis, Best identified the whare wānanga as a formal educational institution dedicated to the preservation and transmission of highly specialised sacred knowledge 'free of any alteration, omission, interpolation or deterioration' (Best, 1959, p.6). The teachers and students of this institution were exclusively male, selected for intellectual capacity and their status as members of high-ranking families. They met in full-time sessions held at certain times of the year in places remote from ordinary life and settlement. Their behaviour was regulated by tapu restrictions (relating especially to contact with women and food), which protected the confidentiality of the knowledge transmitted and punished breaches.

Working among Māori in the 1950s, I heard occasional mention of whare wānanga operating independently in parts of the North and South Islands early in the twentieth century but gathered that they were no longer active. Later I learned that pūkenga from these whare wānanga had lifted the tapu from parts of their teaching and that some had even agreed to publication. For example, after Himiona Kamira, the rangatira of Te Wananga o Tai Tokerau, died in 1953, his daughter Akata Taahana and Tia Waipouri, said to be 'the only surviving member of the waananga of North Hokianga', gave Bruce Biggs, lecturer at Auckland University College, permission to publish Himiona's account of the story of Kupe. It appeared in the *Journal of the Polynesian Society* in 1957 under the title 'Kupe, nā Himiona Kaamira o Te Rarawa' with Biggs' English translation (Kaamira and Biggs, 1957). In November 1970 Eruera Stirling of Te Whānau-a-Apanui, the last student inducted into that tribe's wānanga, recorded 'Te Kirieke Whare Wānanga o Te Whānau-a-Apanui' in Māori on tape.

With the establishment of Māori Studies at Auckland University College in 1952 and Victoria University of Wellington in 1965, Best's model of the whare wānanga came under academic scrutiny. Questions were raised about the provenance of certain teachings in the Tane-nui-a-Rangi papers and in *The Lore of the Whare Wananga* by S. Percy Smith, and also about Best's assertion that wānanga teachings could neither be questioned nor modified in any way. Early fruit of this scholarship was 'The Sources of *The Lore of the Whare Wananga*' by David Simmons and Bruce Biggs (1970) in the *Journal of the Polynesian Society*.

Maori Marsden and Te Wananga o Tai Tokerau

Maori Marsden spoke at length about his personal experience as an initiated member of Te Wananga o Tai Tokerau in one of three interviews on Māori methods of learning and teaching recorded in 1982.* To appreciate Maori Marsden's engagement with Te Wananga o Tai Tokerau fully, it is important to know his family background and numerous whakapapa connections with the iwi of Tai Tokerau. Maori was born into a leading whānau of Ngāi Takoto. A small iwi occupying the shores of Rangaunu Harbour in the Far North, Ngāi Takoto had a close relationship with the Anglican Church dating from the 1830s. Through his parents and grandparents, Maori had whakapapa links with the kaumātua of all the iwi of Tai Tokerau.

> My grand-uncles, of which there were about a dozen, were all lay readers in the church, so they were knowledgeable in the Scriptures and in our whānau we had four Anglican priests and we also had several school teachers who were trained in the Mission Station in Kaitāia and at the school in Awanui ... Most of these grand-uncles and my father's cousins were in general above average in terms of Pākehā education. They all spoke fluent English, they also spoke fluent Māori, Māori being their first language. Many of them had gone away to secondary schools such as St Stephen's, Te Aute and the theological college Te Rau in Gisborne.
> *(Maori Marsden)*

---

* This interview was recorded at the Maungārongo Retreat Centre in Te Kōpuru on the Kaipara Harbour. In editing it I have omitted repetitious passages and slightly varied the order of presentation to make connections clearer. In particular I have relocated the debate about the waka (canoe) Mataatua after his description of wānanga procedures, where it serves as an illuminating example. A text which draws on this interview, edited and amplified with family knowledge, was published in Royal, 2003, pp.xxi–xxxviii.

The Wananga's Early History
Māori began his account of Te Wananga o Tai Tokerau by summarising what he had learned as a member about its beginnings and kaupapa (purpose).

> As far as I can gather, the Whare Wananga o Tai Tokerau originated in the early 1850s because of a general concern at the erosion of Māori culture and its traditions, with the impact of missionary teaching and the tremendous social upheavals and changes that took place in the Bay of Islands, Hokianga and the Kaitāia-Awanui area . . . with the coming of the missionaries and other Pākehās from about 1800 onwards. It was soon realised by many of the tribes that with the many changes taking place, unless some positive steps were taken to preserve their history, their culture, their lore and traditions, then much of what went for Māori culture would be displaced by the Western cultures that were now seeping into the country. It seems as if there were a spontaneous revival of the early forms of teaching . . . and a concerted attempt by all the tribes to begin recording their particular traditions . . . There were also people like Āperahama Taonui who advised against the signing of the Treaty of Waitangi and who began his own wānanga which largely denigrated Pākehā culture and sought to promote Māori religious values in opposition to Christian values, so much so that he was banished from Hokianga and . . . finally settled in the Aratapu area.
>
> It was against this general background that many of the northern tribes decided to form a wānanga with the specific objective of preserving their culture and traditions. So the messages went out through the tribes to appoint the experts from their various tribes, so that they could meet together and begin to collate information that the different tribes had, for instance, regarding the canoes of the North, the history of their own particular tribes, the history of the battles, and also the genealogies of their tribes,

and to have these recorded. The first written records that I have seen myself were compiled in 1857, and it must have taken three or four years for the tribes to organise themselves. So I would put the revival of the wānanga as between 1850 and 1853.

From then on they met regularly, at least twice a year, sometimes three or four times a year. But not only did they meet together as a confederation, representing the various tribes, but they met together in particular areas to collate the work of that area, so that for instance in Te Rarawa men like Wairama Marsh, Teri Puku and Ngakuru Pene Hare had their own small wānangas in which they got together to deal more particularly with their region. Ngāi Takoto, Ngāti Kurī and other segments of the large Te Aupōuri tribe met together, and sometimes in the Kaitāia area elements of Te Rarawa, Ngāti Kahu and Ngāi Takoto because they were so closely related. But the wānanga itself, Te Wananga o Tai Tokerau, comprised one or two official members from the different areas, who together with members from other tribes throughout the North met once or twice a year in order to collate and correlate all this sort of information. . . .

In ancient times the original whare wānanga concerned two main schools: the whare kura and the whare maire. The whare kura was concerned with very much the things we were concerned with in the wānanga, whereas the whare maire was concerned with the more esoteric type of knowledge and with what I suppose you would term witchcraft. But it wasn't witchcraft in the Pākehā sense: it dealt with the occult and the mystic arts.

In contradistinction to the whare kura and the whare maire, the Tai Tokerau wānanga, because of its particular concern to preserve the culture and Māori tradition, evolved its own pattern. It became more the tutorial type of institution rather than the earlier whare kura or whare maire, which were concerned with specialisation in various fields. Whilst our wānanga was to some extent specialised,

it covered a broader field. It included elements from both schools, but the main emphasis was on the whare kura type of lore.
(Maori Marsden)

Early Personal Experience

My own entry into the wānanga resulted largely because from an early age I exhibited interest in these sorts of subjects. When I was young I attended many huis together with my father, and at that time every marae had several elders – kaumātua – and the majority of them were steeped in their culture . . . Later, as I travelled more extensively to various maraes, sometimes with my parents, . . . I began to identify with these maraes, . . . the people in these maraes accepted me as part of themselves . . . That was the background which moulded me and I suppose fitted me for the [Tai Tokerau] wānanga itself when it eventually came . . .

These years were broken by my leaving home to go to Wesley College. Wesley College was a Methodist college and there I met a number of people from the Methodist Church who were elders of the Ngāpuhi tribes as well. There was Eru Te Tuhi who was a Methodist minister and an elder in his own right both in Ngāti Whātua and in Hokianga. There were people like Hira Rogers who during my time had two sons there and was also a visitor to that college . . . As I moved out of Ngāpuhi in amongst the other tribes there were links already established through my schooldays . . .

I left Wesley College and it was my father's hope that I would go to university. At that time I was too young to be enrolled at university, although I had completed my University Entrance and Higher Leaving Certificate, so I stayed home for a year. During that time war had broken out and most of my older brothers, five of them, had gone overseas with the Maori Battalion . . . Even though my father was still alive, he began to delegate a lot of his functions to myself. So I soon found I was speaking on the marae at the early age of fifteen, nearly sixteen. Because two of us in the tribe, from about the age of eight, had been taken in hand by the elders and taught the genealogies of Te Aupōuri and Ngāti Kahu, when I spoke on the marae it soon became apparent to some of the elders at the huis that I had this sort of bent. So three of the elders, relations of my father, approached him to ask me to come on to the wānanga... or at least for me to attend so that they could gauge my reactions. I went to my first wānanga and my main sponsor was a distant cousin of my father, Nopera Otene from Mangamuka. And because my reactions were favourable, Perei Tauhara and Tuki Shepherd from Ngāti Kahu and Nopera Otene decided to initiate me. I am not going to discuss the initiation ceremonies. Anyway they vary from tribe to tribe: the different elders have their own modes of initiation. Sufficient to say that I was put through an initiation ceremony similar to baptism in water. And as I recall, that was the one and only meeting that I had attended when I decided that I would join the Army. So I left home where I was known and went to Auckland and managed successfully to bluff the authorities that I was of age and so I found myself in the Army. *(Maori Marsden)*

Post-war Experience

After the war I didn't attend the wānanga until a couple of years after we had arrived home in 1948. So I began to attend the wānanga when I could. I found at this point that the ranks of the wānanga had been seriously depleted. Many of the faces that had been there in 1940 were now missing. I felt the loss for myself, remembering that one wānanga [session] I had attended in those early days and having come to know some of these elders myself personally...

It was the common practice that a person who felt that death was close or that there was a risk of his dying sponsored an understudy, choosing a younger man from his tribe to accompany him to the wānanga, and when he bowed out it was understood that the pupil he sponsored would take his place as a member of the wānanga. So there was this continuity of a member of the wānanga of a particular tribe. They were the guardians of the lore of that tribe and in a wider sense the guardians of the Tai Tokerau wānanga . . . These elders were fairly careful in choosing who were to be their understudies. They knew all the young men and they knew their attitudes, generally speaking, so they would look for the qualities of humility and integrity and love. These are the qualities they expected in the pupil or disciple they chose, the ones who would best guard and promote the interests of the tribe. A person who took up this position within the tribe as the official representative on the wānanga received status and mana. They could use or misuse their position. So far as my own elders were concerned, they drummed into me the fact that I was to use the knowledge that I received as a means of knitting the members of the tribe together and trying to generate harmony between the various members. One of the tasks that I understood from my association with these elders, especially the three who sponsored me, was that in land matters I was to put the interests of the tribe first, never my own interests. . . .

If you recall, I said at the beginning that it was concern at the erosion of cultural values that had been the main motivating force for the setting up of the wānanga . . . And so the wānanga wasn't open to everyone: it was selective. The tribal representatives were expected to use their discretion in regard to what they imparted but it was clearly understood that they would impart general knowledge, and when promising or interested youngsters came on the scene and showed potential, then they were also expected to move into the deeper levels of the lore of the wānanga. Sad to say many of them didn't do this and so future generations have been deprived of their heritage . . .

The Wananga o Tai Tokerau went into recess in 1958 when Takou Kamira* called a meeting at Taha and Ruka Herewini's home in Mt Albert where he put the proposition to us – there were half a dozen of us left at that time – asking whether we should not go into recess. And we decided at that point to agree, with the proviso that the records of the wānanga should be distributed to the tribes. And so apart from the six of us, where certain tribes lacked representatives we chose people to whom Chairman Takou Kamira could give the books, so that in hope of resurrecting the wānanga we could recover these books and begin again.
(Maori Marsden)

Te Wananga o Tai Tokerau in Action

Now I want to make some general observations regarding the wānanga I attended. It was held at least once a year, sometimes three or four times per year, depending on the circumstances and how urgently the members felt that certain things should be dealt with. The wānanga moved from marae to marae and different tribes hosted the wānanga. It was generally held on the marae and the locals were the ringa wera [workers] who provided meals. We generally met on a Friday evening or a Thursday evening, depending on the pressure of work to be done, so generally it spans over three or four days ... When we met we were welcomed by the hosting tribe, we had a few mihis and then we had dinner. That evening, after dinner, we had Evensong followed by more mihis, then the first session was convened. The person in charge was the Tiamana. During my association with the wānanga the chairman was Takou Himiona Kamira. We had a secretary/recorder: during that period it was Moa Hare or Harris. Takou Himiona Kamira came from

---

* Takou Kamira's formal name was Himiona Kamira. He died in 1953 so Maori's memory was at fault regarding the year.

Mitimiti and Moa Hare came from Rāhiri in between Ōkaihau and Mangamuka.

The normal procedure was this. The chairman outlined the topic for discussion during a particular session and he opened up the subject and then it was thrown open for discussion. A person wishing to speak on the matter would get to his feet and ask permission to speak. At that point he was challenged by the chairman with the words 'Ko wai koe?', 'Who are you?' If the particular case we were discussing was the Ngātokimatawhaorua canoe, of which the captain was Nukutawhiti, it was encumbent upon the speaker to trace his direct descent from Nukutawhiti, otherwise he was not recognised by the chair . . .

If there was any conflict, conflicting or controversial statements made by any speaker, then it was open for challenge . . . A speaker [who disagreed with any point] usually asked permission of the chairman to speak and . . . he was challenged with the same formula, 'Who are you?', 'Ko wai koe?', and even though he was well known to members of the wānanga, he then had to trace his genealogy. And there were enough elders there expert in genealogy to be able to adjudicate whether the recital was in fact correct, and if the speaker made a mistake, then he forfeited his right to speak. If his recital was correct, then the chairman gave him permission and so the debate took place. He gave his version and after he finished then it was thrown open for general discussion. And so other members of the wānanga from other tribes made their contribution. To substantiate your statement not only did you have to know the facts, they brought evidence through the waiata, the karakias, to reinforce their particular contention. Many of these karakia and songs would be known by the various members of the wānanga. And finally, when the discussion had exhausted itself, the chairman would summarise, and then the wānanga members would try to reach a consensus and when that consensus had been agreed to by at least 90 per cent of the wānanga, then that became the official version. And when one session was completed, . . . they moved on.

There were various levels of discussions, various topics. The general historical knowledge fairly common throughout the North – it was felt we could impart that to members of our own tribe, and where it concerned a particular person his genealogy, if he came to you for information. But there were certain karakias that it was understood you did not impart readily. In the final analysis it was left to the discretion of the various representatives to impart what they thought would be of benefit to their particular tribe or to members of it. You can gauge from what I have already said that the wānanga was both a teaching institution and a sharing institution. Knowledge was imparted by your experts in certain fields and other members of the wānanga also contributed if they had something . . . relevant in that particular field. And so, through each one contributing, it was a sharing process. It resembled the tutorial session that has been developed in Western universities. I am grateful for having sat at the feet of the elders of the various tribes, men like Wairama Maihi from Ahipara, Te Rei Puku from Whāngāpē, Takou Kamira from Mitimiti, Ngakuru Pene Hare and old Hepara from the same area, Toki Pangari from the Ihutai area, Nopera Otene, Piri Mokena, Tuki Shepherd, Pereiha Tauhara, Winika Hetaraka, Rekauere, Hira Rogers, Whautere, Ripi Wihongi, old Kemara from Waimamaku, Nika Anihana from Utakura, Brown Muriwai and Ngaronoa Mahanga from Whāngārei, old Boxer Piripi from Ngāti Wai, Riri Kawiti, Moa Tahana, Moa Hare and others too numerous to mention. *(Maori Marsden)*

Debating With a Visitor

Maori's general account of how the meetings of the wānanga were conducted is given vivid life by his story of what happened when he took Dr Maharaia Winiata to one as a guest.*

> I remember taking Dr Maharaia Winiata who belonged to Ngāi Te Rangi [in the Bay of Plenty] to our wānanga in Mangamuka ... I took him as a guest because at that particular meeting we were to discuss the canoes Ngātokimatawhaorua, Māmari, Kurahaupō and Mataatua in that order ... That meeting was scheduled to discuss Ngātokimatawhaorua and Māmari on Thursday evening and the whole of Friday, then the Kurahaupo on Friday evening and Saturday, and the Mataatua canoe on the Saturday evening and the morning of Sunday after the service, and we were to disperse after lunch on the Sunday ... I had warned Dr Winiata that he was not to get up to speak in that wānanga unless he consulted me, and I said he would be allowed to speak if they gave him permission when the Mataatua canoe came up for discussion.
>
> And so on the Saturday evening we began discussions on the Mataatua. The various expert tohungas of the wānanga began to relate their knowledge of that canoe. And at the point at which Toroa and Puhi had their quarrel in Whakatāne, Maharaia said to me 'I disagree' with the Ngāpuhi version. In brief the Ngāpuhi version was that Puhi was the senior and Toroa was junior to him, [whereas] Toroa was the reputed captain according to the [published] books on the Mataatua canoe. I had already introduced him on the first evening and I had asked the wānanga to accept him as an observer because of his interest in the Mataatua canoe.

---

* Maharaia Winiata of Ngāi Te Rangi in the Bay of Plenty graduated MA (UNZ) in 1945, DipEd (NZ) in 1946 and PhD (Edinburgh) in 1952. At the time of his visit to Te Wananga o Tai Tokerau he was employed as Adult Education Tutor at Auckland University College. *The Changing Role of the Leader in Maori Society*, an edited version of his PhD thesis, was published posthumously in 1967.

At that point they had agreed. I had not at that stage asked if he would be permitted to speak and so when he nudged me, I said to him, 'Well, get on your feet and I want you to ask that the secretary not record the discussion until they hear what you have to say on the matter.' And I said to him, 'At that point you will be challenged by the chairman, who will say, "And who are you?" Now, can you trace your genealogy from Toroa down to yourself?' He said, 'Yes.' I said, 'Well, at that point you will trace your genealogy and when you have done that the chairman will ask the meeting whether because you are not a regular member you would be permitted to speak. Unless there is unanimity then you will not be allowed to speak.' 'When he asks that', I said, 'I will stand up and speak on your behalf.' To cut a long story short, he was given permission to speak and he gave the generally accepted version of the controversy between Toroa and Puhi, that is, the version which has been recorded in Pākehā books. I remember at that point where an old man, one of the elders, Toki Pangari, stood to his feet and he said to the chairman, 'Mr Chairman, am I permitted to ask questions of the speaker?' At this point you must realise that Māori logic is different in many ways from Pākehā logic. You'll understand this as I outline the events that followed.

Toki Pangari said, 'First question: was the Mataatua a sacred canoe or was it a food-carrying canoe?' Maharaia said it was a sacred canoe. 'Do you agree, next question, that a canoe can move from its moorings without the karakia or the chants?' 'It cannot.' 'Third question: who held the karakia for the canoe?' Maharaia answered, 'The man or the chief or captain of the canoe', and Toki Pangari then said, 'Final question: If Puhi was not the man of the canoe, how was it that the Mataatua was able to leave Whakatāne and make its way to the North, unless Puhi was both captain and on your own admission holder of the karakia?' Toki Pangari finally finished with these words, 'Well, you Bay of Plenty people stick to your version, we'll stick to ours.'

The point I am illustrating here is that the whare wānanga had its rules of procedure and it had an objective approach. It was concerned with winkling out the truth by various methods, by impartation through the recognised authorities of the day, by debate and discussion, and then through general discussion arriving at a consensus which satisfied everybody as far as possible. Of course, some stubbornly stuck to their guns despite the errors of their position as pointed out by others. The consensus became the official version of the Tai Tokerau wānanga.

The whare wānanga has its own logic, as illustrated above. It is generally accepted in Māoridom that for certain ceremonies, such as taking the tapu off . . . the canoe after launching, a tohunga with his karakia was indispensable, but for navigation and general running the captain and *his* karakia were indispensable. So, accepting this premise, then the logic of Toki Pangari's contention that Puhi was the captain of the canoe was self-evident, and I remember Dr Winiata's comment to me afterwards: he said, 'Well, I have done a doctorate in anthropology and social studies in the Pākehā wānanga, but I can't argue against this sort of logic!' And so I would like to make the point that, from my own experience, the procedure as far as possible aimed at arriving, after debate, discussions and so on, at the truth of the subject under discussion.
(Maori Marsden)

Maori Marsden concluded his account of Te Wananga o Tai Tokerau as he knew it by discussing the form the wānanga might take if it were to be revived. For various reasons, including the greatly increased scope given to the Waitangi Tribunal in 1986, the hoped-for revival did not occur, but Maori Marsden continued to play a prominent part in the transmission of knowledge about Tai Tokerau's history and tikanga at hui, at hearings of the Waitangi Tribunal and in private consultations until his death in 1993.

Maori Marsden and Te Wananga o Tai Tokerau: Comments

Maori Marsden's account of his involvement with Te Wananga o Tai Tokerau is an important contribution to our understanding of a Māori educational strategy that was for a long time veiled in secrecy. Recorded in 1982, his account relates to a particular wānanga operating over a particular time period and should be viewed in relation to wānanga that met in other locations at the same and in earlier times. While it has its origin in one person's experience, that person was widely respected in Māoridom as a pūkenga, knowledgeable in all matters pertaining to Māori history and tikanga.

As described by Maori Marsden, the twentieth-century Te Wananga o Tai Tokerau displayed some features of Best's model of the traditional whare wānanga in a modified form but also incorporated a significant number of new developments. Membership of the wānanga was restricted to adult males descended from the ancestors of Tai Tokerau's several iwi.* Candidates for membership were sponsored by existing members and initiated according to their sponsors' choice of rites. The wānanga met as one body several times a year but members also met on a tribal and regional basis. Meetings of all kinds lasted for three to four days, incorporated weekends and were held at known rather than secret venues, mostly on maraes, but towards the end in private homes in the city.

While the primary aim of Te Wananga o Tai Tokerau was the preservation and transmission of Tai Tokerau history and knowledge to future generations, awareness of the strength of external influences generated a sense of urgency with a particular focus on collection, authentication, consensus and written record-keeping. Far from perpetuating a received body of knowledge unchanged,

---

* Robyn Kamira, who is carrying out research into Himiona Kamira's life and writings, has found the names of women included in his records of wānanga meetings: personal communication.

members of the wānanga engaged in lively debates which tested the reliability of the material presented and achieved consensus by logical argument. They valued the contributions of experts from different backgrounds, treated conflicting versions with respect, and endeavoured to avoid giving offence or hurting others. Far from rejecting knowledge from non-traditional sources, they seem to have brought Christian scriptures, theology and forms of worship into wānanga sessions: Maori mentions Evensong, Sunday services and discussions that drew parallels between traditional and Christian narratives, for example, between Māui's death and the death of Jesus.

Whereas, according to Best, all the teachings of the traditional whare wānanga were kept exclusive to its membership, Te Wananga o Tai Tokerau distinguished between tapu knowledge, which members must keep to themselves (for example, the words of karakia); and general historical knowledge, which members were not merely allowed but encouraged to share with their hapū and iwi. Members were also permitted to share genealogical knowledge with genuine enquirers within their descent groups. Instead of imposing strict rules and sanctions on such matters, the wānanga left decisions concerning them to members' discretion.

Mihi, speechmaking and discussion were governed by the tikanga current in the communities of Tai Tokerau, themselves far from standardised, while certain Pākehā practices were integrated into the wānanga's organisational arrangements. In Maori Marsden's time, management was in the hands of a tiamana (chairman) and secretary. The tiamana was elected to the office by general agreement on grounds of his capacity for administration and the control of meetings. The secretary's main role was that of official recorder, a duty carried out by successive incumbents in beautiful calligraphy in bound books.

Maori Marsden's account of Te Wananga o Tai Tokerau and its history as he knew it raises questions about its connection with the whare wānanga that existed at the time of first contact with European visitors and in the early nineteenth century. In speaking of Te Wananga o Tai Tokerau 'originating' in the 1850s and the tribes 'deciding to found a wānanga' to fight erosion of their culture and traditions, Māori implies that earlier whare wānanga had ceased to exist and that Te Wananga o Tai Tokerau was a separate foundation created to meet new and different challenges.

The way in which Te Wananga o Tai Tokerau (as Maori Marsden described it) combined demonstrable continuities with the past with bold and innovative new goals and practices justifies identifying it as a transformation of the traditional whare wānanga.

Indirect Reports on Whare Wānanga

In addition to Maori Marsden, four of the kai-whakauru reported some knowledge of whare wānanga.

Ephraim Te Paa was one of the workers looking after members of Te Wananga o Tai Tokerau when they met on his home marae in Ahipara. His account supports Maori Marsden's on a number of points.

> When I came back [to Ahipara] in 1929, they had that wānanga throughout this area from Hokianga right through here. They moved around, [meeting] on this marae for instance and in Whāngāpē and in Hokianga and finally a winding-up session in Mangamuka. It was open to the public . . . [JOAN: Did you attend the sessions?] Yes, in the kitchen. [How much did you hear?] A fair bit. [What did the teaching cover?] Te Rarawa, leaving those lines open where the connections to other tribes were . . . The principal authors of the course were elders of Te Rarawa: Takou Kamira from Hokianga, Waru Puku, Okena Hapakuku, Mita Paratene and several others. While they were in session there was an exclusive order. The general public was present but didn't take part, they were there as listeners. Mine was a visual understanding. I was never put through by etiquette [I was never initiated]. I saw these

things happening and you hear things at certain times. I observed and took notes of what must be and what one must do and not do, but it was not direct teaching.

After the wānanga closed, those that took the active part from here had their own little school here. By that time it had achieved the purpose of the wānanga, to unify the general understanding of the whole area. It met for over a year. Unfortunately to me, after the dispensation of that understanding it didn't progress, that was the beginning and the end. Meetings afterward were in the homes and that is where I had my little grasp of the tree, just that little bit, not all of it . . . [There were] several recorders here in Ahipara and in other areas. When the senior lecturers passed on, the records happened to pass into private hands [and] were never dispensed for general information. When they passed on, these records were disposed of as private property, buried with them or disposed of so no one knows where they are. Some were lost in fires.
(Ephraim Te Paa)

Nikora Atama relayed what one of his great-uncles told him about attending a wānanga in Pawarenga. Like Maori Marsden and Ephraim Te Paa, Nikora described how the wānanga was run but discussed the content of the teaching only in general terms.

When he had to go to the wānanga, he'd have to strip, down to nothing, naked, and you weren't allowed to touch women. All the tāne in the whare wānanga, you come home, you are not allowed even to eat kai, touch kai with your hands. That's all the women do, they feed you outside the whare wānanga . . . My uncle went to the last one in Pawarenga . . . They never held it on the marae. This one I know, they held it in an old house . . . they had a special house for it . . . Quite a few from out of the area came to it. All men. The whare wānanga was a place where you learned tapu things. Very tapu. Whakapapa, it was mainly on whakapapa. Of course, tauparaparas, not the tauparaparas that we learn now, the karakias, old Māori karakias, very tapu. Things that you don't just get up and say at any old time. Mind you, of course, you are appointed to it . . . And if you do something wrong or don't carry out their expectations, you are it, the bone is on you. You're gone . . . If I was taught in the whare wānanga I'd swear to you now I wouldn't be sitting here telling you all the things I was taught. No, I wasn't taught in the whare wānanga. *(Nikora Atama)*

On several counts the whare wānanga that Nikora's uncle described was more like Best's model than Te Wananga o Tai Tokerau described by Maori Marsden. Its meetings were held in a house far away from the marae and contact with women and food was prohibited during teaching sessions. These features suggest that it may have belonged to a different network or been held much earlier in the century.

Rose Pere (Tūhoe and Ngāti Kahungunu) recalled her mother telling her that she had learnt whakapapa in a whare wānanga. Rose did not identify its name or the place where it was held.

My mother went to a whare wānanga at the age of eleven, and the main thing she learnt was whakapapa, and she *knew* it. But she never ever spoke about it. The only time she would open her mouth was if someone who was giving the whakapapa made a mistake. She would correct them straight off, even older people than herself, because that is what she learnt . . . She had a terrific memory. When I think of the fact she was so young when she learnt the whakapapa, she still had it. It was a proper wānanga. She said she wasn't allowed to eat food, all sorts of things, and I thought to myself, for such a young person, rigid rules. But she never forgot . . . There were five of them, she told me, and she outlived the other four. *(Rose Pere)*

Chosen for training because of her firstborn status, Rose's mother regarded the whakapapa she learnt as a sacred trust to be used not for personal gain but for the benefit of her people. The fact that there were only five students and that Rose's mother was young and female suggests a situation of specialised teaching, but Rose was adamant that it was 'a proper wānanga' and the restrictions described support that claim. There is growing oral evidence that women *were* taught in wānanga situations. As already noted, the records of Te Wānanga o Tai Tokerau meetings include the names of several women who were attending officially.

Finally, Tawhao Tioke (Tūhoe) told the story of a wānanga that was closed down because students breached the tohunga's rules.

> At one stage Granddad passed me on to his nephew, one of Rua's tohunga. He took me and two cousins to a whare wānanga built by the Mihaia. It was six feet by eight, all ponga trunks lined with raupō and a nīkau roof. It was dark inside, all you heard was the tohunga's voice. One of my cousins played up a bit. We had only three days in it and we were kicked out. Me and the other cousin were keen on it. The whare wānanga was about a mile from the marae, built in the hills. You sat for four hours at a time, you couldn't see a thing it was so dark. My cousin brought a torch and tied it to the roof. We were all expelled. *(Tawhao Tioke)*

It is worth noting that Tawhao associated the term whare wānanga with the use of a special house in the bush.

'Wānanga' Acquires New Meanings

When Best and Smith wrote about the traditional Māori 'house of learning', they always used the full title 'whare wānanga' and emphasised its location in a special building isolated from everyday life. Those responsible for renewing the Tai Tokerau institution in the 1850s called their new foundation Te Wananga o Tai Tokerau and held its meetings on marae where the local people provided hospitality. Maori Marsden sometimes described Te Wananga o Tai Tokerau as a whare wānanga but mostly used the word 'wānanga' on its own. Whatever the reasons for the word 'whare' being omitted from the title Te Wananga o Tai Tokerau, the result was to emphasise the purpose and functioning of this Northland institution rather than its location. 'Wānanga' is a verbal noun formed by the addition of the noun ending -anga to the verb wā. According to *A Dictionary of the Maori Language*, this verb is not used on its own, but with the prefix whaka- acquires meanings associated with the ideas of adjudication, disputation and taking counsel (Williams, 1975, p.472).

From 1960, as wānanga like that of Tai Tokerau went into recession, the word 'wānanga' came to be applied to other situations. First of all, Māori started using it to refer to hui convened specifically to inform whānau and hapū members about their ancestors, land and whakapapa. Wānanga of this kind developed in the context of rapidly increasing migration to urban areas. They were held in both the home community and the city on a regular, often monthly basis and/or during public holidays, especially Christmas. With a focus on strengthening relations among kin and between generations, they lasted for an evening, a day or a weekend, were held in houses, halls and community centres as well as marae, included all ages, both genders and non-experts, and relaxed many of the traditional tapu restrictions on behaviour. In Chapter 5, Hapi Potae recalled the periodic evening gatherings held in the school at Tokomaru Bay when local kaumātua named all the streams in the bay and told the legends that went with them (see page 138).

By the 1970s the word 'wānanga' was being used as a title for hui convened for a variety of purposes, including discussions about the modification and adaptation of tikanga to meet contemporary challenges. Newly appointed as secretary of the Department of Maori Affairs, Kara Puketapu of Te Āti Awa formulated the philosophy of Tu Tangata and reorganised the department's activities to include four kinds of wānanga: 'kaumatua wananga', 'whanau wananga', 'women's wananga' and 'business wananga' (*Reform From Within*, 1982, p.3). In 1980 I attended a Tu Tangata wānanga convened by the Maori Women's Welfare League at the league headquarters in Wellington. This wānanga took place on a single day (31 August) and involved several 'working parties' of around eight women all discussing two pre-set topics: 'Looking at ourselves as parents, grandparents, aunts and uncles in the whanau' and 'Communication with other agencies'. In 1982 the Northern Tu Tangata Advisory Committee sponsored a number of wānanga throughout Tai Tokerau. Prominent among these was a women's wānanga held in the Bay of Islands on 8–10 January at which fifty women studied marae protocol, tangihanga and kawe mate, waiata including apakura, and hapū names and stories.

Some years later, as the logical extension of Kaupapa Māori primary and secondary schools, three new tertiary institutions received government accreditation and funding, including the use of 'wānanga' in their official titles: Te Wānanga o Raukawa based in Ōtaki, Te Wānanga o Aotearoa based in Te Awamutu and Te Whare Wānanga o Awanuiārangi based in Whakatāne.

The Oxford Dictionary of New Zealand English published in 1997 had a long entry on 'whare wānanga' citing examples that all referred to the traditional 'house of learning'; it did not include 'wānanga' on its own. This overlooked the fact that *The Reed Dictionary of Modern Māori* published two years earlier gave wānanga four meanings in English: 'university, wise informant, lore, place of learning' (Ryan, 1995, p.290). In *A Dictionary of Māori Words in New Zealand English*, linguist John Macalister listed the entry as 'wānanga' and gave it three meanings: '1) a meeting, usually on a marae; 2) (shortened form of "whare wānanga") a university; and 3) a project, an occasion for learning' (Macalister, 2005, pp.153–54). A decade later, 'wānanga' standing alone has been fully admitted to the vocabulary of New Zealand English and is used in general as well as in Māori contexts.

CHAPTER EIGHT

Storytelling

Of all the methods of learning and teaching revealed by the kaiwhakauru, storytelling was the most often mentioned and the most warmly remembered. It took place in formal and informal settings, on the marae between as well as during hui, in the home, in the gardens, in the bush and beside rivers and the sea. Sometimes adults tailored their stories for an audience of children; sometimes the children eavesdropped on adult exchanges.

Te reo Māori does not distinguish between the stories themselves and the process of storytelling as English does, but uses the word 'kōrero' to refer to both. As a verb, 'kōrero' means to speak or talk; as a noun it encompasses such varied forms of verbal communication as conversation, formal speechmaking, news, story, narrative and discussion (Williams, 1975, pp.141–42). Native speakers of te reo do not make clear-cut distinctions between different kinds of stories. They sometimes attach the adjectives 'o neherā', 'pūrākau' and 'pakiwaitara' to the word 'kōrero' meaning story, but in speech, print and dictionaries the three terms cover broad and overlapping fields of meaning. Kōrero o neherā (stories of ancient times) refer mainly although not exclusively to stories set in times and places preceding or during migrations from Hawaiki to Aotearoa. Kōrero pūrākau are defined in dictionaries as including legends, myths, incredible stories and fairytales; while kōrero pakiwaitara are defined as including fairy-stories, fiction, legends and mythology (Williams, 1975, pp.254, 312; Ryan, 1992, pp.109, 168, 203).

Storytelling in the Family

In most of the households in which the kai-whakauru grew up, parents were too busy to do much in the way of telling stories but a few recalled their fathers lapsing into storytelling mode when something triggered a memory. These were mainly older men who had nearly completed their families and were approaching kaumātua status.

As George Parekowhai recalled:

> Dad never actually had formal sessions in the sense that he'd say, 'You sit down and I want you to listen to this.' He'd simply get interested in a particular subject and off he'd go . . . From an idle remark he may give a proverb and the proverb would reflect on a family incident. By our response – and I was always interested – he would start off and he'd tell a story, and it would relate to this proverb and it would relate to historical facts. And he would also connect that incident with himself by line of descent . . . It would be a particular rainy day and the mist would come over the valley where we lived – it was a very misty valley . . . we did have probably more than our share of mists. But our particular mist, it was a kind of light, raining mist. Dad used to point it out to us. Eventually I got to identifying it myself. The mist would hang over the valley with a kind of sunglow behind it. And when it misted in that fashion, he would say in Māori, 'That is your ancestress!'; making herself known was understood. You didn't see a particular form but that was the physical manifestation of that ancestress.
> *(George Parekowhai)*

> It was from our father that we learnt our love of poetry and books. He was endlessly quoting and you were expected to pick up quotes and finish them. We also learnt to haka in the same way. We used to leap up and finish the haka. We did it in the kūmara patch.
> *(Keri Kaa)*

Most often the storytellers were older relatives, grandparents, grandparents' siblings and cousins, senior aunts and uncles. They often lived in the same house as the children or else they were frequent visitors.

Tawhao Tioke remembered his mother being 'great on storytelling'.

> When there's nothing doing, she gathers all the mokos in her kitchen and tells stories. We had no electric light, only the light from the fire. You call the youngsters, you sit close to the fire, and the youngsters sit around, even down to toddlers who couldn't understand. *(Tawhao Tioke)*

Hera Motu recalled that she and her siblings and cousins heard many stories from their grandmother as children. She didn't gather them together for the purpose. They would jump into bed with her and then she would tell them stories – or when they sat watching when she was making kits.

Priscilla Manukau had vivid memories of a storytelling uncle.

> The most enjoyable time we had was at night. We had an uncle staying with us and after tea they would take turns telling stories. It was spooky. The uncle was a cousin . . . he was the one, every time we went to bed, he'd come in and tell us stories. If they got too spooky, we'd pull the covers up and go to sleep and he'd pull faces, disgusted because we'd gone to sleep. *(Priscilla Manukau)*

Until he was nine years old Haare Williams lived alone with his Tūhoe grandparents. Looking back, he remembered his grandmother 'forever talking, telling stories'.

> The times that my grandmother spent in talking, in telling stories, in explaining things or giving a lot of love and patience, that kind of things was really done at night or whenever we worked in the

garden. She got up very early in the morning as well and spent a lot of time in the garden. *(Haare Williams)*

Haare remembered his grandfather mainly for his practical instruction and his command of karakia, but a stint teaching at Matauri Bay brought back memories of his grandfather 'telling me little stories when we went out [fishing] at night'.

When grandparents lived elsewhere, their house was a magnet for their mokopuna. This was clearly the case for the Rewi whānau of Te Rarawa.

After kai we'd go up to where Auntie Whenu lived. There was a bank there. They would tell us stories. We didn't know if they were true or not. The tellers were our grandmother, my aunt and uncles. The children were me and my brothers, Sarah, Bella's family, all cousins . . . There would be about twenty gathered together of the family. It was our main place. *(Moira Nepia)*

Harriet Te Paa commented that grandparents had more time for children than their parents.

That's why children like going to their grandparents . . . you are free from them ordering you to do this and that. When you go to grandparents you have a beautiful time, you are king of the castle. They tell you stories. If you want to learn about the Bible, they learn you all these things. *(Harriet Te Paa)*

As a youngster Nikora Atama and two of his siblings often stayed with relatives because their own house was crowded. When they stayed with their mother's mother, they found her approach to life very different from that of their parents.

Her teaching was very close, mainly based on Māori things . . . She sits down and talks a heck of a lot of Māori and Māoridom. She tells

a story every night about the old days . . . Every night, talk about our history, our tūpunas, teach us a lot of things like marae protocol . . . She tells us a lot of stories about Hinerake [a local mountain], stories about tūrehus, stories she used to tell us before we learnt to read books . . . My grandmother never knew to read.
(Nikora Atama)

As well as the stories told to them directly, children often listened in to stories told literally and metaphorically above their heads.

HINEARI: [Telling stories] just happened. Someone would start reminiscing and out it would come. **HAPI:** A lot was told to other adults in your presence. A lot was told in group situations. You listened to stories being told to others. All the kēhua stories my grandmother told, for instance, about a relative who had been mākutu'd, what happened and why. *(Hineari Babbington and Hapi Potae)*

LENA: Mostly they are talking to themselves but the children are all sitting around listening . . . **HONE:** If they know there is a lot of children around they change to English because they want to embrace everybody. I used to love it. It was hard for us to tell whether it actually happened or whether it was just fantasy, a legend or a myth. **LENA:** They get so involved in telling these stories – just at the best part of the story, you get sent back to bed.
(Hone and Lena Pirihi)

When you go to school you have to go to bed early. You are dying to hear the ghost stories. We used to creep under the kitchen table: there you were, shivering with fright. Only when you coughed, they look under the table. They don't growl but they tell you to go to sleep. When you go into the bedroom you are scared stiff. You go into the passage and you can see all these ghosts around.
(Harriet Te Paa)

Storytelling on the Marae

The marae was a prime location for storytelling. It took place on both formal and informal occasions and covered a wide range of genres. During hui children might be admitted to the meeting-house if there was room and the visitors were closely related to the people of the place, but when the stories told were likely to move into tapu territory children were sent home to sleep or bedded down elsewhere on the marae.

> In the marae itself, as the hui gets on in the whare hui itself, they get very emotional. They are telling different stories; it wasn't for our ears, it was for the grown-ups, because it was too deep. We were told by the old kaumātuas that our brains weren't big enough to take those types of kōreros that they were having in the whare hui. *(Nikora Atama)*

When members of the local and neighbouring communities gathered on the marae for communal activities like Sunday karakia or relaxation after planting, the talk was likely to be focused on the local landscape and shared ancestry. On such occasions children were welcome to sit in on the discussion as long as they kept quiet.

> After Evensong during planting, they would have a fair discussion about the service, criticise the preacher. Someone would pop a question: who was So-and-So's father? And that was the signal for them to move into recalling their past. This is where I heard the experts giving the genealogies of the various families, their relationships, and the history. I was one of those who sat at their feet. The elders were fascinating storytellers. *(Maori Marsden)*

The elders of Rangitukia on the East Coast made sure that their children knew at least one of the key myths of their ancestors by setting up regular teaching sessions.

The story of Rangi and Papa was told in the marae over a period of weeks. You would have to learn one bit before you were told the next. *(Keri Kaa)*

Once the visitors left a hui, the local people stayed on to clean up and then sat around talking and telling stories.

When the funeral's over, that's when they sit and talk, after the manuhiris have gone. All the locals. And of course the kids run around. *(Nikora Atama)*

Even between hui, the marae was important as a gathering place, especially for the old and the young.

The old people live on the marae. We'd go and sit with them, and they sit there and tell us about these histories . . . Stories about Tāne-mahuta, a familiar one I see in the books. We started with Tāwhaki, Tāwhaki and Hema. I was only about seven and these old people were telling us . . . about how people got into Pawarenga, the different names for the mountains, how these mountains were named. And of course we are sitting on the marae and we are looking at the different mountains. *(Nikora Atama)*

The Storytellers

According to the kai-whakauru, most of the older members of their whānau told stories to the children either directly or in their hearing, with women figuring as storytellers more often than men. Among the many, however, some individuals were recognised as exceptional. Niki Conrad of Te Aupōuri told me that 'in the old days' the iwi of the Far North had what he called 'professional storytellers, tāngata kōrero tara'. He remembered one in Te Kao, Herewini Waitai.

He would tell stories by the campfire and the children would gather round. Sometimes he told ghost stories and they would all be frightened; yet they were attracted to him like bees to a honeypot. Some years ago I encountered another gifted storyteller when visiting Pipiwai. An old man started talking about the hautipua [giant] who lived at the top of a local hill. '*That* hill!' he said, pointing it out. This giant rolled boulders down the hill to frighten people and picked off the women he wanted. The young people heard the old man telling this story and gathered round, and in no time he had a crowd. He was talking in Māori and some of them had to ask what he was saying, but he held their attention.
(Niki Conrad)

Fred Ellis, who as a child moved between homes in Manukau and Ahipara, singled out one 'old man' and three kuia for mention by name.

Uncle Wiremu Mete at Manukau was the only old man besides Auntie Raupine who would tell us stories, mostly about Māui and how local places got their names. In Ahipara Granny Putiputi, Gib's mother, was a great one to tell stories, too, and we would get Granny Moutini to come and tell us stories. [Uncle Wiremu told his stories] mostly at home around five o'clock, at night-time, or sitting in the sun. We looked up to him, called him Tupu [Granny]. Uncle Fred Clark's kids and myself went and sat around and listened. He was the storyteller in our family.* *(Fred Ellis)*

Ross Gregory observed that 'some people were good storytellers and some were not'.

---

* Fred Ellis was a storyteller himself in adulthood. He had stories published as Riki Erihi in *Te Ao Hou* and republished in Margaret Orbell's *Contemporary Maori Writing*: see Erihi, 1970, pp.17–50.

STORYTELLING

It was a matter of how they put their words together, whether they could act it out. In Pukepoto the outstanding storyteller was Wira Cameron. After church they would all sit under the big pine tree next to the church and he would keep them laughing from the time he opened his mouth – one laugh after another. He made his stories easy to remember. *(Ross Gregory)*

Good storytellers engaged their listeners on several levels, underlining the words with actions, pulling faces, rolling eyes, waving their arms and singing songs. They kept the children swinging deliciously between shivers and laughter.

My uncle, he would speak, his eyes would roll and the expression he would have on his face! If he was telling spooky stories, his voice would change, he'd move up to the light, his eyes would roll and we'd all get scared . . . Most of the time when he tells a story there is a song – the song is connected to the story. *(Priscilla Manukau)*

Uncle Hapi – some nights he'd have us on. Whether it was true or not we'd get carried away. All of a sudden he'd shout a weird shout and then he'd laugh. We called him Papa . . . My mother would ask, 'Where are you going?' We'd say, 'We are going up the hill.' She didn't mind. We used to look forward to the storytelling. He was so serious about it, didn't laugh till we got carried away. We knew he was making it up but it was so interesting. Our grandmother will be there on a chair with a pipe and her leg shaking; she'd laugh like anything . . . Papa was good – it was a pity he didn't marry. He treated all children alike. He was as good [a storyteller] as Auntie Whenu. We were dependent on him to speak for mihis et cetera at the marae. We never thought that one day he wouldn't be here. Was he strict! But he had a sense of humour. We used to think he was just it. *(Moira Nepia)*

Most communities had several pūkenga who were also good storytellers. Maori Marsden recalled that when the people of his community gathered for an evening meal after planting, the kaumātua vied with each other in lively discussions about whakapapa and the associated local and regional histories.

> The elders were fascinating storytellers, I enjoyed every minute of it. We had amongst them raconteurs with their own techniques: each one had his own particular technique and was fascinating in his own way. Others were extremely funny – you laughed and laughed at them. With these various methods you had a fascinating evening, both a learning experience and an entertaining one. Several of us young ones just sat and listened fascinated round the fireside in the evening gloom. *(Maori Marsden)*

Kinds of Stories

Unexpectedly, the stories published in books as 'Māori myths and legends' figured rarely among those remembered most vividly by the kai-whakauru: only a few even mentioned any. Keri Kaa was taught the story of Rangi and Papa in special sessions on the marae but she was the only one to mention the creation myth. Fred Ellis commented that his Uncle Wiremu told some Māui stories, but only 'odd' ones. On the other hand, Nikora Atama remembered kaumātua telling stories about Tāne-mahuta, Tāwhaki and Hema, sitting on the marae between hui, and was able to tell the story of Tāwhaki searching for his lost wife, with a wealth of detail. (See page 228, later in this chapter.)

The stories most often mentioned by the kai-whakauru, the stories that they called to mind most readily, were of four main kinds: stories about the local landscape, stories of the teller's own childhood, 'ghost stories' and fantastic 'tall tales'. They themselves did not have names for these kinds of stories. The classification is mine.

When the kaumātua told stories set in the local and neighbouring communities, they typically did so from a vantage point from which the features of the landscape could be clearly seen or while walking over or camping on the land.

> All our stories were locally based. Now, for example, when I went to Tōrere with Lena at her parents' place, one morning after breakfast we were sitting on the verandah and her father said, 'See that hill over there, John? That's where So-and-So [took place], a great battle.' It was so real because it actually happened *there*. You became involved because it was right there in front of you. It wasn't out of a book, it wasn't a fairytale. This was the impact for a lot of kids, the use of the local environment as their setting . . . They named the different hills: Mokoia and what happened there and the battle and all that sort of thing . . . When they were telling these stories it actually happened on the place itself. When we used to go to Tūtaetoka and those places up there, going pig-hunting [in the bush], they'd tell us all about these different places. It's amazing even in your own home town, stacks and stacks of history, on one place. *(Hone Pirihi)*

Nikora Atama remembered his grandmother and other kaumātua telling how the ancestor Tohe journeyed along the west coast from Spirits Bay to Hokianga, naming the places as he passed.

> I couldn't remember all [the names]. What interested me was my surroundings, the place I came from and the places further up from us . . . how people got into Pawarenga, the different names they gave for the mountains: Hinerake, Kokoramuka. Kokoramuka to us up north is the pūpū. We have a hill, a little mountain, a kahiwi we call it, and we call that mountain Kokoramuka. You go up that and you'll find all these pūpū shells. How these mountains were named. And of course we are sitting on the marae and we are

looking out at the different mountains. Oruareo – that's coming out to the mouth of the harbour, out into the ocean. Oruareo is 'Echo'; when you are talking it comes back. The names up there – it's full of history. And those are the ones, those are the histories they used to sit and talk about. *(Nikora Atama)*

Moira Nepia grew up in Pukepoto inland from Ahipara near Te Oneroa-a-Tōhē (Ninety-Mile-Beach). Her whānau had relatives and land in Ahipara and after she married she lived there on the road running south towards Herekino. The storytellers in her whānau made sure that the children they were responsible for knew the names of the places in Pukepoto, Ahipara and along the coast, the stories behind the names, which places were tapu and which should be avoided as dangerous.

> Uncle Hapi would tell us about Pātito [an ancestor who lived on the west coast] and when his wife left him, and then about [local] history and legends. When Aunt Whenu moved out to the coast at Te Angaanga, she had two Army huts in front of the swamp on the big flat . . . We used to go out by horse to visit them . . . Whenu used to tell us stories about the caves up top [of the hills behind]. She used to send us to get water where the taros grew. She'd tell us where not to take it from. She'd tell us stories [about that valley, where bodies had been interred]. We'd start giggling – we didn't know if she was trying to frighten us. The yarns she used to tell us were about places where we lived [in Pukepoto and Ahipara]! . . . It was Whenu who told these stories – my mother didn't know history. This is how I know this place [across the road from my current home in Ahipara] is Te Tarahaunga. Whenu reckoned people used to bring bones [of the dead] this way and have a rest at that place. *(Moira Nepia)*

Maori Marsden recalled his father leading the members of their whānau on camps and walks on Ngāi Takoto lands.

My father went out often with members of the family and I tagged along. They even took babies when they went out camping for the weekend. There my father taught us the names of all the bends in the river and the reasons for the various names and the best fishing grounds . . . So here he was passing on the lore of the tribe and what the tribe had learnt over two to three centuries living in the area.
(Maori Marsden)

From what the kai-whakauru said, it seemed that storytellers moved easily between different kinds of stories, especially between local stories, stories of their own childhood on the land, and scary stories about kēhua, tohunga, mākutu, death and dying.

Growing up among Whakatōhea, Hone Pirihi remembered the 'old people' telling stories

> . . . usually at night, when you go out eeling, sitting by the fire, and round a table after all the dishes are done. They start talking about their experiences, how they caught their eels, how they went pig-hunting, the things that they did. Also they talked quite openly about ghost stories. They knew So-and So was dying because he had 'visited' So-and-So last night. Like Selwyn Muru's play on television last night, where the son saw the old man in the shop window. These old people used to tell us all that. It was hard for us to tell whether it actually happened or whether it was just a fantasy, a legend or a myth or whatever. LENA: They'd get so involved in telling these stories – just at the best part of the story, you'd get sent back to bed. HONE: When you do go back to bed you're frightened to sleep in the middle of the bed – you want to sleep on the outside part because they've just told you about kēhuas – 'The kēhuas will take you!' 'You better put the light out and if you make a noise after five minutes the kēhua will come and get you!' *(Hone and Lena Pirihi)*

Recalling the stories his Uncle Wiremu told, Fred Ellis said:

He told us about growing up in Te Kao, about the old days, how things were, only odd stories about Māui. A lot of kēhua stories. Kēhua were almost like *Star Wars* to us. *(Fred Ellis)*

Harriet Te Paa listed 'ghost stories', 'funny stories', 'stories made up in a comical way', 'serious stories' and 'stories that were in the primer books, like Goldilocks'. When her husband emphasised that 'they tell it in their own way, they add to it', Harriet continued:

If there was a ghost in the story you'd just about see this ghost creeping along... They would talk about their younger days, when they used to travel from here to there and they had these experiences. The peculiar signs they see when someone is dying.
(Harriet Te Paa)

Ross Gregory vividly remembered the stories told about the eels in Lake Tāngonge, the swampy lowland north and north east of Pukepoto.

The extent of the lake varied with the rains. In one story, an old couple set off to the lake to catch eels, taking food and a billy with them. The lake seemed a long way out and after a while the old man got tired and said, 'On the next rise let us stop and cook us some kai.' So they did that, and they had just got the billy boiling when there was a rumbling and a heaving under them and the hill moved. It was a giant eel! Another story told how the lake level went down when an eeling expedition caught and landed another great eel. *(Ross Gregory)*

On the evidence of these quotations, it would seem that many stories combined two or more genres and purposes, explaining why any distinction between kōrero pūrākau and kōrero pakiwaitara was difficult to sustain.

Stories with a Purpose

Although one kai-whakauru characterised his grandmother's stories as 'just entertainment', many if not most of the stories told had at least one purpose. In the case of stories attached to features of the landscape, the main purpose was clearly concerned with developing the children's sense of personal identity and connection with their hapū territory. Stories about the storytellers' life experience helped strengthen personal bonds and continuity between the generations. Many stories were concerned to warn children against certain kinds of behaviour, especially behaviour that was dangerous because it breached tapu or attracted the attention of hostile beings.

> **HAPI POTAE:** One of my aunties couldn't have children. I must have asked why her two children were adopted. She told me she had been on the beach and started screaming and yelling. A wave came and knocked her on the rocks and damaged her womb. She was telling me not to shout on the beach . . . Telling me these experiences – maybe it was to all of us, but in a lot of cases she was telling my grandfather about experiences she had at hui. It was like confession. She would recount stories of why people were afflicted with a hurt and how it had been treated at Ringatū hui . . . The story about the aunt was told to me in answer to a question. Another was after [my brother and I killed] the owl, about someone being visited, the owl being a messenger to a certain family where someone has died. These sorts of stories she spoke of a lot, but I don't remember legends . . . They were frequent stories and it wasn't that she was just telling my grandfather. **HINEARI:** At that time they were believing in mākutu. **HAPI:** Very much so. **HINEARI:** A lot of their behaviour was governed by what they thought might happen if they stepped out of bounds of some of the rules.
> *(Hapi Potae and Hineari Babbington)*

Tawhao Tioke was aware even as a child that his grandmother's stories had a teaching purpose, warning children what *not* to do.

She told a story about a man cutting scrub at the back of the hills. This man found a jawbone. He used it as a candlestick. At night he heard a horse crossing the river. A man got off and came in and looked at him lying in his bed. The man said, 'What have you come for?' The other man said, 'Taku kauwae!' [my jawbone]. All the kids jumped with fright, they never forgot. [Such stories warned about] things to watch out for, ngā tohutohu [signs]. I was one who was never afraid of kēhua, but I had cousins who never budged out of the meeting-house after dark. *(Tawhao Tioke)*

Tawhao capped this story with one his mother told when his wife Hurihia and other Tūhoe women were going to the bush to gather material to use in weaving tukutuku panels.

Mum told Hurihia and me how seven women went to gather kiekie. The tohunga told them to beware, to stick together, to know each other and know what time they were coming out [of the bush]. He said karakia. Then they went off and picked kiekie. One woman heard a whistle. A voice said, 'Anei!' [Here!] She thought there was better kiekie there and went over, and there was the kiekie. Then she heard it again. When the time came to leave, the six came out. They went calling but there was no answer, so they went home and told the tohunga. He said, 'Something is wrong!' Her husband stayed up stoking the fire. The door opened; his wife came in carrying kiekie. Her face was all wet and covered with hair. She started work on the kiekie. He said, 'Come and warm yourself!' She never answered or looked up but started weaving. He noticed that the shape she wove was the shape of a coffin. He was frightened. He took off to the tohunga. The tohunga said, 'Go back. We'll go back in the morning. She's not there.' Next morning they went back [to the bush] and found her. She had fallen over a cliff and a tree had gone right through her. Mum said, 'Before you go to the forest, go to the tohunga first or the tūrehu will get you.' *(Tawhao Tioke)*

Tawhao commented that 'the teaching here is respect' for the plant and the craft and to warn listeners to 'beware of evil supernaturals'.

While stories warning against wrong behaviour were often told well ahead of likely breaches, storytellers also took advantage of a dramatic event to tell stories that combined information about local places with warnings against treating them with disrespect.

> Quite often it is a catastrophe, a mate [death], an error is the time for instruction, the time for learning, the time for teaching . . . Someone drowns and all the stories about taniwha or te awa come out . . . and usually come out at the tangi in the whare hui at night, not on the marae [ātea]. *(Wiremu Kaa)*

Storytellers in Full Flight

The quotations that comprise the heart of this book provide ample evidence that the kai-whakauru themselves were skilled storytellers. However, until now these quotations have typically appeared under headings that highlight particular content or purpose rather than the story as such. Now is the time to present two stories so long and complex that they could be filed under a dozen headings. The first is Nikora Atama's telling of the culture hero Tāwhaki's search for his lost wife; in the second Sonny Huia Wilson tells a story he heard as a boy visiting a marae on the bank of the Waipā River and what happened afterwards: a story within a story with a coda. Both tellings display features characteristic of all oral storytelling: discursiveness, frequent use of colloquial expressions, direct speech and the present tense, a wealth of personal and local detail, and digressions explaining the mysterious and the unfamiliar. Oral storytellers work hard to engage their current audience and in doing so use language and illustrations that are meaningful to their listeners (Metge, 2010, pp.29–40).

First, however, I need to point out that the words printed on the following pages convey something less than the full stories as they were told originally, because the music of the speakers' voices, their tones and timing, their facial expressions and gestures were lost in the tape recording and transcription. In spite of that, I hope readers will pick up echoes of these lost elements (as I do) as you read the printed stories.

Tāwhaki on the West Coast

Nikora Atama's story of Tāwhaki's search for his lost wife has particular significance to students of Māori literature because it departs in significant detail from the English version published in Sir George Grey's *Polynesian Mythology* (1961, pp.51–61) and the numerous re-tellings that have been based on it. Grey's version was written down for him by storytellers from tribes inhabiting the forested areas in the centre of the North Island and tells how Tāwhaki ascended into the heavens by climbing up connecting forest vines. In contrast Nikora's telling is localised on the west coast of Te Rarawa territory and tells how Tāwhaki walked across the 'billowy waves' of the Tasman Sea and dived through a bed of kelp into an undersea world (Metge, 2005, pp.153–59).

Talking about the elders sitting on the marae who used to tell the children 'different histories', Nikora mentioned a kaumātua of his grandfather's generation who was 'a tohunga in our area, in the whare wānanga' and launched into the tauparapara with which the old man introduced the story of Tāwhaki and his lost wife.

> Tāwhaki, he used to tell us, Tāwhaki had a wife and his wife was a tūrehu. They used to live in this house and his wife would never come out till night, because tūrehu only go out at night. And he used

to boast about his wife, how nice looking she was, how beautiful. One night they were asleep in their hut. He plugged up all the holes so as daylight comes it wouldn't come into the house, so she wouldn't know it's daylight. He did this while she was asleep, and she slept on and on and on. She got up in the morning, hullo, still dark! She went back to sleep again. As soon as she heard the birds, she woke up. She looked around and she heard the birds again. She knew it was daylight. She knew her husband had tricked her. She heard all the voices outside, the people. Tāwhaki had already told all the people that 'in the morning you come and have a look, you'll see how beautiful my wife is'. She went to open the door and there they were. A lot of people were standing there, looking at her, at how beautiful she was. She pointed up. Everyone turned to have a look. When they looked back, she had gone. She disappeared. She never ever came back. She said to Tāwhaki, 'I will never come back. You have betrayed me.' He cried and begged her to stay, but she wouldn't stay. She disappeared. She took off.

Tāwhaki went to this tohunga, to his auntie, she was a great tohunga. He told her what had happened. And she said to him, 'You were arrogant, and your wife was fed up with your arrogance.' He cried and cried, of course. She felt sorry for her nephew. She said, 'Alright. Go, go out to sea, haere, haere, ki runga i te moana tōu haerenga, e kite koe i te repo, te rimu i te wai, ka ruku ki roto, ka kite koe i tōu hoa i reira.' What she meant was, 'You go out to sea and as you go out to the ocean, you'll see the kelp; as the kelp goes out, you dive in between the kelp, and that's where you'll see her.' And he said to her, 'How will I get there?' She said, 'Walk on the [crests of the] waves. Don't go between the waves', and she'll chant it, chant a karakia. So he said, 'OK.' So he took off. He went on the first wave; it was nice and he walked across. And as he got further out, he was – he wanted to try everything. He thought, 'This is good. I must try to go in between, to see what happens.' Of course, when he went in between, the spell broke and he sank. And he swam ashore. He got there and his auntie said, 'No! No more! You will never see your wife again. I tried to help you but you went against my wishes.' So he came back, and he went back and pestered her again. She wouldn't do it. Until he really, really got sick, and he went over there and he begged her. She said, 'Alright, but this time don't try anything!'

So he went, on the waves. As he stepped over the waves till he got out into the open sea, he came to this kelp. And the kelp came in and out. As the kelp went out towards the open sea he saw the opening and he dived. As he went through he fell into this green patch. He looked around and there were some people chopping trees, making canoes and whatever. He went up to this person who was felling a tree and he told him that he came to look for his wife. Na, 'Ko mea, ko mea, ko mea taku wahine, e haere mai ki te rapu.' This man said, 'Yes, you'll find her in that house.' This old man came out. He introduced himself, and he told this old man he came to look for his wife. And this old man said, 'I'm the father, and that woman is in the house.' So he walked in. He begged that woman to come back with him. She wouldn't. So this woman said, 'You stay here with me.' So Tāwhaki stayed there with her, and that's how that tauparapara went: 'Ko ahau, ko ahau, ko Tāwhaki. Ruia he makauri e te moana waewae.' That's where he walked on the waves. 'Puta ki te Wheiao, te Ao-mārama!' That's where he went through the kelp and then he came out to the world of light. He came out to the real blue, blue skies, the skies that open out to the heavens. Where they are pointed out, that would be the gods. He came and saw his wife and approached the people of his wife, and he had victory, because he found her. And from there he ascended to 'te maunga o Te Matua-kore, i rirohia ngā kete tohu o te whare wānanga', got the baskets of knowledge, of wisdom, and he came back with those baskets of wisdom, but he never came back with his wife. And he was a god, one of the Māori gods, Tāwhaki-Hema, who controls the waves, controls the sea. He took the mana of his auntie. *(Nikora Atama)*

The Drowned Girl, the Taniwha and the Marae

This story was taped during a three-cornered discussion I had with Sonny Huia Wilson and Wiremu Kaa. Our discussion having been mostly in English, Sonny told the story in that language but switched to Māori at key points; he took time to explain certain things to listeners unfamiliar with the place but left some that he himself took for granted unexplained, for example, the difference between Oneparepare (the sandbank) and Ruaparepare (the taniwha's cave). Sonny was brought up on ancestral land in Māngere in Tainui territory but from childhood was a frequent visitor to his grandmother's marae in Whatawhata on the Waipā River, between Hamilton and Raglan.

> There was a tangi [on Whatawhata marae] for an old lady who had been drowned. Now when we got to this tangi, we all sat round and mihimihi'd in the evening, then someone got up and told this story of this previous drowning, years before, of this young girl. I'll just give you a little bit of background first. There is a meeting-house at Whatawhata called Papa-o-roto and down below that is the Waipā River and just below the marae there is a big sandbank, white sand, and that's called Oneparepare, and that was reputed to be one of the homes of Tūheitia, the taniwha of that river, the Waipā, all the way up to Taupiri. And really the story had a warning in it, and that is that the people always said, 'Kaua e haere ki a Ruaparepare mimi ai i te wai', 'Don't go down to that place and mimi there because it's a tapu place, it's the home of Tūheitia.'
>
> And then this story was recounted, where this young girl had gone down and wanted to go for a swim and of course somehow or other when you are stripped off, naked, and you see water, you automatically want to do a mimi before you go in and have a swim. So this girl did, right on Ruaparepare. So this girl went in and she was drowned of course. And they had the tangi, they had her body lying in state, and it was a long time before the advent of coffins, and so this girl was lying in state, and suddenly, she sat

up. And everybody looked at her, and of course those people, who didn't know what was going on, were scared and mad because there was this tūpāpaku – ! And this girl sat up and the first thing she asked for was hot water. And so they brought her some hot water and she had a drink. They took her off that bed where she was lying in state and stuck her on another bed and covered her over with blankets because she was cold. Nobody left that hui house all night, not one person; not even one person went out for a mimi or anything, because they were so scared.

When it was light this girl woke up and she said, 'I'm going to tell you people something.' And she told the story of how she went down to the river, and she took all her clothes off, and she wanted to mimi, so she went on to Oneparepare, because the rest of the bank was covered with blackberries and reeds and all sorts, and if she sat down she'd get prickles in her nono [bottom], and so the clearest part was Oneparepare. And she went down and squatted on the sand and had a mimi, and then she went for a swim. And she waded up to her knees, and then she thought she was going to be cold, so she did a plunge in. She dived in, and when she dived in she opened her eyes, and there she saw this tuna [eel], a huge tuna, and it was staring at her, and she knew it wasn't an ordinary tuna because there was whakairo [ornamental tattoo] around the middle. Now Tūheitia himself is reputed to be a tuna, with whakairo around his middle. So this tuna just looked at her and it turned round and its head just pointed in a certain direction, and she knew she was meant to follow it. So she followed it, and they went for a long way, until they got to this marae. And this tuna stopped, and when she looked round she couldn't see the tuna anymore, but she saw a whole lot of people standing outside this meeting-house, and they started to karanga.

And she started to walk in slowly, and she saw her mother, and her mother took hold of her and ka hongi i ia tāna māmā, ka mutu, ka kī tāna māmā, 'Haere mai, me haere tāua.' [Her mother hongi'd her – pressed noses with her – and when she had finished she said, 'Welcome, let us two go!'] And they went in and there were a whole lot of people sitting, a place laid out on the ground, a great long place set out as an eating place, so they sat down. Her mother told her to 'sit here', and over on that side, on to her left, she saw her mother sit down, and there was an old man, and she didn't know why but she knew that was her mother's father, and he was sitting there with a walking stick. And so everybody was having a kai, and they would reach over and take something and put it in their kono [small basket for cooked food]. So she just sat there. She got hungry too and started to reach over the table. And the old man got hold of his tokotoko and whacked her hand and said, 'Kaua koe e kai!' [Don't eat!] So she sat there. And again she got hungry, and she reached over to get something to eat, and he whacked her hand with his walking stick, and he said, 'Kaua koe e kai!' So when everybody had finished they all got up and went away, and he said, 'Haere mai, e kōtiro!' [Come here, girl!] So she stood up and he said, 'Me haere tāua!' [Let us two go.] And he went back to where she came from, and he said, 'Haere iho! Ka tae atu koe ki te kāinga, kei te kai tuatahi māu he wai wera.' [Go down! When you come to the village, let hot water be the first food you take.] So he said, 'Ko tētahi te huarahi' [That's the way!] and he pointed the way out, and when she looked down she saw this tuna again. And this tuna took her all the way back to Oneparepare. And she climbed up on the sand and she didn't know anything more. And from that time on the people found that she was drowned, and so they took her back.

She asked why her grandfather had told her not to eat. And all the old people who were sitting round her said, 'If you had eaten anything, you would be stuck there for good, you really would have been drowned. But he told you to come back here, and the first thing to ask for was hot water, and the steam from the hot water was to take the tapu off you, and make you live again.' So that's the story. And the story behind that is, 'Don't go and whakanoa the tapu that is already there, don't go and mimi on a place or tiko on a place where you shouldn't.' And boy! that was a good lesson for people. That night, all that day, people wouldn't go anywhere near the river at all. And good enough, too, because that girl had desecrated a tapu.

[As a child] the impression was really made on me because Ruaparepare is *there*, and whenever we go to visit Whatawhata we always go down to the river, you know to whakairi [sprinkle ourselves with water]; we always go down there after a tangi, after the hongi, go down there and wash our hands, and sprinkle ourselves with water. And I always remember this story because of that. And if anybody who is new to Whatawhata is with me I would say, 'If you want to mimi, get up there in the blackberries, don't do it here!' Then they'll ask why and I'll tell them.
(Sonny Huia Wilson)

Having told and commented on the story as he heard it as a child, Sonny went on to talk about recent developments at Whatawhata and the way they had impacted on children's learning.

You were talking about Sir Peter Buck's people coming along and saying, 'You've got to adopt Pākehā sanitary ways!' That's right, and I can see the reasons for it, but in doing that – ! Now . . . a few years, just a little bit more than ten years ago I think, when we used to go to tangis at Whatawhata, we always used to go down to Ruaparepare, after the hongi, after the mihimihis, and whakarite ourselves with water from the river. And those people always observed [the tapu] of Ruaparepare, because they knew that was the home of Tūheitia . . . Now in recent times, something very important has happened. They've built right next to the meeting-house an ablution block, where people can go and wash and shower. Now, all right, we realise that you should go and wash after you have observed all the tapus of the marae. But young kids I think don't

know that, and by going down to the river we used to talk about it. But now, because the wash-basins are right there in the toilet block, you just go and automatically do this, but you don't explain to your children why you are doing it. And on top of that, you miss out on talking about Ruaparepare if you don't have the opportunity to go down to the river, so you miss out on talking about Tūheitia if you don't go down to the river, and you miss out on seeing Waipā itself and talking about and remembering the traditions that went on that river, the transport during the Land Wars and all that sort of thing. These are the things we are missing out on, not only Māori things but historical things, because the new wash toilets have been provided for the people to use.
(Sonny Huia Wilson)

A Story to Close With

Recalling the way her kaumātua often told a story instead of answering her questions as a child, Keri Kaa reported incorporating storytelling into her teaching as a lecturer in Māori Studies at Wellington Teachers' College. Instead of answering the questions students asked directly, she told stories that challenged them to work out answers for themselves. As an example she remembered telling this story in response to a question about the mānuka tree, too often dismissed in the past as scrub and clear-felled in favour of grass or pines. Another story within a story, it illustrates the way a narrative can convey several messages at once, stimulate curiosity and facilitate communication between the generations.

> It's to do with what happened in an incident which took place one day in 1962. I went with my parents to a great church gathering in the Waikato on the Māori Queen's marae. Knowing the history of the place and what happened during the Land Wars, I was astounded

that the Anglican Church was going to be formally welcomed on to the marae. My father phones us up and said that we were to come to help Ngāti Porou take their offering. And my brother and I turn up and all the tribal church groups were lined up with young people at the heads of the delegations carrying the gifts. Some tribal groups had very elaborate things to carry and others had wonderful woven baskets and some had small carvings. And our tribe had a branch of a tree and tied on to the small branches were rolls of money, banknotes. I didn't want to carry the tree and neither did my brother want to carry this old tree. Our friends were carrying these beautiful presents and we had a dead branch of a tree. The thing was, the tree was the mānuka tree, which is a very tough native tree which grows here [on the East Coast] and its wood is beautiful for smoking fish, and if you keep bees they feed off the nectar of the flowers which have particular healing qualities when you want to make the honey. So it is a tree which has many uses. There was enormous significance in tying the banknotes to the branches of the tree. So we suddenly appeared at the gates with our biggest branches and then the old people arrived and started tying the money on it. You could see who's giving it. You see, each wad of notes represented each little area of the tribe. It was getting most competitive. I think we had something like two hundred pounds sterling tied to the money tree. In 1962 that was a lot of money. And then we decided it was OK to carry this tree.

And our father's younger brother turns up. He was a very quiet man but he realised that we were not too pleased about carrying this branch along. So he came up to us and he started chanting. What he called to us with this ritual chant was 'E rere te mānuka! Tomokia!' [The mānuka will come forward! Bring it in!] Some years later we asked him about the significance of that, because he assumed we knew. I said to him one day, 'Do you remember with the money tree?' 'Yes.' 'Do you remember how we didn't want to go?' 'Yes,' he said, 'I remember.' I said, 'Do you remember what you said?' He said, 'Yes, I do', and then he started to tell us the symbolism. The mānuka grows in its natural state, and its job in the bush, actually it nurtures other seedlings, and when those seedlings reach a particular height where they can take on and grow on their own, then the mānuka dies away, only to live again. It goes through this cycle... The money [on the tree] was a gift. The money was less important than the symbolism. *(Keri Kaa)*

CHAPTER NINE

Learning in the School System

The main focus of this book has been on Māori methods of learning and teaching as revealed by the kai-whakauru talking about their childhood learning experience in households, whānau and rural communities. The research agenda did not include their experience of formal schooling. However, in the course of our discussions, seven of the kai-whakauru volunteered comments on that subject which illustrate both the variety and the complexity of the relation between school and community while they were growing up.

Community Attitudes to Schooling

Work colleagues Wiremu Kaa and Sonny Huia Wilson revealed that even within their own home communities there were conflicting and ambivalent attitudes to schooling, especially at secondary level. As a child Sonny Wilson lived with his parents in Māngere East in Auckland. His parents both belonged to Waikato iwi which had a history of opposition to their children attending secondary school. As Sonny recalled:

> My grandmother went further than that. None of her children went to school at all, from the eldest to the youngest of seven kids. My mother, being a little bit forthright and a little bit stubborn, wouldn't have all of this, so she made sure to send my brother and

me to school. And it was towards the end of my Form 2 year, she and Dad talked to my grandmother about sending me to a private school, to Wesley College, if they could find the money. She was dead against the idea, she wouldn't have me going to secondary school at all. If I did attend secondary school, I would have been the first in the whole of the extended family to do that. So Mum argued, and she turned round and said to her mother, very disrespectfully mind you, 'Whether you like it or not, my son's going to go to a secondary school.' And she argued and argued, and cried, and at the end my grandmother gave in. So she said, 'Send for that boy. I want to talk to him. Send for my moko.' So I sat there, all formal and stiff, and this was one of the very first times that I was scared of my grandmother, and I was a little bit whakamā, because I didn't know what was going to happen. So she turned round to me and she said, 'Kia ora ana koe, e tama. Ko te pīrangi o tō whāea kei te haere koe ki te kura kia mōhio koe i te mōhioranga Pākehā. Āe, e whakaae atu ana au, engari ko taku kōrero ki a koe, haere atu ki te kura Pākehā, engari kaua e hoki mai ki te kāinga nei ki te whakapākehā i a koe. Hoki mai koe ki konei he Māori koe. Nō reira, haere, haere atu koe ki ngā mātauranga o te Pākehā, whakahokia mai ki konei, huihuia mai ngā taonga o te Māori, hei oranga māu. Haere mai nei.' And these were the words – this has had a big effect on my life. My grandmother had said, 'OK, go to the Pākehā, learn the Pākehā education, but don't come back here to make a Pākehā of yourself. Remember you are a Māori. But go to the Pākehā, learn his ways, bring it back here to combine with the ways of your own life, on which to build your future life.' And I think that this had a very big influence on my thinking, in that, sure, when we started secondary school a lot of the things Māori got knocked out of us: we hardly ever spoke Māori until we went home. My home was at Māngere East near Ōtāhuhu, and I attended Otahuhu College. But my grandmother lived at Ihumātao about seven or eight miles away. And every Sunday we would go home to see Nanny.

'Home' – there, I'm saying 'home' now. We'd go home to see Nanny. No Pākehā language was used at all because she wouldn't use it, and she couldn't anyway. We older kids, before I started secondary school, used to laugh at some of the English words she used to say because she couldn't speak English and she used to say it just to be funny and to make us laugh . . . Her philosophy had a big influence in my life in that I've tried to remember that I'm a Māori, I've tried to remember that I'm looking for the Pākehā way of life to build my own life on, and I can see now that not only my own life but the lives of other people are influenced by the work I do.
(Sonny Huia Wilson)

Brought up in the Waiapu River Valley, closely associated with Sir Āpirana Ngata and the heart of Ngāti Porou territory, Wiremu Kaa capped Sonny Wilson's account of the transition to secondary school with his own.

When I went to Te Aute, the whole village went with me. It used to worry me in a way . . . the expectations of the people. When we came back, everyone was happy to see you. They went out of their way to welcome you into their houses, to talk to you and to hear you talking, and to miri you, rub you, touch you like this, and when they kiss you, the old people, they feel your face. I remember when they put on a hākari [feast] for all the children who were away at secondary school, and this was their way of showing their pleasure at what their children were doing . . . There were seven of us from Rangitukia. They had a hākari for us. That was my first year at Te Aute. *(Wiremu Kaa)*

While they did not go as far as putting on a hākari in his honour, Sonny's whānau took a keen interest in his progress.

Being the first in the extended family to go to secondary school, I knew by the talk that went on with the family that they had their eyes on me, and they wondered how I was going to do at school, how I was going to be among all these Pākehā children, because at that time Ōtāhuhu didn't have very many Māoris . . . about three of them altogether on the roll . . . I knew this talk was going on and . . . I enjoyed being discussed, especially when I heard nice things being said. And then towards my School Certificate year – now my father had been working for a farmer, Walter Massey the farmer's name was. Walter Massey was at that time Chairman of the Board of Governors [of Otahuhu College] and Dad used to have long discussions with him and Walter Massey told Dad the sorts of things I could do that were open to me once I got School Certificate. So Dad came home and . . . said, 'What do you want to be when you grow up?' . . . I said, 'I want to be a teacher.' He flew off the handle. But then I think I was a little bit of a stubborn person like my mother, that was born in me, and whether he liked it or not, by hook or by crook, I was going to be a teacher. But Dad didn't like it because he said all teachers do is sit on their bums all day and that is not a way to earn a living, because as a kid he could plough when he was nine, and he was milking cows earlier than that. So he believed the way to work for your living was with your hands, not sitting on your nono. I got older, I got what was required to get into training college, and I did that, and then as soon as I was trained and going out on my PA [probationary assistant]* year, he said, 'Where are you going to teach? . . . I want to know, are you going to teach here in Auckland?' And I said, 'No, I want to get right out of here.' So I applied for my first job as a PA and got it. And I told him and he was thrilled to bits – there was a whole change of attitude now . . . Mum was pleased all the way through when I said I wanted to be a teacher. One of the things my grandmother said to me again,

---

* First year of teaching required for completion of Dip. Tchg.

she reminded me, 'You're not a Pākehā, you're a Māori.' The reason why my father was so pleased was because I was going to do my PA at Rākaumanga, right next to Waahi marae, where the King lived. The school was next to the King's farm. And then he sat me down and talked to me seriously. Not about teaching, not about my career. He said, in Māori, 'You are going to the marae of your ariki. Whatever you do, put your foot down correctly, don't you set your foot in the wrong place.' Now that took a little figuring out. I understand what that means now. What he was really saying was, 'You are going back to the people of the rangatiras of Waikato. Be careful how you handle yourself, be careful how you talk to people, and be careful most of all how you handle their children.' I think this is what changed my father's attitude, because at last I was going to do something useful in his eyes. *(Sonny Huia Wilson)*

Wiremu Kaa's experience of visiting home after qualifying as a teacher involved a similar ambivalence on the part of the whānau. In particular they were keen that the newly qualified should bring their skills back home.

[When we qualified as teachers] our parents were pleased, but they didn't know how to handle it, their young teenagers. I don't know what the expectation was. But there *was* an expectation, because of the way they would miri you, talk to you, look up to you. But in some ways they found it difficult to cope with it. The older ones were very tolerant, for instance, at mates [deaths]. . . . The old kuias would do this [beckon] to me and I'd go and sit by the tūpāpaku, I'd sit with them, maybe for half an hour, sometimes for a whole hour. They'd have their tangi, they'd talk away and forget about my presence, and when I wanted to go away they'd pull me to sit down. Then they'd ask me to buy them a half brandy . . . The girls were a different kettle of fish. One kuia, referring to one of the cousins, the comment went something like, in an off-handed manner, 'He kai tērā mā te wai.'* They looked towards us, towards me and August, as the people for Rangitukia. *(Wiremu Kaa)*

The School System and its Effects

Happy enough attending the local convent school in his early years, Nikora Atama struggled to cope with the very different environment of state schools in the outside world.

> In 1951 we shifted from Pawarenga to Broadwood. It would be about an hour's drive to Pawarenga. It was the first time we had lived in an outside area, an area that felt to us at the time as predominantly European. There weren't many Māori families in Broadwood. [We went] to a high school, and the teachings were very different, different in a way, that is, to me. Looking at a teacher talking, it made no sense to me. The school we went to in Pawarenga was a convent. They, the nuns talked, but the majority of stuff we did over there, the teachings that they went through, was a practical way of teaching. They showed us how to do things. If we didn't know how to write a name, they came up and made our hands go the way which the pencil should go to form whatever letter or word we wanted to write. That was the only way we were taught. And to go into a public school, that was different. I felt that these people were just standing there talking to us and writing on the blackboard and they never came down and showed us what to do. It was a different world of teaching. From then on, that was where I lost . . . I was good at my figures, I was good at artwork, anything practical I was good at. English – no good. I couldn't spell. I couldn't even read . . . I struggled, I struggled right to the day I left school. I was used

---

* Literally, 'that one's food for whomever', reflecting the idea that girls were expected to 'marry out' into other places and whānau establishing kinship links, while boys with leadership potential were expected to come home to serve their own people.

to the practical way of teaching where I was shown what to do and once they had shown me a thing to do, I'll never forget it... When I went there and all they did was talk and write it on the blackboard and talk again and cross it out and write it down again, I didn't know what the heck was going on for a start. Teachers came home to see Mum and Dad to see if they could take me to a special school where I could pick up a lot, but Dad knew I couldn't because of the way they taught me. I was very practical and whatever they taught me they had to show me. But our home life, the way we were taught at home, it still existed at that time... I shifted from there, I went to Whangarei Boys' High School and there my life really changed. I made a lot of friends in Whāngārei. I saw trains, I saw buses, I saw everything. It was the last stage in my schooling. That was when I found out education was really something important. It was too late, I was finishing school. *(Nikora Atama)*

Tawhao Tioke was born in the Urewera bush and spent his earliest years in kāinga in the bush, as he put it, 'living on berries and fernroot'. That was his way of pointing out their subsistence way of living. When the government started to open up a road into the bush from Waimana, the menfolk took jobs on the road project and came out of the bush to live in Waimana but it was a long time before their families joined them.

When the paymaster came to the kāinga, the women would take the kids and go deep into the bush. I was six in 1926, the first time we came out into the open, to Whakarae. That is where my adopted brother had his first schooling at fourteen at Hoani Laughton's mission school.* I didn't start school until I was ten. I went to the Pākehā school. Six boys and six girls were chosen to listen for any Māori children who spoke Māori. The names were written on the

---

* Reverend John Laughton was a Pākehā appointed to work as Māori missioner among the Tūhoe people by the Presbyterian Church.

blackboard, we were called out and given three cuts and kept in. Our parents started to enquire why we were late home and when they found out they took us away. Because we were getting too much strap for talking Māori and Hoani had opened another mission school at Tanatana, our parents sent us there. It was arranged by the teacher: 'I'll leave the Māori to you, you leave the Pākehā to me.' We were sorry to leave our friends. At the mission school we spoke only Pākehā in school but Māori outside.
(Tawhao Tioke)

In contrast to Nikora and Tawhao, the other kai-whakauru who talked about their experience of the school system found that the learning habits instilled in their homes and community stood them in good stead at school. Maori Marsden started school at five in the school closest to his home, a school administered by the North Auckland Education Board.

I started school at five, went to Awanui School. Probably because of my father's constant reading to us – we had Bible readings in the evening then prayers followed by the reading I mentioned before – by the time I went to school it wasn't long before spelling came easily and arithmetic, the three basic Rs. Then I fell foul of one of the teachers. I suspect now, looking back, it was because I consistently headed the class and my Pākehā teacher resented this Māori heading the class all the time. She had favourites, Pākehās, she had that superiority complex. I suppose I was a puzzle to her, and the rest of the family, because we spoke good grammatical English. I began to switch off and my father realised what the problem was, so he switched me to Paparore School which was three and a half miles from [our home at] Maimaru . . . Here I was at the age of seven or eight leaving Maimaru. I cut through paddocks, swam the Awanui River and made a bee-line for Paparore School and went over obstacles rather than around . . . [Later] I began to ride to school on a horse but I also enjoyed walking, so 50 per cent of the time I walked or rather ran all the way in the morning . . . As the days drew in I stayed at Waimanoni . . . but always on Friday evenings I made a bee-line for home.

    A little bit about Paparore School. We had a man called Robert Shutt as headmaster. His wife was also teaching and I had a couple of cousins who were assistants in that school. The school was about 80 per cent Māori. There were a few Pākehās, Dalmatians, and a fair sprinkling of half-caste Māori-Dalmatians. At Paparore School I soon settled in. I could relate to that sort of situation where I couldn't to the Awanui School which was really a Pākehā school, about 60 per cent Māori and 40 per cent Pākehā. Our headmaster [at Paparore] was a Christian and very advanced in his methods of teaching. He understood us Māoris, he had a tremendous relationship with the Māori community. Whenever there were any jobs around the school, he got Māoris to do them, especially parents. The school committee was nearly all Māori; I think it had one Pākehā. Mr Shutt was part of the community. We had quite a number of children who lived up on the gumfields, at Kauri Flat, in rather poor conditions. They tended to be covered with scabies. I remember they had an evil-smelling brown ointment and one of the jobs I had to do was to stoke up the boiler on Friday afternoons and shepherd all the boys through a hot bath and cover them with this evil-smelling brown ointment. His wife supervised the girls. To me this was quite tremendous that he should take such an intimate interest in the general welfare of the children. Every morning we opened with prayers. We always had the impression that for him it was something meaningful, not just a formality. I remember gaining a Native Scholarship. One of the things the tribe made a big thing of was sending their children away to secondary school. *(Maori Marsden)*

When Maori won a Native Scholarship, his father planned to send him to St Stephen's School in Bombay, south of Auckland, but Maori enrolled himself in Wesley [Methodist] College in Paerata.

> There at Wesley it was about 70 per cent Māori and Islander and about 30 per cent Pākehā. I was brought up in that Māori environment as far as my education was concerned. The third year I managed to scrape through University Entrance, the next year I got Higher Leaving Certificate. I was too young to go to university. My father wanted me to. He himself had been closely involved with the Young Maori Party* when he was at Te Rau Kahikatea [Māori theological college] in Gisborne. It was his ambition that as many as possible in the family should have tertiary education. I went home and he enrolled me at Kaitaia High School just to mark time till I was old enough to go to university. He died before this and that was my opportunity to sign up and get away overseas with the Maori Battalion. I managed to bluff the authorities that I was old enough and I found myself shortly afterwards in the Middle East.
> *(Maori Marsden)*

After spending his early years living alone with grandparents, Haare Williams made a difficult but eventually successful adjustment to the formal education system.

> For the first six years of my life I internalised very, very deeply those Māori things. Culturally I was very much a Māori, in the way I felt about things, the way I was brought up, the cooking of the kai and the sleeping with my grandparents . . . At Ōhiwa we were very much isolated from the rest of the community and I was the only grandchild brought up in that fashion . . . The emphasis that

---

* This was not a political party but a coalition of young, tertiary-educated Māori at the end of the nineteenth century and the beginning of the twentieth, led by Āpirana Ngata, Te Rangi Hīroa, Rev. Rēweti Kōhere and Dr Wī Repa.

my grandparents gave to my informal Māori learning I suppose carried on to my formal education within the Pākehā system of learning within the school . . . My grandfather had a Bible and he would read from texts. There were certain parts of the Bible where I would pick it up and read it myself over and over again, particular favourites of mine. And there were some encyclopaedias of Greek mythology; I really enjoyed some of this. He didn't read any of that to me. I used to go through the pictures and familiarise myself, and some of my uncles would come and tell me a little story about Greek mythology. Fascinating stuff. Of course, my koroua all the time was talking about Māori mythology and all the stories about Te Kooti . . . I found that very fascinating too. So there was an informal process of my beginning to read and things like that before I started school. And my uncles would bring me comics . . . I'd read them page by page and picture by picture, and even now I can still see the images of the drawings and the little balloons, the way they spoke, and the words as English became part of me before starting school . . . I went to a Pākehā school at Kutarere. I was about six and a half, a big kid. Imagine the whakamā associated with being a big kid among all these primers when my peers were already in the standards . . . I wasn't punished for speaking Māori. I remember sitting in a classroom, very much afraid to say anything, completely overwhelmed by the situation I was in. There was a subtle sort of inference there that things Māori weren't really relevant, for example, if I stayed home for the Twelfth, the Tekau-mā-rua, or the First of July, the Hūrae, these very important Ringatū hui and tangihanga. While my grandparents insisted that I went to these huis with them, I felt totally whakamā about going to school after a spell like that, away from it all. I can't recall whether I was punished, but I think there was a subtle feeling that these Māori kids are wasting their time going to these hui . . . At the small school at Kutarere I was able to skip three classes in the first two years. Then I went back [to my parents and the school at] Te Karaka [on the East Coast]. But I found that interrupted my own programme because of the lack of interest that was shown by my own parents towards school work. My father certainly showed a very real interest in me and my older brothers getting on and joining the shearing gang with him. But somehow I had this internal feeling that I wanted to do something else. As young as fifteen or sixteen I wanted to be something more than just a shearer . . . I attribute a lot of that to my maternal grandmother, Waioeka Brown. She made it quite clear she wanted her mokopunas to succeed in the Pākehā world as well, but she also wanted them to be up to date with the teachings of Te Kooti and the Ringatū Church. Looking back on it now, my time on the marae and my time in the schools, although they weren't related, they weren't wasted times in my life. . . .

When I went to high school I spent a whole year in the third form among all my mates, not aspiring too high, to place myself above all my mates and to be cut off from them. Towards the end of the first year, my third form year, the principal took me into his office and said to me, 'Williams, you've got more intelligence than you are showing at the moment: we're going to put you in an academic form', and so I restarted again in my third form year. But thank goodness I managed to scrape through and get School Certificate and I ended up at Ardmore Teachers' College as a student. And during all that process I guess I was very much beginning to be materialistic in my approach. I didn't understand a great deal, you know. I wrote a brilliant essay at high school on the Industrial Revolution; I didn't know until I had been teaching a couple of years what the Industrial Revolution meant. I rattled off these words, off by heart, so the Māori thing more or less became adjunct to the processes that I was going through. I went through teachers' college relatively easily, I found the work I enjoyed. I suppose that is what really helped me to succeed. *(Haare Williams)*

George Parekowhai attended both primary and secondary school in Te Karaka. Looking back, he gave equal credit for his later success at tertiary level to his family and to his teachers.

> [With regard to] my motivation at secondary school – I was keen to do well for my kin-group, for Dad and Grandmother, but just as keen to do well for my teachers. It seemed to me that my secondary school teachers took a close personal interest in my personal achievement. My secondary school [at Te Karaka] was somewhat exceptional. It was the first experimental school – Form One to Six – in the North Island. It was in the transition stage from District High School to a form one to six Area School when I was at school, and Lopdell, who was a pretty bigwig educator from Wellington Teachers' College, had a great hand in picking the schools he wanted for the experiment. He picked one which was ours at Te Karaka and the other one was at Geraldine in the South Island. We were the two prototype schools for Area Schools. Rose is right, he got a team of specially good teachers. But I know that my teachers were very personally involved in my education and I think I worked just as hard for them as I did for my parents. I saw the teachers as lighting the way – they weren't the way of education for me but they sort of held a torch and lighted the way. They held the torch up high enough above me for me to see the vision of their view and it was still up to me to go ahead if I wanted. In the case of my own children, they can hardly give the names of their teachers at different levels. Yet I remember these people as having a faith in my own future and I shared that faith with them. They did all they could. *(George Parekowhai)*

While not all Māori children were as fortunate in their school teachers as Maori, Haare and George, it is important to acknowledge that the school system of the time included teachers of high calibre and sensitivity.

Comments on Learner–Teacher Relations

Having qualified as a certificated teacher and spent many years teaching in primary schools, Wiremu Kaa commented thoughtfully on his experience of teacher–learner relations in school and whānau settings.

> [At school], if one kid that was Māori was down in the dumps, generally all the other Māoris would feel with that child down in the dumps. So if the teacher tells that one kid off, he's really told the whole class off, he's got twenty-nine other enemies. I'm saying the same thing about rewards – it's a shared thing amongst the group rather than by the individual. Same thing with punishments. It's a whānau context thing . . .
>
> The other thing about Māori learning is, the transmitter is not really overly perturbed if there isn't immediate feedback, whereas in the school situation, when you transmit information or knowledge you expect at some point, maybe two or three days later, you can measure feedback. If there isn't any feedback or the feedback is incorrect, then either the recipient is not with it or didn't do any homework about that information you [the teacher] gave them – they usually get the blame. But sometimes it is the transmitter really at fault – but they are not going to admit that. In a Māori context there's no threat about whether you have achieved a skill or not. But there *are* some things that you need to achieve. In certain Māori projects, they make them practise, they demand excellence, for instance, in a taiaha drill, in the haka or an action-song.
> *(Wiremu Kaa)*

CHAPTER TEN

Educational Practices and Principles

The seven chapters that form the heart of this book are resonant with voices from the past as speakers who collaborated on the research remember and reflect on their own personal experience of growing up in the middle of the twentieth century. Whether read singly or as a body, these chapters project a clear impression of variety allied with a body of shared practices and principles.

The variety is easy to discern. In talking about their childhood, the speakers reveal significant differences in personality, interests and achievements; their home communities differed widely in terms of size, location and resources; and they came from many different iwi with markedly different histories of relations with other iwi, government and non-Māori generally. Here in this chapter their variety needs only to be acknowledged and valued.

The practices and principles the speakers shared are less accessible to readers because they were not clearly articulated in a formal system with standardised curricula and teacher training. Knowledgeable adults decided for themselves with whom, when and how to share their knowledge, mostly by reference to the examples provided by previous generations and the dictates of the tikanga, the rules and guidelines, prevailing in their communities. Almost everybody was a teacher at some stage to some extent, while most communities included knowledge-holders who restricted access to their special field. In this chapter, drawing on the evidence provided by the kai-whakauru, I attempt to identify and briefly characterise the practices and principles they share.

Educational Practices

In recounting their learning experiences as children, the kai-whakauru revealed a number of educational practices so widespread that they might be identified as 'typically Māori' for that time.

Learning by Doing

Prominent among these practices was an emphasis on learning by doing with a minimum of verbal instruction and explanation. Over and over again the kai-whakauru recalled parents, grandparents and other relatives saying 'Haere mai, titiro mai, whakarongo! Me pēnei!' [Come here, look, listen! (Do it) like this!] Learners sat or stood side by side with their teachers, watched what they did and copied it. Once they had mastered the basics, their teachers left them to carry on at their own pace, intervening only to correct mistakes and demonstrate the next steps. In this context the teacher was a kai-tohutohu, 'one who shows', a demonstrator.

Importantly, this applied not only to practical skills but also to basic values such as respect for people and the natural environment, hospitality to visitors, and aroha to kin and the unfortunate. Such values were absorbed by osmosis from relatives who practised what they preached: the seafood gatherers who took only the fish and shellfish they needed, cleaned them away from the beach and shared them with others on the way home; the household heads who sent farm and garden produce to the marae every time there was a tangihanga and planted extra for the marae, the widows and the poor; and the kuia who invariably spoke kindly and gave practical help to the less fortunate.

According to one kai-whakauru, 'whatever they did, there was a teaching point in it'. However, hidden lessons were not always recognised as such nor appreciated at the time by children who resented sharing scarce resources such as food and their parents' time. Often the impact was delayed until many years later when as mature adults they found themselves behaving in the same way and worked out what the lesson had been.

Learning and Teaching in Context
According to the kai-whakauru, much of their learning took place in settings where the relevant materials, instructors and opportunities for application were already in place. Girls learnt to weave flax mats and kits in the corner of the family living quarters where their mothers kept a mat or kit 'on the go'. When the meeting-house began to look shabby, the girls were recruited by the women of the community to weave new floor mats and tukutuku panels in the meeting-house itself. Boys and girls learnt about the location, species and habits of fish and shellfish in season on adult-led fishing and gathering expeditions, and about the needs and care of crops as helpers in their planting, weeding and harvesting. Kai-whakauru chosen to accompany experts into the bush learnt the appearance and purposes of plants with craft and medicinal uses while helping in their gathering. Many remembered being told stories about what their ancestors did while they themselves 'walked the land' where their ancestors had lived and worked and sat on vantage points overlooking it.

While in most cases learners were encouraged to practise developing skills, the kai-whakauru recalled a rule internalised in childhood that the tangi and the karanga should be performed only 'for real' in appropriate circumstances, not practised beforehand. In most iwi these practices were the prerogative of women.

Teaching and Learning in a Group
Much of the learning of the kai-whakauru was carried out in the context of relationships that were both personal and co-operative.

In the first place, children spent a lot of time in groups of siblings and cousins. In large families the older children were deputed to look after two or more of the younger ones. The kai-whakauru recalled hanging out together in 'gangs' of age-mates through primary school and 'chewing over' their experience of the adult world, especially with regard to things adults did not discuss such as kin relationships, religious beliefs, marae etiquette and sex. Pooling their knowledge, they had worked things out – not always accurately – in discussion among themselves.

From time to time children were incorporated into groups comprising a range of age-grades and expertise. Young recruits were supported to do simple tasks to begin with and were close enough to competent practitioners to observe what they were doing. They were watched to assess their ability and responsibility, and as they mastered one task they were moved on to more complex ones. Eventually some were promoted to roles as supervisors of their juniors and leaders among their age-mates.

Hui at marae required a large and varied workforce. Children were fitted in where qualified or needed, some ranging widely while others settled into particular areas: dining-hall, kitchen, hāngī area, more rarely the meeting-house. They began by running errands, fetching and carrying, moved on to washing dishes and laying tables out of public sight, and were finally promoted to responsible tasks like peeling vegetables, waiting on tables, helping to make hāngī and making up beds in the meeting-house, always under the eagle eyes of adults.

Children were similarly involved in the workforces that handled the preparation of aggregated gardens for crops, the actual planting and harvesting, and the gathering of seafood for hui. While the bigger and stronger boys helped the men to cut scrub and break up the earth with ploughs, the younger ones dragged the cut branches out of the way and attached and rode the harrows. The complementarity of varied tasks was particularly evident during planting when children helped count the kūmara tupu into hundreds, the men formed the long mounded rows, the kuia formed the holes for planting the tupu, the younger children fetched and poured water into the holes, the older children laid the tupu with the correct east-west orientation, and the women heeled the tupu in.

Restrictions on Access to Learning
The guardians of special kinds of knowledge protected the children by restricting access to particular people: to members of certain descent-lines, to one sex or the other, and to those who had demonstrated their capacity to learn and to treat knowledge-holders with respect. In general, they delayed teaching whakapapa into late adolescence or adulthood. While they allowed both boys and girls to learn traditional as well as modern waiata if they were interested, they restricted tutoring in whaikōrero and karanga (the women's form of whaikōrero) to adult men and women respectively, and screened applicants for readiness, aptitude, whakaiti and willingness to serve community needs.

There were, however, exceptions to these restrictions. Especially in widowhood, many kaumātua chose a mokopuna as a companion who slept with them and accompanied them everywhere until it was time to go to school. In the course of such close companionship, these moko taura (tethered grandchildren) were privy to much that was beyond their comprehension and denied to other children. They buried much of what they saw and heard during their school years, only to have it resurface years later when it became relevant.

Memorisation
When they were young, the kai-whakauru memorised many combinations of words and music without conscious effort simply by joining in their constant reiteration in the course of family and group life. In this way they built up extensive repertoires of songs, hymns, karakia and Bible verses in both Māori and English. Several reported that as

children they had paid little heed to the traditional waiata their grandparents sang in the early morning, but as adults had found themselves singing some they were unaware they had learned.

In the case of haka, songs and dances performed on public occasions, learning and practice were combined in group sessions open to all comers. These were usually held on the marae ātea or in the dining-hall, under the direction of expert instructors who stood at the front facing the rows of performers and rehearsed them through constant repetition of words and actions. Haka perfected in this way were performed during the reception of visitors on the home marae and on trips away. On such occasions the instructors typically selected those they considered competent to represent the community.

In contrast, experts in tapu fields of knowledge such as karanga, whakapapa and whaikōrero taught selected learners on their own or in small groups. While their teaching styles varied in some ways, they all emphasised repetition as the technique of central importance. Typically they would start by modelling the first phrase in the work to be learnt and set their pupils to repeating it over and over until they were satisfied with pronunciation, rhythm and tone. Then they repeated the process with the following phrases, returning periodically to an earlier point to run through those already learnt in sequence. Some teachers gave little or no explanation of the content of what was learnt until the whole had been fully memorised; others stopped at appropriate points to explain the meaning of individual words and the context in general. One kai-whakauru reported that his teacher had sent him away to learn the words on his own and spent their sessions together in exposition, but this reflected confidence in his pupil's abilities rather than a common tactic.

Whatever the subject and ultimate purpose, rote learning was clearly not an end in itself but the first step towards the goal of meaningful performance. A kai-whakauru experienced in teaching waiata likened the relationship between learning and performance to a pianist learning and playing a musical score on the concert platform.

Knowing the words of a waiata well enough to sing or recite it was not enough on its own. Far more important was choosing appropriate waiata for any given occasion, and that depended on knowing a range of suitable choices, sizing up each particular situation, choosing appropriate waiata, and presenting them with understanding and feeling.

Handling Questions

The kai-whakauru agreed that in their experience the ways in which adults responded to children's questions depended on the circumstances. If they considered that the questioner was not mature enough for a full answer or that a question was inappropriate in that particular setting, they might refrain from answering entirely, divert attention in another direction or supply a partial, stop-gap answer, deferring a full one to another time. In general, adults tended to limit how many questions they would answer at any one time. Not infrequently they told children to stop asking questions in no uncertain terms: 'Kāti! Hōhā i ōu pātai nā.' (That's enough! I'm sick and tired of your questions!) On occasion this discouragement of questions was due to impatience or more pressing concerns, but it could also be a deliberate ploy to test the depth of the questioner's desire to learn and make them think for themselves instead of seeking knowledge the easy way.

Sowing Seeds for Future Learning

Looking back, the kai-whakauru remembered the adults in their lives dropping 'snippets of information' which made no sense at the time. Often these snippets took the form of whakataukī and metaphorical references to people and natural phenomena. Sometimes the kai-whakauru had been intrigued enough to ask for elucidation but more often they simply filed such snippets in the backs of their minds until later learning provided a context that gave them meaning. Thoughtful teachers used this tactic deliberately to stimulate curiosity, enquiry and a search for meaning.

Warning of Problems and Dangers

Several kai-whakauru complained that the adults in their lives often failed to warn them of possible mistakes and contingencies beforehand. Certainly, when danger was a real possibility, adults issued strong verbal warnings and told stories about the consequences of breaching tapu or offending taniwha, tupua or kai-tiaki (see Glossary), but in everyday life they often left learners to make mistakes and even to flounder for a while.

The kai-whakauru variously explained this avoidance of direct warning as a preference for a positive approach to minor problems and a belief that children learnt more from their own mistakes than from verbal warnings. In their experience, the adults involved usually extricated the blunderer sooner or later and had a quiet word of explanation and advice in private. However, if adults thought the child was or had been whakahīhī they might compound the pain with a public rebuke. Looking back, the kai-whakauru acknowledged that the consequences of a mistake, including the resulting whakamā, fixed the event in their memories and made them less likely to make that mistake again.

Practising in Safe Contexts

Where the skills and knowledge imparted were physically or spiritually dangerous if misused, responsible adults restricted children to practising their performance in safe contexts before allowing them to work on their own. They did this by providing supervision and monitoring each learner's passage through a series of stages. Thus children were introduced to equipment used on the farm, at sea or in the bush as members of work groups under constant supervision, and were only promoted to more complex tasks as they demonstrated maturity as well as competence. Experts in whakapapa, whaikōrero and karanga did not begin to train students in these fields until they were nearly or fully adult and helped them develop their skills in the local community among close kin before allowing them to perform in the presence of outsiders.

Emphasis on Readiness

The kai-whakauru repeatedly commented on the extent to which adults and especially pūkenga emphasised readiness over absolute age as the criterion for admission to more advanced learning and practice. This was particularly evident in the more esoteric fields of knowledge and could lead to differentiation among siblings and age-mates. It was sometimes associated with the idea that individual family members inherited different attributes and roles from their forebears.

Expressing Approval and Disapproval

In the communities in which the kai-whakauru grew up, the responsibility for applying positive and negative sanctions to their behaviour as learners was shared widely across the whole community. Whatever their exact relationship, adults did not hesitate to intervene if they saw children in difficulties or behaving badly. There was, moreover, a division of labour between the roles of parents and those of other, especially older, relatives. Parents were mainly concerned with checking bad behaviour and signs of whakahīhī: they refrained from praising their children to their face and typically ignored or disparaged their achievements. In contrast, other relatives, especially those from senior generations, were generous with expressions of love, praise and encouragement.

As well as expressing approval and disapproval in words, adults often did it non-verbally, with a look or a touch, and indirectly, by accepting them into or excluding them from more responsible tasks and special tuition.

Whatever they did in private, in public adults usually directed praise and criticism to the group as a whole rather than singling out individuals. They were aware that public praise in particular ran the risk of making children whakamā and upsetting their relations with their peers. While children were grateful not to be singled out in public whether for praise or blame, they did not always recognise expressions of approval as such when they were given indirectly.

Taking Advantage of Opportunities

The kai-whakauru reported that the adults who were their teachers when they were children recognised and took advantage of opportunities for learning as they arose, even if this meant diverging from existing plans. In particular, pūkenga responded to crises by telling and re-telling stories about local ancestors and events that held lessons for present and future behaviour. Told in times of heightened emotion, for example, at the celebration of a notable success or when mourning a death, such stories made a lasting impression.

Summing Up

The educational practices described in this and previous chapters developed organically in the context of home and community life. They were not expressed as explicit prescriptions nor taught as such. Some community members simply replicated patterns of behaviour remembered from their own childhood or did what was possible or seemed best in particular circumstances; but many others, especially koroua, kuia and pūkenga, thought deeply about the educational goals they wished to achieve and both used and modified traditional methods to achieve them.

Thinking back to their childhood, the kai-whakauru realised that many important lessons were not presented as such but were conveyed indirectly in the course of doing something else. Storytelling and the dramatising of social encounters and interpersonal relations at hui on the marae successfully impressed information and ideas on their young minds. Several of the kai-whakauru were certain that their parents and grandparents deliberately turned a blind eye to them hovering on the fringe of adult conversation as adolescents, allowing them to pick up information the older generations were reluctant to address directly. Learning by eavesdropping, one of them called it.

As far as the kai-whakauru were concerned, the cumulative effect of the educational practices of their childhoods was to reinforce their identity as Māori and their capacity to play effective roles as adults both at home and in the wider society.

Educational Principles

The learning and teaching practices highlighted by the kai-whakauru are undergirded by a set of generative educational principles (kaupapa). After several readings of our recorded conversations I venture to identify the following as principles of key importance.

Knowledge as a Taonga

The kai-whakauru were united in valuing knowledge in general as a taonga or more accurately a collection of taonga, to be cherished, added to and passed on. Originating with God or the gods, knowledge had mana and conferred mana on its holders. It was to be aspired to, actively sought and attained only with effort.

The Complementarity of Tapu and Noa Kinds of Knowledge

Different kinds of knowledge were either tapu or not-tapu (noa). Tapu kinds of knowledge were protected by restrictions on access and practice: by and to whom they might be taught, where and before whom they might be presented. Noa kinds of knowledge were concerned with ordinary everyday experience and were generally open and available to all who were willing to learn. Far from being opposities, alternatives or ranked in value, tapu and noa kinds of knowledge were complementary to each other, intertwined in practice and thought of as constituting a single whole. Noa kinds of knowledge were associated with te oranga o te tinana – survival and bodily well-being. If their value was less publicly proclaimed it was in some ways more fundamental, a value expressed in whakataukī that stressed the importance of food-providers and child-bearers.

Knowledge as a Group Possession

Knowledge belonged to the group (whānau, hapū, iwi, churches, kapa haka and various voluntary groups) rather than to individuals. The idea of knowledge as a group possession went with emphasis on the use of knowledge in the service of the group rather than individual ambition. Learning to be an acceptable group member and to work in groups, learning the skills of interpersonal relations and co-operation, were more important than individual achievement. Educational strategies stressed learning in the context of relations with people, working alongside and in interaction with others. Learning was a very personal project in which affection, respect, awe, and a degree of competition between learner and teacher were key features.

Storehouses of Knowledge

Certain kinds of knowledge were stored by the group in individuals described as pūkenga, a word translated as 'a repository' and 'a storehouse of knowledge' (Williams, 1975, p.307; and Ryan, 1995, p.200). Pūkenga were seen as trustees charged with preserving, increasing and handing on the knowledge entrusted to them. While they held knowledge in store, pūkenga were expected to use it for the benefit of the group; doing so won them recognition and status in the community. They were also expected to select and train their successor or successors. In making this selection a pūkenga took account of a range of factors including kinship, aptitude and appropriate attitudes.

Shared Responsibility for Learning

Learning and teaching were joint enterprises in which responsibility for learning was shared and the development of good interpersonal relations and co-operation was as important as or more important than individual achievement. As the custodians of knowledge, teachers were worthy of respect and learners were expected to treat then accordingly; but teachers whose knowledge proved inadequate could expect to be abandoned by their pupils. Learners were given considerable freedom to choose whether and what to learn. If they did not take advantage of the opportunities offered, that was considered their responsibility and loss. Where tapu kinds of knowledge were concerned, their custodians actively discouraged would-be learners in order to identify those who were committed enough to persevere.

Hinengaro – Combining Head and Heart
Learning and teaching involved recognition of the importance of the emotions as well as the intellect. Te reo Māori includes both thinking and feeling in the word 'hinengaro', defined as 'the seat of thoughts and emotions' (Williams, 1975, p.51) and traditionally located in the chest. When speaking English, the kai-whakauru used 'head' and 'heart' interchangeably when translating 'hinengaro'.

Using All the Senses
Verbal expression and expressiveness (kupu, kōrero) were highly valued in association with (and not in isolation from) full development of all the senses. Learning to look and see with the eyes, to listen with the ears, and to co-ordinate bodily movement in both music and dance were fundamental skills best mastered young.

Adaptation, Debate and Creativity
The preservation, protection and presentation of knowledge, including that tuku iho nō ngā tūpuna, did not preclude adaptation and change. On the contrary, knowledge must be kept relevant and useful in the present by the continual adjustment of both form and content to the needs of the people and the present time. Once the basics of a skill or knowledge store were acquired, there was plenty of room for debate, synthesis and creativity.

Achieving Understanding

The ultimate aim of education was understanding of people and the world, in short, the attainment of wisdom. Understanding required a foundation in factual knowledge but it also required experience, the amassing of an extensive range of cases and precedents. The true pūkenga did not simply reproduce what they knew factually, did not simply sing a waiata or recite a whakapapa. They reviewed all the similar situations they had witnessed and on that basis decided how to act in the present, which waiata to sing, which ancestor to begin with, by a rapid computing of all the variables involved.

Continuing Education

Education was essentially continuing education, an ongoing life-long process passing through a series of stages. Learners had to learn certain things and show signs of competence before being allowed to progress further.

The Importance of Readiness

Readiness, both actual and as assessed by the teachers, was of key importance in learning. There were things some people would never be 'ready' for but there was always a niche for them to find where they could make a contribution. On the whole children (tamariki) were expected to be concerned with exploring and developing their senses rather than the intellect. In the past, adults actively discouraged children and even young people (taitamariki, nowadays called rangatahi) from showing what they considered a premature interest in subjects that required maturity. Pūkenga might capitalise on children's capacity for rote learning and teach them waiata and short whakapapa, but they regarded this more as sowing seeds to lie dormant to come to fruition in later years. Certain things (whakapapa traced from the gods or celebrated ancestors, whaikōrero before visitors) should not be approached until middle age and beyond.

Wholeness and Connectedness

The view of education that emerges from the discourse of the kai-whakauru emphasised wholeness and connectedness. It put together things that Western thinking separates, tackled several subjects and pursued several goals at once. It aimed at nothing less than the education of the whole person.

He Kupu Whakamutunga

In talking with such openness about their childhoods, the kai-whakauru give modern readers privileged access to the learning contexts, teaching practices and bodies of knowledge that obtained in Māori rural communities between 1920 and 1960. In doing so they clearly establish that these communities were misjudged by the educational authorities of the time, and share ideas and insights into the educational process that could and should make a useful contribution to current debates about educational theory and practice, whether in the home or at school.

In a recent letter Haare Williams summed up his experience of growing up Māori in just three sentences. The other kai-whakauru who have read this statement endorse it as true of their experience also. It makes a fitting last word.

> I learned in those early childhood years by observation and imitation, then by affirmation and approbation. Learning was connected to all things, a joint enterprise with nature, ancestors, the elders and with the communities we lived in, all involving the heart, the body, the mind and the spirit in unison. Learning was a journey without end. *(Haare Williams)*

GLOSSARY

The primary purpose of this glossary is to extend the understanding of readers unfamilar with te reo Māori. It is particularly complex because it involves two languages, Māori and English, each with its own grammar and vocabulary.

The Māori words and phrases listed in the left-hand column all occur in the main text glossed on first appearance with an English 'translation' chosen as the most appropriate in that context. But more than this is needed for full understanding. Sometimes a Māori word and an English word share exactly the same meaning, but more often the match is inexact: the Māori word has other meanings or (to put it another way) other English words are needed to translate it fully. For this reason, the right-hand column uses English to explore the meanings attached to each Māori word, together with its metaphorical applications, dialect variations and changes in usage over time. These explanations are derived from several sources: *A Dictionary of the Maori Language* (H. W. Williams, 1975), chosen as the dictionary known and used by the kai-whakauru in the early 1980s and closest to traditional Māori usage; the dictionaries edited by H. M. Ngata (1993) and P. M. Ryan (1995), which include later developments in meaning and usage; the writer's own field-based knowledge and consultation with the kai-whakauru; and the *Guidelines for Māori Language Orthography* booklet published by Te Taura Whiri i te Reo Māori.

Te reo Māori has its own grammatical categories that differ significantly from those of the English language. However, for the sake of readers not familiar with Māori grammar, this glossary continues the long-standing convention which identifies Māori words as belonging to the grammatical categories used in dictionaries of the English language: as nouns (n.), locational nouns (loc. n.), transitive and intransitive verbs (v. tr. and v. intr.), adjectives (adj.), adverbs (adv.), personal names (pers. name), prepositions (prep.), phrases (phr.), pronouns (pron.) and metaphorical usages (metaph.). It also uses numbers to distinguish several meanings of a word, beginning sometimes with the root meaning (for example, 'straight' for 'tika'), sometimes with the most common. Readers interested in the in-depth study of te reo are referred to Bauer (1997) and Te Taura Whiri i te Reo Māori (2008).

In te reo Māori, the length of vowels is significant for both meaning and pronunciation. In this work, long vowels are marked with a macron where these are known or in well-established usage. Names of organisations and institutions that existed before the use of macrons became widespread are not given macrons, e.g. Te Wananga o Tai Tokerau.

a/o, ā/ō	prep. of, belonging to. Whether 'a' or 'o' is used depends on and indicates the nature of the relationship between what comes before and after (see Te Taura Whiri i te Reo Māori, n.d., pp.7–8).
aha	pron. 1. what; 2. he aha? why, for what purpose; 3. hei aha! never mind.
āhuatanga	n. 1. likeness; 2. circumstance, e.g., ngā āhuatanga o te wā (the circumstances of the time). From āhua (form, appearance) + tanga.
aituā	n. 1. misfortune; 2. trouble; 3. disaster; 4. accident; 5. death.
ako	v. tr. 1. learn; 2. teach; 3. advise.
ākonga	n. 1. learner; 2. pupil, student; 3. disciple.
ānei	= ēnei, pl. of tēnei.
anei	adv. 1. here; 2. in this case.
apakura	n. a sung poem of lament for the dead (McLean, 1996, pp.145–46).
ariki	n. 1. firstborn in senior descent-line in an iwi and thus inheritor of special mana; 2. chief of chiefs in an iwi with special ritual status and duties; 3. spelt with upper case 'A', meaning 'Lord', Ariki is reserved for Jesus Christ.
Arikinui	n. title for heads of the Kīngitanga and Ngāti Tūwharetoa respectively.
aroha	n. 1. caring, compassionate love for others, especially relatives; also used to convey 2. sympathy for those in sorrow or trouble; 3. gratitude; 4. approval.
ātea	adj. clear (of space).
atua	n. 1. thing or person imbued with mana and tapu; 2. spirit; 3. god; 4. with upper case 'A', Atua means God. adj. extraordinary.
awa	n. 1. river; 2. channel; 3. gully, gorge; 4. groove.
awhi	v. tr. 1. embrace; 2. foster, cherish.

GLOSSARY

haka	n. 1. generic term for dances performed to chanted words; 2. dances of this type performed by men before war-like activities, e.g., challenge to visitors, rugby match (McLean, 1996, pp.44–46, 57–67; Kāretu, 1993).
hākari	n. 1. gift, present; 2. feast accompanying exchange of gifts; 3. climactic meal during a hui, following the main activity.
hakihaki	n. skin disease characterised by itchiness and scabs.
hāngī	n. 1. earth oven, a means of cooking food in a pit by means of steam; 2. food cooked in a hāngī.
hāhi	n. transliteration of English 'church'.
hapū	adj. pregnant. n. a descent group associated with a particular territory that was politically independent until mid-nineteenth century but is now referred to and treated by government as a sub-tribe subordinate to the iwi (Ballara, 1998). In-married spouses and non-descendants resident on hapū territory are excluded in theory but take part in hapū activities under the hapū name.
hara	n. 1. violation of tapu; 2. offence; 3. sin.
harakeke	n. 1. New Zealand flax, *Phormium tenax*; a flax bush (pā harakeke) consists of multiple fans of flax blades and is used as a metaphor for the whānau.
hararei	n. transliteration of holiday.
hau	n. 1. wind; 2. breath; 3. breath/wind that comes from the supernatural realm (hauora); 4. the force believed to accompany the gift of a taonga to ensure its return to sender; 5. dew, moisture.
haukāinga	n.1. home settlement; 2. the home people; 3. the hosts at a hui on their home marae = tangata whenua
hautupua	n. a supernatural being of fearsome proportions, a giant.
he	indef. article both singular and plural.
hē	adj. 1. wrong; 2. erring; 3. mistaken; 4. perplexed, at a loss; 5. in trouble or difficulty; 6. baleful; 7. dead. n. 1. error; 2. mistake; 3. fault; 4. trouble, difficulty.
Hema	pers. name, father of mythical Māori hero Tāwhaki.
hī aka	phr. fishing, especially with line and hook.
hiki	v. tr. 1. lift up, raise; 2. remove, take away, e.g., tapu or rāhui. Hīkina is the passive form.

hīmene	n. transliteration of 'hymn'.
hine	n. 1. girl, chiefly used in address as 'e hine'; 2. daughter, see tamāhine.
Hinenuitepō	pers. name, the goddess who presided over the realm of the dead in Māori mythology.
hinengaro	n. 1. an internal organ, possibly spleen; 2. seat of both thought and emotions.
hōhā	adj. wearied with expectation, importunity, anxiety etc.; according to context, exasperated, irritated, fed-up, impatient, can't be bothered.
hongi	v. tr. to greet by pressing noses. n. the action of pressing noses, signifying trust and friendship because it brings the parties close enough to mingle breath (see hau above). The details of performance vary slightly between tribes.
hopuhopu	v. tr. catch frequently or one after the other.
hui	v. tr. put or add together. v. intr. gather, congregate, come together. n. 1. generic term for a Māori gathering, typically held on a marae and organised according to the tikanga of that marae; 2. in other situations, meeting or gathering.
huia	n. a native bird now extinct, *Heteralocha acutirostris*. Huia feathers were prized by Māori as hair ornaments.
huti, huhuti	v. tr. 1. hoist, pull up (e.g., anchor; 2. pull off the rocks (e.g., limpets).
ika	n. generic term for fish
iri	v. intr. 1. be elevated on something; 2. rest on something; 3. hang, be suspended from.
iriiri	v. tr. 1. sprinkle with water, especially as a ritual act; 2. baptise.
iwi	n. 1. bone; 2. stone of fruit; 3. people, as in te iwi kāinga (the local people); 4. a large-scale socio-political grouping defined by descent from a named ancestor, usually translated as 'tribe'.
kā	v. tr. take fire, be lighted, burn.
kahawai	n. a fish, *Arripis trutta*.
kai	v. tr. 1. eat; 2. consume, e.g., by fire. n. food.

GLOSSARY

kaimoana	n. seafood.
kai-	prefix indicating 'one who (does something)'.
kai-karanga	n. a woman trained to do the karanga; see below.
kai-kōrero	n. one who makes formal speeches, especially on the marae and as the representative of a group, e.g., whānau.
kai-tiaki	n. 1. guardian, protector; 2. 'guardian animal' associated with a whānau, hapū or iwi; 3. members of land-holding descent groups with responsibility to care for and protect taonga, especially land.
kai-tonotono	n. one who obeys command: 1. formerly slave; 2. today, dogsbody, gofer.
kai-whakauru	n. participant; in this book, research participant.
kāinga	n. 1. kā (burn) + inga, hence place where fires have burned, e.g., for cooking; 2. unfortified settlement, village; 3. house, home; 4. any place of abode.
kamokamo	n. fruit of exotic gourds; possibly a transliteration of cucumber.
kanohi	n. 1. eye; 2. face. Kanohi ki kanohi = face to face.
kānga	n. corn, maize.
kānga kōpūwai, kānga pirau	n. porridge made of fermented corn.
kao	n. sundried kūmara.
kapa haka	n. 1. performance of both sung and recited song and dance styles in rows; 2. group formed to perform such.
kapu tī	phr. cup of tea; transliteration from English.
karaka	n. a native tree, *Corynocarpus laevigata*, with glossy green leaves and orange fruit with a poisonous kernel. Māori removed the poison by steaming.
karakia	n. 1. ritual chant; 2. prayer(s) (McLean, 1996, pp.35–38).
karanga	v. tr. 1. call, summon; 2. welcome. n. 1. chanted calling by women, used to invite visitors to enter marae, to reply to such an invitation, and to acknowledge a koha; 2. relative, in expressions karanga rua (relatives related two ways) and karanga maha (relatives of many kinds).
kaukau	v. tr. 1. bathe; 2. swim.
kaumātua	n. 1. adult; 2. in past, the head of a whānau; 3. a male or female person of senior social status, knowledgeable

	about tikanga Māori; 4. a male or female person of grandparental or equivalent age.
kaupapa	n. 1. level surface, applicable to floor, stage, platform; 2. layer; 3. groundwork of a feather cloak; 4. basic idea, principle; 5. topic; 6. plan.
kāuta	n. cooking shelter or shed.
kauwae/kauae	n. 1. jaw; 2. chin; 3. chin tattoo.
kawa	n. 1. tapu-lifting chant involving use of sprig of greenery; 2. tapu-lifting ceremony; 3. the rules/protocol obtaining on a marae or comparable setting = tikanga.
kawakawa	n. 1. a native shrub, *Macropiper excelsum*, with medicinal uses; 2. a dark variety of greenstone.
kawe mate	n. literally 'carry the dead'; the ritual visit paid by the bereaved to reciprocate visits to a tangihanga by other groups and to thank them for their attendance.
kēhua	n. ghost, spirit; identified as 'a modern word' by Williams (1975, p.112) and translated as 'ghost, Jack of cards, apparition, gremlin, phantom, banshee' by Ryan (1995, p.92).
kete	n. a flat rectangular container with handles, made by weaving long strips of flax together; 'kit' in New Zealand English.
kī	v. tr. 1. say; 2. tell. n. saying, word. See whakataukī below.
kiekie	n. a native climbing plant with long narrow leaves, *Freycinetia banksii*; used in tukutuku panels and superior kete.
kimi	v. tr. seek, look for.
kina	n. sea-egg, *Evechinus*.
kino	adj. 1. bad; 2. evil. Opposite of pai (good).
Kīngitanga	n. Kīngi + tanga = the King Movement based at Tūrangawaewae on the Waipā River.
kiore	n. rat, especially the species brought to New Zealand by Polynesian voyagers.
kiri	n. 1. skin, bark; 2. person, self.
kirimate	n. near relative of a person who has died.
kiritea	adj. fair-skinned.
koha	n. 1. parting instruction; 2. gift given in reciprocation for gifts, services or hospitality received; may take form of money, goods or services.

kōhanga reo	phr. literally 'language nest'; pre-school centre based on Māori principles and using Māori as the language of instruction.
kohi	v. tr. 1. collect, gather together; 2. collect one's thoughts.
kohu	n. 1. mist; 2. fog.
koko kahawai	phr. a large, spoon-shaped net for landing kahawai fish.
kono	n. a small flax basket for serving cooked food = rourou.
kopakopa	n. an exotic plant, plaintain.
kōrero	v. tr. 1. tell, say. n. 1. conversation; 2. news; 3. story; 4. speech; 5. discussion.
kōrero-ā-whare	n. peacemaking discussion inside the meeting-house.
kōrero pakiwaitara	phr. a wide range of stories traditional and modern, often fictional. See Chapter 8, p.XX
kōrero pūrākau	phr. a wide range of stories, especially those of significance, e.g., origin stories, myths, stories of the ancestors.
kōrerorero	v. intr. talk much or frequently, discuss. n. discussion.
koromiko	n. a species of shrub, *Hebe salicifolia*.
koroua	n. a male kaumātua; shortened to koro as form of address. In some tribes koro is used to describe and address grandfather.
korowai	n. a finely woven flax cloak with twisted black flax thrums.
kotahitanga	n. kotahi (one) + tanga. 1. unity; 2. union, association, committee; 3. with upper case 'K', Māori Parliament of late nineteenth century; 4. healing movement with widely dispersed practitioners.
koti, kokoti	v. tr. cut in two, divide
kotinga	n. 1. the process of dividing; 2. boundary line or zone.
kōtiro	n. 1. girl; 2. daughter in northern iwi.
kōuka	n. 'cabbage tree' in New Zealand English, *Cordyline australis*.
kōura	n. crayfish, both seawater and freshwater species.
kōwhai	n. 1. native tree with golden flowers in spring, *Sophora tetraptera*, *S. microphylla*; 2. the colour yellow.
kōwhaiwhai	n. painted scroll patterns, especially on the rafters and ridgepole of the meeting-house.
kuia	n. a female kaumātua; shortened to kui as form of address.

	In some tribes kuia is used to describe and address grandmother.
kuku	n. mussels, *mytilus planulatus*.
kūmara	n. sweet potato, *Ipomoea batatas*.
kupu	n. 1 anything said; 2. word; 3. saying; 4. message; 5. talk.
kura	n. 1. the colour red; 2. valued possession; 3. school, a transliteration from English.
kura kaupapa Māori	phr. primary or secondary school based on Māori principles and using Māori as the language of instruction.
kuta	n. a rush, *Scirpus lacustris*, used for weaving mats and kits.
mahi	v. tr. 1. work; 2. make; 3. do, perform. n. 1. work; 2. occupation; 3. doing(s), e.g., ngā mahi a ngā tūpuna (the doings of the ancestors), mahi-ā-ringa (manual work).
mako	n. 1. mako shark, *Isurus glaucus*; 2. shark tooth worn as ear pendant.
mākutu	n. 1. the use of mana to harm or punish others; 2. chant used for that purpose.
mana	n. power originating in the spiritual realm conferred from above (by the gods) and endorsed from below (by the people); 2. authority stemming from the indwelling of spiritual power (Marsden, 1975, pp. 193–94); 3. prestige, standing; 4. proven ability to do and get things done.
manaaki	v. tr. 1. show respect for; 2. show kindness to; 3. care for, look after; 4. show hospitality to; 5. bless, in prayer 'Mā te Atua koe e manaaki' (God bless you).
manawa	n. 1. belly, bowels; 2. bowels of the earth; 3. the (physical) heart; 4. the heart as seat of the affections; 5. breath (hē manawa = short of breath); 6. patience; 7. mind, spirit (manawanui = stout-hearted, manawa pā = grudging, reluctant); 8. encouragement, support.
manono	n. shrub, *Coprosma australis*.
mānuka	n. trees popularly known as 'tea-tree', *Leptosperm scoparium* and *L. ericoides*.
manuhiri, manuwhiri	n. visitor, guest.
māngai	n. 1. mouth; 2. mouthpiece; 3. with capital, title given to the prophet Wiremu Tahupōtiki Rātana.

māngoingoi	v. tr. to fish with a line from the shore.
māori	adj. normal, usual, ordinary, familiar cf. unusual, extraordinary; as in wai māori (fresh water cf. wai mātaitai, sea water), rākau māori (ordinary trees cf. forest giants like kauri and tōtara).
Māori	n. Māori person. adj. pertaining to Māori, e.g., te reo Māori (the Māori language). In the nineteenth century the indigenous people distinguished themselves as tāngata māori in comparison to the extraordinary visitors who had come from overseas. The latter identified the adjective (which in Māori follows the noun) as the noun. They called Māori 'New Zealanders' for a long time, then 'Natives', adopting 'Māori' as official nomenclature in the late 1940s.
Māoritanga	n. 1. Māoriness; 2. pride in being Māori; 3. Māori ways = ngā tikanga Māori.
māra, māranga kai	n. area under cultivation, 'gardens' = plantings of kūmara, potatoes, pumpkins, corn, etc.
marae	n. 1. open space in front of a meeting-house, best described as the marae ātea; 2. combination of marae ātea with meeting-house, dining-hall and related buildings on land reserved for the purpose, usually associated with a hapū and used for communal gatherings; sometimes identified as a marae complex; 3. community focused on a marae, especially in the Waikato area. adj. generous, hospitable.
marama	n. 1. moon; 2. month.
maramataka	n. lunar calendar
mārama	adj. 1. light (not dark); 2. clear of sight or sound; 3. transparent; 4. easy to understand.
māramatanga	n. mārama + tanga. 1. enlightenment, illumination; 2. highly developed understanding.
mata	n. 1. face; 2. eye; 3. headland.
mātāmua	n. the firstborn (in some iwi the firstborn male) in a sibling set.
mātau	v. intr. 1. know, be acquainted with; 2. understand; 3. feel certain of.
mātauranga	n. mātau + -ranga. 1. knowledge; 2. understanding.

mate	adj. 1. dead; 2. extinguished; 3. sick, ill, unconscious; 4. injured, damaged, suffering; 5. in want, lacking; 6. overcome with emotion. n. 1. death; 2. sickness etc.; 3. hui mourning the dead = tangihanga (Williams, 1975, p.185).
matū	n. 1. fat; 2. nourishment; 3. gist, kernel (of a matter).
matua (sing.), mātua (pl.)	n. 1. parent of either sex in most iwi; 2. parents' siblings and cousins of the parents' generation and both sexes.
Māui	pers. name, demi-god hero of a Māori myth cycle.
mauri	n. 1. life principle of human beings, natural resources and many artefacts; 2. material object holding and representing the mauri of something else, e.g., stones representing the mauri of a forest or a meeting-house.
mea	n. 1. thing; 2. reason, cause; 3. fact, event. With capital, Mea = So-and-so.
meeting-house = whare hui	n. a building maintained as a gathering place for a group, usually a hapū; ideally rectangular with gabled front decorated with carving and typically named after an ancestor.
mihi	v. tr. greet. n. 1. greeting; 2. speech of greeting; 3. welcome ceremony which includes speeches of greeting.
mihingare	adj. in Te Hāhi Mihingare = the Anglican Church. Transliteration of 'missionary'.
mimi	v. intr. urinate. n. 1. urine; 2. stream, creek.
mingimingi	adj. curly, twisted. n. shrubs of a twisted divaricating growth, *Cyathodes juniperina*.
miri	v. tr. 1. rub; 2. stroke; 3. soothe. n. massage
miro	n. tree with berries attractive to birds, *Podocarpus ferrugineus*.
moana	n. 1. sea; 2. lake.
mōhio	v. tr. 1. know; 2. understand; 3. recognise. adj. 1. intelligent; 2. wise. n. a knowing person (*too* clever).

mōhiotanga	n. mōhio + -tanga. 1. knowledge; 2. understanding.
moko	n. 1. tattooing on the face or body; 2. general term for lizard; 3. abbreviation of mokopuna.
moko taura	phr. grandchild attached to a grandparent as if by a cord.
mokopuna	n. 1. grandchild of either sex; 2. all relatives of the same generation as grandchild.
mōteatea	n. generic term for poems composed in traditional style, both sung and chanted.
mua	loc. n. 1. of place, the front; 2. of time, the past.
muka	n. 1. prepared flax fibre; 2. a strand of flax fibre.
muri	loc. n. 1. of place, the back; 2. of time, the future.
muru	v. tr. take compensation from an offender. n. the ritualised process of taking compensation from an offender and his whānau or hapū.
na	adv. used at beginning of sentence to call attention to point being made.
nīkau	n. New Zealand palm, *Rhopalostylis sapida*.
noa	adj. 1. free from tapu and restrictions; 2. free from anxiety, relaxed; 3. ordinary, of no moment. adv. without limitations or conditions, to be translated according to context.
nono	n. 1. (coll.) bottom; 2. anus; 3. vagina.
ngākau	n. 1. viscera, guts; 2. seat of affections and/or feelings, heart (metaphorical); 3. sometimes mind.
ngākihi	n. general term for limpet.
ōhākī	n. farewell speech bestowing gifts, especially when delivered by one about to die.
ora	adj. 1. alive; 2. well, in health; 3. healthy (whole) in body, mind and spirit. n. life and health in full measure, in body, mind and spirit.
oranga	n. ora + -nga. 1. food; 2. livelihood; 3. wellbeing, (good) health.
oranga ngākau	phr. comfort.
pā	n. 1. traditionally, a fortified settlement; 2. in twentieth century an unfortified settlement.
pae	n. 1. horizon; 2. region; 3. direction; 4. horizontal range of hills; 4. any transverse support, e.g., hen roost.

pāeke	n. rule governing speaking order in pōwhiri in which host speakers speak first followed by all visiting speakers, and a host speaker closes the speeches.
paenga	n. margin, boundary, especially between natural and supernatural worlds.
paepae	n. 1. beam, bar, especially across the front of a carved meeting-house; 2. threshold, doorsill; 3. horizontal bar of old-time latrine; 4. bench or row of seats occupied by host speakers on a marae (= taumata in Tai Tokerau).
Pākehā	n. 1. non-Māori New Zealanders of British and European descent, especially those who feel that their roots are in New Zealand; 2. when used in the pairing Māori and Pākehā, all non-Māori New Zealanders.
pakeke	adj. 1. hard, stiff; 2. obstinate, difficult; 3. adult. n. 1. old person; 2. adult; 3. used in certain iwi as synonym for kaumātua.
pakiwaitara	n. 1. scandal; 2. subject of gossip; 3. fiction, legend, folklore; 4. light-hearted stories told to entertain.
pao	n. a poem of derision composed and sung in traditional style (McLean, 1996, pp.117–23).
pāpaka	n. crab
papakāinga	n. papa (anything broad, flat and hard) + kāinga. 1. piece of land held by hapū on collective title on which hapū members can build houses but do not own their house site; 2. a settlement resulting from this arrangement.
Papatūānuku	pers. name, 1. female partner of primal pair in Māori mythology; 2. the earth, literally and metaphorically.
parāoa	n. 1. flour; 2. bread; a transliteration of 'flour'.
parareka	n. 1. the horseshoe fern, *Marattia salicina*, cultivated for its starchy rhizome; 2. potato.
parengo	n. edible seaweed, *Porphyra columbina*.
paru	n. 1. dirt, mud; 2. excrement. adj. dirty.
paruparu	n. 1. mud, dirt; 2. particular kind of mud used in dyeing flax.
pātai	v. tr. 1. question, inquire; 2. provoke, challenge. n. question.

pātaka	n. storehouse raised on posts for storing special foods and other taonga.
pātere	n. song composed by women in reply to gossip or slander (McLean, 1996, pp.41–43).
patu	v. tr. 1. strike; 2. beat; 3. ill-treat; 4. kill. n. stone club
pāua	n. generic name for species of *Haliotis*, a univalve mollusc with iridescent inside to shell.
pawhera	v. tr. split open a fish for smoking or cooking.
pikopiko	n. a fern, *Polystichum richardi*; 2. young curved fern shoots.
pipi	n. bivalve shellfish, triangular in shape.
piri, piripiri	v. intr. 1. stick, adhere, cling to; 2. keep close to; 3. be attached to.
piupiu	n. skirt consisting of patterned dried flax cylinders hanging from a woven waistband; long for women, short for men.
poka	n. hole, pit, well.
pokanoa	v. tr. to do anything at random, without authority, thus breaching tapu and damaging mana.
pokapoka	v. tr. pit with holes.
ponga	n. a tree fern, *Cyathea dealbata*.
pono	adj. 1. true; 2. bountiful, abundant. See whakapono.
pononga	n. 1. slave; 2. servant.
pōrangi	adj. 1. out of one's mind, 'mad'; 2. hurried; 3. distracted; 4. headstrong.
poroiwi	adj. emaciated, skeletal. n. bone.
poroporo	n. plant species Nightshade, *Solanum nigrum*, *Solum aviculare*.
poroporoaki	v. tr. leave instructions on departing. n. last speech of a dying chief to his people; 2. farewell chant addressed to a dead person by a male mourner; 3. ceremonial exchange of speeches initiated by visitors before departing from a hui.
pōtiki	n. youngest child in a sibling set.
pou	n. 1. post, pole; 2. (metaph.) support; 3. teacher, expert.
pōua	n. male grandparent in certain iwi.

poupou	n. carved slabs lining the walls of a meeting-house.
pōwhiri	v. tr. 1. wave; 2. beckon someone to come forward; 3. welcome, especially visitors to a marae. n. 1. action-song of welcome typically involving women waving greenery; 2. welcome ceremony including action-songs of welcome, a case of a part standing for the whole.
pūhā, pūwhā	n. 1. sow thistle, *Sonchus oleraceus*; 2. any green vegetable.
pūkenga	adj. skilled in a branch of knowledge. n. a person who is a storehouse of special knowledge; synonym of tohunga without the sometimes negative connotations of the latter.
puku	n. 1. abdomen, stomach; 2. swelling; 3. seat of affections; 4. memory; 5. appetite.
puna	n. 1. spring of water; 2. source; 3. ancestor.
pūpū	n. general name for volute molluscs of the winkle type, coll. 'cat's eye'.
pūrākau	n. 1. legend; 2. myth; 3. stories of serious significance.
pūriri	n. tree with small pink flowers and berries and very hard striated wood, *Vitex lucens*.
rāhui	n. 1. a temporary ban imposed by kaumātua on a particular area or activity to protect natural resources or show respect after a death; 2. physical object, e.g., post marking a rāhui.
rakaraka	n. implement to break up ground for cultivation, rake or harrow.
rākau	n. 1. tree; 2. timber; 3. wood; 4. stick; 5. anything made of wood, e.g., mast, weapon, walking stick.
Rākaunui	n. the nights of the full moon in the maramataka.
rangatahi	n. 1. a certain kind of fishing net about 10 fathoms long; 2. key metaphor in the proverb 'Ka pū te ruha, ka hao te rangatahi' (the worn out one is cast aside, the new net goes fishing). This proverb was used originally to refer to the replacement of a dead chief by another chief but was adapted at the end of the nineteenth century to refer to the replacement of old-style Māori leaders by leaders of a new kind, young, educated and bilingual (e.g., Āpirana Ngata and Te Rangi Hīroa). It was then further adapted to identify young people between children and kaumātua.

rangatira	n. 1. member of senior descent-lines in hapū or iwi constituting the aristocracy; 2. chief of a hapū, chosen on basis of senior descent and leadership capacity = *the* rangatira; 3. captain (of a ship).
rangatiratanga	n. rangatira + tanga. 1. evidence of aristocratic breeding and leadership; 2. the role and attributes of a chief; 3. a group's right and capacity to manage its own affairs. Tino Rangatiratanga: Māori self-determination.
rangi	n. 1. sky; 2. day; 3. tune of a song-poem.
Ranginui	pers. name, 1. male partner of primal pair in Māori mythology; 2. sky; 3. heavens.
raranga	v. tr. weave mats and kits from flax and other plant materials.
rātā	n. a forest tree with red flowers, *Mitrosideros robusta*; begins life as a parasitic vine.
raupatu	v. tr. conquer, overcome. n. 1. conquest; 2. with capital, the government's confiscation of land in the Waikato as punishment for alleged rebellion.
raupō	n. bulrush, *Typha angustifolia*.
reo	n. 1. voice; 2. tone; 3. speech; 4. language, dialect; 5. a speaker of a language; 6. spokesperson. Used with and without adjective to refer to the Māori language: te reo Māori, te reo rangatira, te reo.
reti	n. a board with rod at right angles towed through sea by a person walking on shore, used to tow kahawai hooks.
rēwena	n. home-made yeast, transliteration of leaven.
ringa wera	n. literally 'hot hands', the workers behind the scenes at hui on the marae, especially the cooks.
Ringatū	n. church founded by Te Kooti Rikirangi that sets aside the First and Twelfth days of the month for gathering and worship (Tarei, 1978).
riroriro	n. the grey warbler, *Gerygone igata*.
ritenga	n. 1. likeness; 2. customary action, practice or ritual.
rongoā	n. 1. medicines made from plants; 2. the plants from which Māori make medicines.
rourou	n. small flax basket of cooked food.

rua	n. 1. pit, hole; 2. store for provisions, generally a shallow excavation with low walls and a roof.
rūnanga	n. 1. gathering of hapū or iwi members to discuss particular issue(s); 2. formally constituted group set up by hapū or iwi to manage its affairs, including interaction with outsiders, especially government.
ruru	n. owl, morepork, *Ninox novaeseelandiae*.
taha	n. 1. side; 2. edge; 3. margin; 4. part, portion; 5. dimension. Te taha whānui: the broad, visitors' side of a meeting-house; te taha wairua: the spiritual dimension.
Taha Māori	phr. the Māori dimension, introduced into the school curriculum in the 1970s and 1980s.
tāhuhu	n. 1. ridgepole of a meeting-house; 2. rods used in specialised equipment, e.g., bird snares and kites; 3. first weft row in weaving a cloak; 4. direct line of ancestry; 5. eldest son of the senior family in a descent group.
tāhuna	n. 1. seaside, beach; 2. sandbank.
tai	n. 1. the sea; 2. the coast as opposed to inland (uta); 3. the tide; 4. wave.
Tai Rāwhiti	phr. the East Coast.
Tai Tokerau	phr. Northland.
taihoa	adv. 1. by and by; 2. 'hang on!', 'wait a bit!'
tākaro	v. intr. play. n. general word for sport.
take	n. 1. root; 2. stump; 3. base of a hill; 4. cause; 5. reason; 6. origin, beginning; 7. subject of discussion; 8. chief, head of hapū or iwi.
tākirikiri	v. tr. to pluck repeatedly.
tama	n. 1. child, usually male; 2. own son; 3. son of siblings and cousins of own generation; 4. eldest son; 5. man, person, in metaphors and proverbs, e.g., tama tū, tama ora, tama noho, tama mate/a man on his feet is fit and well; a man sitting down is sick or dying.
tamāhine	n. 1. own daughter; 2. daughter of siblings and cousins of own generation; 3. girl.
tamaiti (sing.), tamariki (pl.)	n. child, children of either sex.
tāmure	n. a fish, *Pagrosomus auratus*, 'snapper'.
tāne	n. 1. male; 2. husband/partner.

GLOSSARY

Tāne-mahuta — pers. name, son of Rangi and Papa, responsible for separating them in the Māori creation story; creator of the first woman and progenitor of human beings, progenitor and guardian god of the forest and its resources, god responsible for obtaining the baskets of knowledge from Ranginui.

Tāne-whakapiripiri — pers. name, another name for Tāne-mahuta, a reference to the meeting-house, traditionally made of forest products (wood, cordage etc.) and used for peacemaking and whaka-whanaungatanga, binding people together.

tāniko — n. a form of weaving used for borders of the finest cloaks, belts and piupiu tops.

taniwha — n. 1. a supernatural creature imbued with mana and tapu, having its own name and history, sometimes taking a physical form, e.g., as a log or eel, associated with particular whānau or hapū and with important natural resources and performing protective and warning functions; 2. used metaphorically to refer to chiefs representing their followers.

Tangaroa — pers. name, son of Rangi and Papa, guardian god of the sea and its resources in Māori mythology.

tangata (sing.), tāngata (pl.) — n. human being, including both male and female.

tangata whenua — phr. 1. sing., 'person of the land' = member of a marae community or locality through a line of occupying ancestors, ideally owning Māori land in the vicinity; 2. collective, the host group ('hosts') at a hui on a marae; 3. with upper case 'T' and 'W', the Māori people of New Zealand, as opposed to non-Māori New Zealanders.

tangi — v. tr. 1. weep; 2. lament.
n. 1. a stylised lamentation in which women express grief after a death and when meeting after separation; 2. a gathering held to mourn and bury the dead.

tangihanga — n. tangi + hanga; a gathering held to mourn the dead, usually lasting several days and including the successive arrival of mourning parties, mourning expressed in tears, tangi and speeches, funeral service, feast, and the lifting of tapu from the deceased's home.

taonga	n. 1. something highly valued; 2. treasure. May be tangible or intangible, animate or inanimate, e.g., a greenstone ornament, the Māori language, a mokopuna, a landmark.
tapu	n. 1. a state of being deriving from close contact with beings or forces from the supernatural realm, especially the indwelling of mana: sacred or polluting according to context, set apart under ritual restriction and closely associated with ideas of danger, anxiety and restriction of freedom; 2. a prohibition on doing something, e.g., taking fish from a tapu area.
taro	n. a plant cultivated for food, *Colocasia antiquorum*, brought to New Zealand by Polynesian settlers and grown mainly in the north of the North Island.
tātou/tātau	pron. we many, inclusive of two or more groups, including the speaker and the group or groups being addressed.
tau-	adj. strange, used only in a few compounds.
tāua	pron. we two.
tāua	n. female grandparent in certain iwi.
tauira	n. 1. teacher; 2. student; 3. pattern; 4. copy.
tauiwi	n. 1. strangers; 2. people other than the tāngata whenua of a marae, including other Māori individuals and groups; 3. with capital, non-Māori. Cf. tauwhenua, foreign land.
taumata	n. 1. brow of a hill; 2. mound reserved as chief's seat; 3. host speakers' bench in Tai Tokerau.
tauparapara	n. traditional-style composition recited by men before or after making a formal speech (McLean, 1996, pp.39–40).
taura	n. 1. rope; 2. cable; 3. cord.
taura here	phr. 1. a cord/rope metaphorically connecting individuals or groups; 2. commonly used to describe members of whānau, hapū or iwi living outside their own group's territory.
taura whiri	phr. 1. a rope plaited of many strands; 2. used metaphorically to refer to the interweaving of whānau, hapū and other groups.
Tāwhaki	pers. name, mythical Māori hero.
tāwhara	n. flower brachts of kiekie.

teina/taina (sing.), tēina/tāina (pl.)   n. 1. younger sibling(s) of the same sex; 2. cousin(s) of the same sex and generation in descent-lines junior to speaker.
tiaki   v. tr. 1. guard; 2. look after; 3. protect.
tika   adj. 1. straight, direct; 2. just, fair; 3. right, correct.
tikanga   n. tika + nga. 1. rule, plan, method; 2. customary way of doing something; 3. anything normal or usual; 4. reason; 5. meaning; 6. purpose.
Tikanga Māori, Ngā   phr. Māori ways of thinking and doing = Māori culture.
tiko   v. intr. evacuate the bowels.
tinana   n. 1. body; 2. trunk; 3. main part of anything; 4. the physical aspect of the human person.
tipu/tupu   v. intr. grow, increase.
n. shoot, bud.
toheroa   n. a bivalve mollusc, *Amphidesma ventricosum*.
tohu   n. 1. sign; 2. mark; 3. proof.
v. tr. 1. point out; 2. show.
tohutohu   v. tr. 1. mark; 2. show, point out; 3. direct, guide; 4. instruct, advise, recommend.
tohunga   n. 1. expert/specialist, qualified to indicate specialisation, e.g., tohunga whakairo (carving expert); 2. commonly used without qualifier to refer to a Māori religious expert who uses karakia and rongoā (herbal medicines) to heal or harm; 3. ritual expert in the Ringatū Church; 4. dismissively translated as medicine man, faith healer.
tōihi   n. plant tendril.
tokotoko   n. 1. staff, rod; 2. walking stick, especially the carved stick used by male kaumātua.
tono   v. tr. 1. bid, command; 2. send; 3. demand. See kai-tonotono.
tōnui   adj. prosperous, prolific.
tōnuitanga   n. prosperity.
tōpū   adj. assembled in a body; hui tōpū, regional, national or annual conference.
tū mai, tū atu   phr. rule governing speaking order in pōwhiri in which host and guest speakers speak alternately.
tuahine (sing.), tuāhine (pl.)   n. 1. sister(s) of a male; 2. female cousin(s) of same generation as a male speaker.

tuakana (sing.), tuākana (pl.)	n. 1. older sibling(s) of the same sex; 2. cousins of the same sex and generation in descent-lines senior to speaker.
tuangi	n. a shellfish, *Chione stutchburyi*, cockle.
tuatua	n. a bivalve mollusc, *Amphidesma subtriangulatum*.
tui	v. tr. 1. fasten by passing a cord through holes; 2. lace; 3. sew (e.g., a hem).
tūī	n. a native bird, *Prosthemadera novaeseelandiae*, the 'parson-bird' because of the white feathers at its throat; the tūī eats berries, fruit, insects and nectar.
tuku	v. tr. 1. let go, give up; 2. allow, let; 3. present, offer a gift of value or significance in gift exchange.
tukutuku	n. lattice work on the inside walls of the meeting-house, positioned between carved wall slabs.
Tūmatauenga	pers. name, a son of Rangi and Papa who tried and failed to separate his parents in the Māori creation story; Māori god of war.
tumuaki	n. 1. crown of the head; 2. head of a group or organisation; 3. school principal.
tuna	n. eel, *Anguilla dieffenbachii* (long-finned), *A. australis* (short-finned).
tungāne	n. 1. brother of a female; 2. male cousin of same generation as female speaker.
tūpāpaku	n. 1. dead person, body; 2. sick person, invalid.
tupu/tipu	v. intr. grow, increase. n. shoot, bud.
tupu noa	adj. growing wild, uncultivated.
tupua/tipua	n. 1. supernatural being of fearsome aspect; 2. synonym for taniwha; 3. human being of extraordinary powers.
tupuna/tipuna (sing.), tūpuna/tīpuna (pl.)	n. 1. ancestor(s); 2. grandparent(s); 3. relative(s) of grandparent's generation.
tūrangawaewae	n. 1. literally, a standing place for (one's) feet; 2. one's home base; 3. one's home marae; 4. with initial capital, Tūrangawaewae, official headquarters of the Kīngitanga in the Waikato.
tūrehu	n. 1. ghost, fairy; 2. a race of pale-skinned 'fairy' people.
tutū	v. intr. be stirred up (of dust, disturbance etc.).
tutūanga	n. the stirring up (of dust etc.).

Twelfth	*see* Ringatū
umu	n. earth oven = hāngī.
uru	v. tr. 1. enter; 2. associate oneself with; 3. participate in; 4. arrive.
urupā	n. 1. burial place; 2. cemetery.
utu	n. 1. return for something received; 2. principle of reciprocity; 3. compensation; 4. countergift; 5. price.
wahine (sing.), wāhine (pl.)	n. 1. woman; 2. female; 3. wife/partner.
wai	n. 1. water; 2. liquid, oil etc.; 3. vessel to hold water etc.; 4. abbreviation of waiata.
waiata	n. generic term for poems composed in Māori in both traditional and non-traditional styles and both chanted and sung. v. tr. sing.
waiata aroha	n. song-poem mourning lost or unrequited love.
waiata tangi	n. song-poem mourning death or loss, lament.
wairua	n. 1. spirit = the incorporeal aspect of the human being.
waka	n. 1. generic term for (Māori) canoe, qualified to indicate type; 2. any long narrow receptacle, e.g., box for feathers, trough; 3. vessel = container; 4. woman (metaphorical); 5. federation of iwi stemming from ancestors who travelled to Aotearoa in the same sea-going waka.
wānanga	n. 1. specialised knowledge of pūkenga; 2. wise person; 3. hui for sharing traditional knowledge; 4. tertiary institution based on Māori principles (from whare wānanga, traditional house of learning).
wātea	adj. clear, free, open, especially after the lifting of tapu.
wehi	n. 1. awe, reverential wonder especially of the metaphysical; 2. an attribute of or response to a powerful performance, e.g., of kapa haka. adj. awesome.
wero	v. tr. 1. spear; 2. throw a spear; 3. challenge an enemy by throwing a spear; 4. challenge visitors by laying down greenery or carved stick(s).
whaea	n. 1. mother and mother's siblings of the same generation; 2. woman fulfilling mother's/aunt's role. Whāea in the plural in some iwi.
whaikōrero	n. 1. speechmaking; 2. art of oratory.

whaka-	causative prefix. to make someone do or be something.
whakaaro	n. whaka + aro (desire, mind). 1. thought; 2. intention; 3. opinion; 4. understanding; 5. plan.
whakaako	v. tr. teach = make to learn.
whakahīhī	whaka + hī (v. tr. rise) doubled. adj. 1. lofty; 2. enterprising; 3. conceited, arrogant.
whakairi	v. intr. 1. be elevated on; 2. hang, be suspended from. v. tr. 1. sprinkle with water, baptise.
whakairo	v. tr. 1. ornament with a pattern. n. 1. object ornamented with a pattern; 2. a carving.
whakaiti	whaka + iti (adj. small) v. tr. belittle, humiliate. adj. 1. modest; 2. belittled, humiliated.
whakamā	adj. whaka + mā (adj. white, pale, without tapu); used to describe a range of inward feelings from shyness through embarrassment to shame, and behaviour involving varying degrees of withdrawal and unresponsiveness (Metge, 1986).
whakamomore	v. intr. remain expressionless; from adj. momore, smooth, bare.
whakamōwai	v. intr. behave modestly, be unassuming.
whakanoa	v. tr. whaka + noa, to lift tapu from something (synonym of whakawātea, to make free, clear away).
whakapapa	v. tr. whaka + papa (n. anything broad, flat and hard) 1. place in layers; 2. recite genealogies and associated stories. n. 1. descent-line(s) tracing connection between ancestor(s) and descendants; 2. study and recital of descent-lines and associated stories and kinship linkages.
whakapono	v. tr. 1. believe; 2. admit as true. n. 1. faith; 2. creed.
whakarite	v. tr. 1. make (to be) like (something); 2. compare; 3; put right; 4. put oneself right spiritually by a ritual act e.g. sprinkling with water.
whakatau	v. tr. to address in formal speech. n. welcome ceremony free of restrictions observed on marae.
whakataukī	n. whakatau + kī (to say), proverb, saying.
whakauru	v. tr. 1. participate in; 2. ally oneself to; 3. assist.

whānau	v. intr. be born. n. 1. group of descendants stemming from recent, named ancestor(s); 2. this group plus spouses and adopted/foster children = extended family; 3. term of address for people gathered for a common purpose.
whānau pani	phr. bereaved family.
whanaunga	n. 1. relative, related by descent and/or by marriage; 2. a person regarded as being like a relative. From whanau (v. intr. incline, bend down) + nga; note short first vowel.
whanaungatanga	n. whanaunga + tanga: kinship in the widest sense, including descendants of common ancestors, affines, friends and strangers treated as kin.
whāngai	v. tr. 1. feed; 2. bring up (of children). adj. and n. used to identify parents and children linked in adoptive/foster relationships.
whare	n. 1. building, house, qualified to indicate particular type, e.g., whare hui, meeting-house; whare kai, dining-hall; whare karakia, place of worship; 2. people living in a house, household; 3. group of co-descendants, synonym for whānau.
whare kura	phr. traditional school of learning specialising in benign knowledge.
whare maire	phr. traditional school of learning specialising in occult lore.
whare mate	phr. 1. shelter for the tūpāpaku and mourning family during a tangihanga; 2. the mourning relatives of the deceased.
whare nui	phr. literally the big house = meeting-house.
whare ngaro	phr. a family or descent-line that has died out.
whare paku	phr. lavatory, toilet; from euphemism 'little house' when the toilet was detached from house.
whare puni	phr. house of superior construction, e.g., a meeting-house; puni (adj. stopped up) indicates no draughty gaps or cracks.
whare rūnanga	phr. house used for debate, 'council house'.
whare tangata	phr. 1. the house which produces human beings = the womb; 2. a woman, women in general.
whare wānanga	phr. traditional 'house of learning'.

whāriki	n. woven flax mat.
whati	v. intr. 1. be broken (of anything rigid, e.g., bone); 2. be broken off (e.g., of the chanting of a karakia).
whatu	v. tr. weave garments, kits and mats from flax and other plant materials. n. 1. stone; 2. kernel; 3. pupil of eye, eye; 4. core of a boil.
whekī	n. a tree fern, *Dicksonia squarrosa*.
whenua	n. 1. land = country; 2. ground, earth, above and below water; 3. placenta = afterbirth.
whiri	v. tr. 1. twist; 2. plait; 3. weave flax and other plant materials.

NGĀ KAI-WHAKAURU/BIOGRAPHIES

This section provides brief biographies of the twenty-five kai-whakauru who constituted the core group of speakers on learning and teaching in general, and basic information about fourteen who contributed comments on some aspects only. The name by which each speaker is best known is highlighted in bold.

The Core Group
Each biography focuses on key aspects of the kai-whakauru's life histories under the following headings: birth and death dates; home community; iwi; secondary school; tertiary education; qualifications and awards; employment; community service; date(s) of research interview.

Atama, **Nikora**: b. 1942; Pawarenga; Te Aupōuri; Whangarei Boys' High School for one year. Leaving school at fifteen, Nikora worked as a quarryman in Whāngārei and Auckland and as driver and foreman for a road construction firm in Auckland for twenty years, all the while organising activities including kapa haka for urban Māori youth. Headhunted for his skills, he worked as social worker and cultural adviser for the Departments of Maori Affairs, Social Welfare and Health for another twenty years. He is sought after as pūkenga, kai-kōrero and teacher of whakapapa. Interviews recorded on 30.9.82, 21.10.82, 28.10.82 in Auckland.

Babbington, **Hineari** Riria Kahumaraki, née Ratapu: b. 1929; Tokomaru Bay; Ngāti Porou, Te Whānau-a-Rua; Hukarere Maori Girls' College; Wellington Teachers' College, Dip. Tchg 1953. Before entering Teachers' College Hineari spent two years as a junior assistant at Ruatoki District High School where local kuia helped her extend her knowledge of te reo Māori. In 1954 she and her husband married and settled in Masterton close to relatives. Beginning soon after her children started school she held a succession of teaching positons at Masterton East Primary School and retired as Assistant Principal in 1990. Closely involved with the establishment of kōhanga reo and kura kaupapa Māori, Hineari also served as Itinerant Teacher of Maori in Wairarapa schools for several years. In retirement she is Nanny Hineari to a large whānau and the many local children she taught over the years. Interviews recorded on 5.3.82 (with other Itinerant Teachers of Maori) and 17.8.82 (with Hapi Potae) in Wellington.

Hohaia, **Wiremu**: 1922–89; Whatuwhiwhi and Ahipara; Ngāti Kahu, Te Rarawa. Wiremu spent his working life travelling round Northland as a linesman with the Post and Telegraph Department. He retired to Ahipara where he farmed family land, shared his knowledge of land and sea with rangatahi as supervisor of a horticultural training scheme, and became kaumātua and kai-kōrero on Roma marae. Interview recorded on 24.4.82 in Ahipara.

Hunkin, Elizabeth (**Liz**) Mana: b. 1937; Nūhaka; Ngāti Kahungunu (Ngāti Rākaipaka); Turakina School for Maori Girls; Wellington Teachers' College, Dip. Tchg 1957; Te Wānanga o Raukawa, MA 2000. Liz taught in Wellington primary schools (1957–80), was on the staff of Wellington Teachers' College (1981–82) and Acting Maori Adviser with the Department of Education (1983–84). Returning to Nūhaka she worked in support of kōhanga reo and kura kaupapa Māori and served as Itinerant Teacher of Maori from that centre. She founded the private training establishment Te Kura Motuhake o Te Ataarangi in Nūhaka in 1996. Her continuing leadership of this college was recognised with a New Zealand Tertiary Teaching Excellence Award in 2012. Liz served the NZQA on the Kaitūhono Advisory Board and as moderator of Te Reo Māori and is a member of the Ngāti Kahungunu Māori Advisory Committee. Interview recorded on 5.3.82 (with other Itinerant Teachers of Maori) in Wellington.

Kaa, Hohi Ngapera Te Moana **Keri**: b. 1942; Rangitukia; Ngāti Porou, Ngāti Kahungunu; Queen Victoria School for Maori Girls, American Field Service scholar, Auckland Girls' Grammar School; Ardmore Teachers College, Dip. Tchg 1964; Te Wānanga o Raukawa, MA 2013. Keri taught in primary schools in Rangitukia, Wellington and Hawke's Bay, in secondary schools in the Hutt Valley (Wellington), and for fifteen years as a lecturer at Wellington Teachers' College where she played a key role in the founding and running of the college marae Te Ako Pai. Returning home to Rangitukia she has been both teacher and student at

Te Wānanga o Raukawa campus at Hicks Bay. Her services to Māori education were recognised with a CNZM and QSO. Her children's book *Taki Ki Ro Wai* won the New Zealand Post Māori Language Award in 2014. Interviews recorded on 25.1.1981, 2.2.1981 and 9.2.81 in Wellington.

Kaa, Mateohorere **Jossie**: b. 1934; Rangitukia; Ruawaiapu, Ngāti Porou; Tikitiki High School, St Joseph's Maori Girls' College; Wellington Teachers' College, Dip. Tchg 1956. Jossie taught in primary schools until 1972, was Itinerant Teacher of Maori in the Hutt Valley (1972–87) and worked for eleven years as editor, writer and translator for School Publications and Huia Publishers. She is currently educational adviser and kuia for Rangitukia and Ngāti Porou. Interviews recorded on 5.3.82 (with other Itinerant Teachers of Maori) and 19.8.82 (with Wiremu Kaa) in Wellington.

Kaa, **Wiremu** Mangai: b. 1934; Rangitukia; Ngāti Porou, Ruawaiapu; Te Aute College; Wellington Teachers' College, Dip. Tchg 1957. Wiremu taught in primary schools in Northland and on the East Coast from 1958 to 1972. He was employed by the Department of Education as Schools Adviser, Education Officer and Director of Maori, Pacific Islands and Migrant Education (1973–89), and by Victoria University of Wellington as lecturer, senior lecturer and chairman of the Māori Studies Department (1992–2000). Wiremu then returned home to Rangitukia where he works as writer and translator of books in Māori and English, negotiator for Ngāti Porou with the Crown, educator and Archdeacon in the Tairāwhiti Pīhopatanga of the Anglican Church (Tikanga Māori), and is kaumātua for Rangitukia and for Ngāti Porou when needed. Interviews recorded on 11.9.81 (with Sonny Huia Wilson), 12.2.82 (with Rose Pere) and 11.8.82 (with Jossie Kaa) in Wellington.

Manukau, Pirihere (**Priscilla**) Terehia: 1924–2003; Te Kūiti, Mangapēhi; Ngāti Maniapoto. Priscilla, her husband and three children joined the Māori migration to the city in the early 1960s. They settled in Papakura in Auckland and were deeply involved in community development in the rapidly growing suburbs of South Auckland. Priscilla worked with the Maori Women's Welfare League and the Department of Maori Affairs as weaving tutor and co-ordinator of youth programmes teaching skills and employment readiness, helped police provide victim support, patrolled streets and hotels as a Maori Warden, and supported a local kapa haka group. Having spearheaded the drive to establish a marae in Papakura, she served as one of its trustees until her death. Widely known in South Auckland as Nana Priscilla, she opened her home to all in need and was remembered as always leading by example. Interviews recorded on 20.8.81 and 3.9.81 in Papakura.

Marsden, **Maori**: 1924–93; Maimaru; Ngāi Takoto, Patukoraha; Wesley (Methodist) College; Auckland University College 1952–54, St John's Theological College, LTh 1957. After ordination in the Anglican Church, Maori served in parishes and pastorates in Taranaki, Waikato and Auckland and as a New Zealand Naval Chaplain at the Devonport Naval Base. He founded and led the community at the Maungārongo Retreat Centre at Te Kōpuru on the Kaipara Harbour. He was recognised throughout Māoridom as a storehouse of knowledge, one of the last initiates of a whare wānanga, a writer and kai-kōrero (Royal, 2003). Interviews recorded on 9.11.82 and 11.12.82 at Te Kōpuru.

Matete, Te Aomarama **Joe**: 1918–94; Puketawai (near Tolaga Bay) and Manutūkē; Te Aitanga-a-Hauiti, Rongowhakaata. Leaving school at fifteen, Joe worked as a farm labourer at Māhia, then lived in Mangakino with his wife and family for thirteen years while he worked for the Ministry of Works as a quarryman and roadmaker during the building of the Waikato River dams. He then transferred to Auckland where he worked on building the airport in Māngere. He and his wife Vi played important roles as kaumātua in the development of the South Auckland community, with special reference to the building of the Anglican marae-church in central Māngere. Interview recorded on 22.7.82 (with Vi Matete) in Auckland.

Matete, Violet (**Vi**) Matakorihi, née Wairoa: 1920–94; Mōhaka; Ngāti Kahungunu. Vi married Joe Matete in 1941 and moved with him and their family to Mangakino and then Auckland. She was recognised in her own right as a kuia in the Māngere community and the Manukau Anglican Pastorate. Interview recorded on 22.7.82 (with Joe Matete) in Auckland.

Parekowhai, **George**: b. 1933; Puha (in Poverty Bay); Rongowhakaata, Te Aitanga-a-Māhaki; Te Karaka Area School; Wellington Teachers' College, Dip. Tchg 1955; Victoria University of Wellington, BA 1973, Dip. TESL 1979. George taught in several primary schools, including seven years as headmaster of Parikino Maori School on the Whanganui River with his teacher wife Rose as infant mistress. George and Rose lived in Wellington for several years while George taught Māori at the Correspondence School and completed his BA. A year teaching Māori at St Stephen's Maori Boys' College was followed by positions as Lecturer-in-charge of the Maori Language Section at Akoranga North Shore Teachers' College, lecturer in Māori language and then Director and Dean of Te Punawaihanga at Auckland Teachers' College. In retirement George serves as kaumātua and whakapapa expert for the Parekowhai whānau and its home marae Whakarongo. Interview recorded on 8.8.82 (with Rose Parekowhai) in Auckland.

Pere, Rangimarie Turuki **Rose**: b. 1937; Waikaremoana; Rongowhakaata, Ngāi Tūhoe, Ngāti Ruapani, Ngāti Kahungunu; Hukarere Maori Girls' College; Wellington Teachers' College, Dip. Tchg; Victoria University of Wellington, Hon. D. Litt.; CBE for services to education. Rose taught in primary schools from 1958 to 1975, held a Visiting Teaching Fellowship at Waikato University in 1982, worked for the Department of Education as Adviser in Maori and Island Education and Senior Education Officer from 1983 to 1989. Her book *Te Wheke* was one of the first on the subject of Māori education by a Māori. She now runs her educational consultancy Ao Ako Global Learning (founded in the late 1980s) from her home base in Waikaremoana. Interviews recorded on 12.2.82 (with Wiremu Kaa) in Wellington, 11.3.82 and 23.3.82 in Hamilton.

Pihema, **Ani** Masefield: 1924–2002; Haranui (near Helensville), Ōkahu Bay; Ngāti Whātua; Auckland Teachers' College, Dip. Tchg 1953.
Ani served as secretary of the Orakei Tribal Committee from 1948 to 1951 while the government worked towards the eviction of the Māori residents from Ōkahu Bay. She taught in primary schools in Helensville and Auckland and then joined the Department of Maori Affairs. As a Maori Welfare Officer (1956–70) covering the area from Wellsford to Auckland, she was involved in the establishment of the Maori Community Centre in Auckland and worked closely with the Maori Women's Welfare League

in their campaign of support for Māori migrants to the city. Returning to teaching she taught in Palmerston North, Whanganui and at Hillary College in South Auckland. After retiring she continued to serve Ngāti Whātua as a member of the Ngāti Whātua Trust Board and the Ōrākei Marae and Educational Trust. Interviews recorded on 17.3.82 and 30.3.82 in Auckland.

Pirihi, Hirini Teuanga **Hone**: 1934–96; Te Rere, Ōpōtiki; Whakatōhea; Opotiki College; Auckland Teachers' College, Dip. Tchg; University of Auckland. When Hone and Lena married in 1959, Hone was working as a laundryman at Opotiki Hospital. He began training at Auckland Teachers' College while commuting between Ōpōtiki and Auckland but it proved too taxing and he moved his family to Auckland in 1966. After finishing his training Hone taught in two primary schools in Māngere, completed relevant papers at the University of Auckland and was appointed as a foundation member of the staff at Ngā Tapuwae College in South Auckland. With his wife Lena he was a leading member of the marae-church whānau in Māngere. A gifted artist, he provided the artwork for both covers of *In and Out of Touch* (Metge, 1986). Interview recorded on 26.7.82 (with Lena) in Auckland.

Pirihi, Mamaerangi **Lena**, née Herewini: 1931–87; Tōrere (Bay of Plenty); Ngāi Tai. Lena married Hone in 1959 and they moved to Auckland with three children in 1966. While Hone completed his training she supported the family by working handling freight on the Auckland wharf; later she worked as a cleaner at a Māngere primary school. In partnership with Hone she was a kuia for the whānau at the marae-church in Māngere. Interview recorded on 26.7.82 (with Hone Pirihi) in Auckland.

Potae, **Hapi**: 1929–2014; Tokomaru Bay; Ngāti Porou; Dannevirke High School (chosen for its rugby football); Ardmore Teachers' College, Dip. Tchg 1949. Throughout the 1950s Hapi taught in primary schools in the Bay of Plenty and pursued his passion for rugby: as a Māori All Black he played against a touring South African team. From 1961 Hapi worked for the Department of Education as Adviser in Maori and Island Education, spent two years teaching in Samoa and served as an Itinerant Teacher of Maori in Wellington. He also acted in the TV series *Close to Home* and worked as a translator for Learning Media.

After retiring in 1994 he worked in Tokomaru Bay helping establish the kōhanga reo and kura kaupapa Māori, and after ten years in Auckland returned home for good to farm family land and serve on the boards of several Māori land trusts. Interviews recorded on 5.3.82 (with other Itinerant Teachers of Maori) and 17.8.82 (with Hineari Babbington) in Wellington.

Reedy, New Amsterdam (**Amster**): 1943–2014; Ruatōria; Ngāti Porou; Wellington Teachers' College, Dip.Tchg 1964; Victoria University of Wellington, BA (Hons). Amster taught in primary and secondary schools up to 1973 and as lecturer and head of the Maori Department at Wellington Teachers' College from 1974 to 1986. He returned to the East Coast as principal of Ngata College in Ruatōria (1986–90), established Radio Ngati Porou in 1986 and honed his acting skills in the dramatisation of the signing of the Treaty of Waitangi presented during the sesquicentenary in 1990. Setting up his own consultancy Ngā Kete o Te Mātauranga in 1991, he worked as a consultant and mediator between Māori and non-Māori groups including government and the Waitangi Tribunal. He was Māori adviser to the New Zealand teams attending the Olympic Games in Greece (2004), Italy (2006), China (2008) and Britain (2012), and the Commonwealth Games in Melbourne (2006). Interview recorded on 2.3.82 in Wellington.

Tangaere, **August**: 1932–97; Rangitukia; Ngāti Porou; Te Aute College; Wellington Teachers' College, Dip. Tchg. With his wife Ruth, August taught in rural primary schools including Whāngāpē in Northland and for several years in Nauru and Fiji. After holding several positions teaching in secondary schools he worked as Adviser in Maori Education for the Education Department and as Education Officer for Te Puni Kōkiri in Wellington. Interview recorded on 5.3.82 (with other Itinerant Teachers of Maori) in Wellington.

Tangaere, **June**: b. 1935; Ōtoko (Whanganui River); Ngā Ruahine; Turakina Maori Girls' College; Wellington Teachers' College, Dip. Tchg. June taught in rural primary schools including Rangitukia (home to her husband Cassidy Tangaere) and Tikitiki on the East Coast, and in urban schools in Wellington, where she was appointed as an Itinerant Teacher of Maori. She wrote children's books in Māori for Learning

Media. Interview recorded on 5.3.82 (with other Itinerant Teachers of Maori) in Wellington.

Te Paa, **Ephraim**: 1904–1990; Ahipara; Te Rarawa; St John's Theological College (1924–27). After Ephraim and Harriet married in 1928, they took up farming in Ahipara on land developed by the Department of Maori Affairs under Ngata's land development scheme. Over the years Ephraim grew into the role of kaumātua and kai-kōrero in Ahipara and became known on the national and international stage as a prominent member of the Bahá'í community. Interview recorded on 29.4.81 (with Harriet Te Paa) in Ahipara.

Te Paa, **Harriet** (Nane) née Okena: 1910–1995; Pawarenga; Te Rarawa. Pawarenga Native School to Standard 4. Nane worked with her husband Ephraim as a farmer, raised a family of six boys and ten girls, and was loved and respected as kuia in the Ahipara community. Interview recorded on 29.4.82 (with Ephraim Te Paa) in Ahipara.

(Te) Tioke, **Tawhao**: 1920–2009; Waimana; Ngāi Tūhoe (Ngāi Tama, Ngāi Tūranga). Tawhao spent years learning bushcraft under his uncle Ereatara Manukau (Binney, 1979, p.78) and one year as a ten-year-old at the Presbyterian Mission School at Tanatana in the Urewera. He worked as a shepherd, fencer and horse-breaker on a sheep station on the East Coast, then returned to Waimana where he married Hurihia and raised a family. In 1955 they moved to Whakatāne where Tawhao spent three years studying at Te Wananga a Rangi, the Maori Presbyterian theological college. Tawhao served as a Presbyterian minister in parishes in Te Teko, Auckland and Wellington until his retirement in 1986. Tawhao and Hurihia then settled in Auckland where for twenty years Tawhao was active as kaumātua and cultural adviser to the New Zealand Heart Foundation and the Auckland University Medical School, sharing his deep knowledge of native plants and rongoā. His lifetime of achievement was honoured before his death by awards from Te Wananga a Rangi, the Māori Synod of the Presbyterian Church, Te Waka Toi (the Māori arm of Creative New Zealand) and the University of Auckland. Interviews recorded on 10.9.81 and 26.2.82 (with Hurihia) in Wellington.

Williams, **Haare** Mahanga Te Wehinga: b. 1936; Karaka on Ōhiwa Harbour, Bay of Plenty; Ngāi Tūhoe, Te Aitanga-a-Māhaki, Rongowhakaata; Opotiki College; Ardmore Teachers' College, Dip. Tchg 1956; University of Auckland, BA 1975. Haare taught in primary schools in Tauranga, Northland and Taupō until 1969, held lectureships at Ardmore and Auckland Teachers' Colleges, and was community director at a South Auckland college (1970–74). A stint as TV and radio reporter for the New Zealand Broadcasting Corporation led to the position of general manager of Radio Aotearoa in Auckland and work with the 1990 Commission and a film and television training organisation.
In recent years Haare has held a senior lectureship at UNITEC and acted as cultural adviser and kaumātua to the Manukau and Auckland City Councils, three Auckland museums and the New Zealand Association of Psychotherapists. Interviews recorded on 18.10.82, 22.10.82, 4.11.82 and 12.11.82 in Auckland.

Wilson, **Sonny** Huia: 1930–1983; Ihumātao, Auckland; Ngāi Te Ata, Waikato; Otahuhu College; three years as an apprentice shoemaker; Auckland Teachers' College, Dip. Tchg. Sonny taught in various schools in Auckland and the Waikato, then spent four years in Rarotonga as an organising teacher. He joined the Department of Education in Auckland in 1973 as one of the first specialist advisers in Māori. Two years later he was transferred to head office in Wellington where he provided national leadership to the growing number of advisers in Māori until his death eight years later. In his joint eulogy to Sonny and Alan Smith in Wellington Cathedral, the Director of Education William Renwick paid tribute to Sonny as 'our songbird, one of the most gifted Māori orators of his age group and an inspired teacher. He had an enviable gift for communicating with people of very different ages and very diverse backgrounds. He was always warm and encouraging, ... endlessly inventive in helping his students grasp what he wanted them to understand about Maori or Maoritanga ... In everything he did he lived by the highest standards ... he was a great storehouse of knowledge of Māori language and culture.' Interview recorded on 11.9.81 (with Wiremu Kaa) in Wellington.

Other Kai-whakauru

Of the fourteen other kai-whakauru, two (Cambridge Pani and Wi Tarei) were interviewed in 1979 (before the research programme began) on the teaching of whaikōrero; two (Rose Parekowhai and Hurihia Tioke) spoke briefly during interviews with their husbands; and the other ten contributed brief comments on particular aspects of learning.

Conrad, **Niki**: Te Kao; Te Aupōuri; farmer, conservationist, bus driver, kaumātua. Conversation recorded 16.6.81 in Kaitāia.

Ellis, **Fred** (Riki Erihi): 1928–c.1990; Manukau, Ahipara; Te Rarawa; writer, mental health worker (manager of community homes in Auckland and Ahipara). Interview recorded 28.7.81 in Auckland.

Gregory, **Ross**: b. 1939; Pukepoto; Te Rarawa; secondary school teacher, educational consultant, public speaker, kaumātua. Interviews recorded 13.5.81, 5.12.81 in Pukepoto.

Maihi, Ani (pseudonym): Te Aupōuri; kuia. Interview recorded 26.4.82 (with Raiha Paraone) in Karepōnia.

Motu, **Hera**: 1920–?; Ngāwha; Ngāpuhi; Maori Welfare Officer, kuia. Interview recorded 4.5.81 in Ngāwha.

Nepia, **Moira**: Pukepoto; Te Rarawa; farmer, kuia. Interview recorded 24.11.81 in Ahipara.

Pani, **Cambridge**: 1919–94; Nūhaka; Ngāti Kahungunu; farmworker, shearer and fencer; pūkenga, kaumātua and kai-kōrero for Ngāti Rākaipaka. Interview recorded 28.3.79 in Nūhaka.

Paraone, Raiha (pseudonym): 1917–?; Te Aupōuri; kuia. Interview recorded 26.4.82 (with Ani Maihi) in Karepōnia.

Parekowhai, **Rose**: b. 1931; Auckland; Ngāti Pākehā; primary school teacher. Interview recorded 8.8.82 (with George Parekowhai) in Auckland.

Penfold, **Merimeri**: 1920–2014; Te Hāpua; Ngāti Kurī; teacher, university lecturer, Vice-President Maori Women's Welfare League 1970–78, Hon. D. Litt. (Auckland) 1999, CNZM 2001, kai-karanga, kuia, writer, translator. Interview recorded 5.10.81.

Tarei, **Wi**: 1924–?; Māpou (Bay of Plenty); Ngāti Awa; Ngāi Tūhoe; tohunga (minister) of the Ringatū Church. Interview recorded 24.10.79.

Thompson, Ngaio (pseudonym): Waikeri, Ahipara; Te Rarawa; community worker in Auckland and Ahipara, kuia. Interview recorded 1.10.82 in Ahipara.

Tioke, **Hurihia**: Tūpāroa; Ngāti Porou; Presbyterian minister's wife and co-worker, kuia. Interview recorded 10.9.81 (with Tawhao Tioke) in Wellington.

Tuoro, **Mavis**: 1924–?; Rotorua; Ngāti Pikiao; teacher, kuia at Hoani Waititi marae. Interview recorded 3.8.82 at the marae in Auckland.

BIBLIOGRAPHY

Allen, R. E. (ed.), 1990. *The Concise Oxford Dictionary of Current English*, Clarendon Press, Oxford.
Ballara, Angela, 1998. *Iwi: The Dynamics of Māori Tribal Organisation*, Victoria University Press, Wellington.
Bauer, Winifred, 1997. *The Reed Reference Grammar of Māori*, Reed Books, Auckland.
Best, Elsdon, 1959. *The Maori 'School of Learning': Its Objects, Methods and Ceremonial*, Dominion Museum Monograph No. 6, Government Printer, Wellington (first published 1923).
Binney, Judith, 1979. *Mihaia: The Prophet Rua Kenana and His Community at Maungapohatu*, Oxford University Press, Wellington.
Blank, Arapera Hineira Kaa, 1968. 'One Two Three Four Five' and 'Postscript: O nga ao e toru', in Erik Schwimmer (ed.), *The Maori People in the Nineteen-Sixties*, Blackwood and Janet Paul, Auckland, pp.85–96.
Brougham, A. E., A. W. Reed and T. S. Kāretu (eds), 1987. *Māori Proverbs*, rev. edn, Reed, Auckland.
Erihi, Riki, 1970. 'The Proper Little Devil', 'The Forbidden Tree', and 'A Different Kind of Man', in Margaret Orbell (ed.), *Contemporary Maori Writing*, A. H. & A. W. Reed, Wellington, pp.17–50.
Evans, Miriama and Ranui Ngarimu, 2005. *The Art of Māori Weaving*, Huia, Wellington.
Grey, Sir George, 1928. *Nga Mahi a Nga Tupuna*, 3rd edn, ed. H. W. Williams, Board of Maori Ethnological Research, New Plymouth (first published 1854).
___, 1961. *Polynesian Mythology*, ed. W. W. Bird, Whitcombe & Tombs, Auckland (first published in English, 1855).
Haami, Bradford, 2013. *Ka Mau Te Wehi: Taking Haka to the World. Bub and Nen's Story as told to Bradford Haami,* Ngapo and Pimia Wehi Whanau Trust, Auckland.
Hohepa, P. W., 1964. *A Maori Community in Northland*, Anthropology Department, University of Auckland (reprinted 1970, Reed, Wellington).
Ihimaera, Witi, 1972. 'A Game of Cards', in *Pounamu Pounamu*, Heinemann, London, pp.1–5.
___ (ed.), 1998. *Growing Up Maori*, Tandem, Auckland.
Kaa, Arapera Hineira, 1995. *nga kokako huataratara: the plumes of the kokako*, Waiata Koa, Auckland (comprising prize-winning essay on kūmara growing first published in 1958, and poems first published in 1986).
Kaa, Hone, 1998. 'It's all that Haka in the Kumara Patch', in Witi Ihimaera (ed.), *Growing Up Maori*, Tandem Press, Auckland, pp.104–9.
Kaa, Keri, 2013. *Taka Ki Ro Wai: He Korero Purakau mo Tetahi Hoiho,* www.taniaandmartin.com

BIBLIOGRAPHY

Kaa, Oho, 1992. *Kua Hikina te Rāhui*, Learning Media, Wellington.
Ka'ai, Tania M., 2008. *Ngoingoi Pewhairangi: A Remarkable Life*, Huia, Wellington.
Kaamira, Himiona and Bruce Biggs, 1957. 'Kupe na Himiona Kaamira o Te Rarawa', *Journal of the Polynesian Society*, 66 (3), pp.217–48.
Kāretu, Tīmoti, 1993. *Haka! Te Tohu o te Whenua Rangatira: The Dance of a Noble People*, Reed, Auckland.
Kohere, Reweti, 1951. *He Konae Aronui: Maori Proverbs and Sayings*, A. H. & A. W. Reed, Wellington.
Macalister, John, 2005. *A Dictionary of Māori Words in New Zealand English*, Oxford University Press, Melbourne.
Marsden, Maori, 1975. 'God, Man and Universe: A Maori View', in Michael King (ed.), *Te Ao Hurihuri: The World Moves On*, Hicks Smith & Sons, Wellington, pp.191–219.
McLean, Mervyn, 1996. *Maori Music*, Auckland University Press.
McRae, Jane, 2011. *Ngā Mōteatea: An Introduction*, Auckland University Press.
Mead, Hirini Moko, 2003. *Tikanga Māori: Living by Māori Values*, Huia, Wellington.
Mead, Hirini Moko and Neil Grove, 2001. *Ngā Pēpeha a Ngā Tūpuna: The Sayings of the Ancestors*, Victoria University Press, Wellington.
Metge, Joan, 1964. *A New Maori Migration: Rural and Urban Relations in Northern New Zealand*, Athlone Press/Melbourne University Press, London and Melbourne.
___, 1984. *Learning and Teaching: He Tikanga Maori*, Department of Education (Maori and Islands Division), Wellington.
___, 1986. *In and Out of Touch: Whakamaa in Cross Cultural Context*, Victoria University Press, Wellington.
___, 1990. *Te Kohao o Te Ngira: Culture and Learning*, Learning Media, Wellington.
___, 1995. *New Growth From Old: The Whānau in the Modern World*, Victoria University Press, Wellington.
___, 2002. 'Returning the Gift: *Utu* in Intergroup Relations', *Journal of the Polynesian Society*, 111 (4), pp. 311–38.
___, 2005. 'Tawhaki Finds His Way to the World of Light: Exploring the Meanings of a Maori Myth', in Claudia Gross, Harriet D. Lyons and Dorothy A. Counts (eds), *A Polymath Anthropologist: Essays in Honour of Ann Chowning*, Department of Anthropology, University of Auckland, pp.153–59.
___, 2008. 'Maori Education 1959–1990: A Personal Memoir', *New Zealand Journal of Educational Studies*, 43 (2), pp.13–28.
___, 2010. *Tuamaka: The Challenge of Difference in Aotearoa New Zealand*, Auckland University Press.
___ and Patricia Kinloch, 1978. *Talking Past Each Other: Problems of Cross-cultural Communication*, Victoria University Press, Wellington.
Ngata, H. M., 1993. *English–Maori Dictionary*, Learning Media, Wellington.

Orsman, Harry (gen. ed.), 1997. *The Dictionary of New Zealand English*, Oxford University Press, Oxford and Auckland.
Pere, Rangimarie Turuki, 1991. *Te Wheke: A Celebration of Infinite Wisdom*, Ao Ako Global Learning New Zealand, Gisborne.
Puketapu, Kara, 1982. *Reform from Within*, Department of Maori Affairs, Wellington.
Radio NZ (Continuing Education Unit), 1981. *Whai-Korero: Ceremonial Farewells to the Dead*, University of Waikato, Hamilton.
Royal, Charles (ed.), 2003. *The Woven Universe: Selected Writings of the Rev. Maori Marsden*, The Estate of Rev. Maori Marsden.
Ryan, P. M., 1995. *The Reed Dictionary of Modern Māori*, Reed, Auckland.
Salmond, Anne, 1975. *Hui: A Study of Maori Ceremonial Hui*, Reed, Wellington.
Schwimmer, E. G., 1963. 'Guardian Animals of the Maori,' *Journal of the Polynesian Society*, 72 (4), pp.397–410.
Scott, Raymond A., 1986, *The Challenge of Taha Maori: A Pakeha Perspective*, Office of the Race Relations Conciliator, Wellington.
Simmons, David R., 1966. 'The Sources of Sir George Grey's *Nga Mahi a nga Tupuna*', *Journal of the Polynesian Society*, 75 (2), pp.177–88.
Simmons, D. R. and Bruce G. Biggs, 1970. 'The Sources of *The Lore of the Whare Wananga*', *Journal of the Polynesian Society*, 79 (1), pp.22–42.
Simon, Judith (ed.), 1998. *Nga Kura Maori : The Native Schools System 1867–1969*, Auckland University Press.
Tarei, Wi, 1978. 'A Church called Ringatu', in Michael King (ed.), *Tihei Mauri Ora: Aspects of Maoritanga*, Methuen, Auckland, pp.60–66.
Tawhai, Wiremu, 2013. *Living by the Moon: Maramataka a Te Whānau-ā-Apanui*, Huia, Wellington.
Te Taura Whiri i te Reo Maori, 2008. *He Pātaka Kupu: Te Kai a te Rangatira*, Penguin, Auckland.
___, n.d. *Guidelines for Māori Language Orthography*, www.tetaurawhiri.govt.nz
Walker, Ranginui, 2001. *He Tipua: The Life and Times of Sir Āpirana Ngata*, Penguin, Auckland.
Williams, Haare, n.d. *Karanga*, Coromandel Press.
Williams, Herbert W., 1975. *A Dictionary of the Maori Language*, reprint of the 7th edn 1971, Government Printer, Wellington.
Williams, Melissa Matutina, 2015. *Panguru and the City: Kāinga Tahi, Kāinga Rua*, Bridget Williams Books, Wellington.
Winiata, Maharaia, 1967. *The Changing Role of the Leader in Maori Society*, Blackwood and Janet Paul, Auckland.

INDEX

The first page number after the name of each kai-whakauru refers to the biographical information in Ngā Kai-whakauru/Biographies.

age: learning at different ages, 21–2, 64–73; changes, 56–8, 80
age-mates, 62–3, 82, 255
ako, ākonga, 7, 268
ancestors, 40, 114, 128, 157–8, 212, 254
Anglican Church, 17, 98–100, 191, 197
apakura, 167–8, 210, 268
approval and disapproval, 260
aptitude, 71, 157, 256, 263
aroha, love, 53–4, 86, 88, 118–19, 130, 196, 268
Atama, Nikora, 291; 11, 16–17, 18, 20, 23–4, 25, 29, 36, 37–38, 41, 43, 45, 64, 66, 67, 70–1, 72, 73, 74, 75, 97, 100–1, 129, 156, 159, 162–8, 181, 183–4, 185–6, 206–7, 214–15, 216, 217, 220, 221–2, 227–30, 243–4
aunt/s, 9, 47, 58–62, 68, 81, 213, 225, 229–30

Babbington, Hineari, 291; 12, 23, 27, 28, 30, 32, 42, 54, 56, 65–56, 67–9, 80–81, 90, 109, 116, 118, 120, 123, 124, 130, 132, 134, 138, 139–40, 161, 184–85, 215, 225
beach, 19, 65–6, 134–6, 225
Best, Elsdon, 189–90, 204, 208, 302
Bible, biblical knowledge, 100, 125–6, 147, 245, 248, 256
birth, 154–5
body language, 49
blessing, 101–2, 141
bread: making, 11, 16, 24; ritual use, 141–2
brooms, mānuka, 10–11, 87–9
Buck, Sir Peter, 234, 247

calendar, lunar, *see* maramataka
caring: for people, 119; for natural resources, 133–6; *see also* manaakitanga
carving, 152
cemeteries, 109, 111
choosing: students, 158, 162; successors, 157, 195–6, 263
Christian scriptures/theology/worship, 80, 97, 204; *see also* Evensong
churches, hāhī/whare karakia, 12; denominations, 96–101; *see also* Anglican Church; Rātana; Ringatū Church; Roman Catholic Church
community: differences in tikanga, 139; resources, 134; settings, 9–13; wānanga, 138–9, 209

conflict, 129; resolution of, 54–5, 198, 201–2
Conrad, Niki, 300; 217–18
consensus, 198, 202, 203
conservation, 66, 133–36
context/s: learning in, 31–33, 43, 64–66, 70–1, 106, 127, 221–2, 234, 254; practising in safe, 259
cooking, 16, 74
copying, *see* imitation
corn, kānga, 26, 121, 271
correction, 84–95, 260
counting: games, 57; tupu, 32, 67
crabs, 19
crayfish, kōura, 19, 53, 136, 138, 273
creation myth, 217, 220
creativity, 173, 264
crops, *see* corn, kānga; kūmara; planting, of crops; potatoes

death, 147, 156; *see also* tangihanga
decision-making, 187
dedication, 101–2
demonstration, 23–6
descent, 34–5, 62, 127–8, 158, 198, 212; *see also* whakapapa
dining-hall, whare kai, 12–13, 30, 43
differences: between persons, 60–62; in natural resources, 134; in tikanga, 139
diving: as sport, 22–3; for kaimoana, 38, 66, 136
discussion, kōrero, 187, 204

eavesdropping, 82–3, 261
education, 8; 'Māori education', 2; Department of Education, 2, 8; continuing education, 138, 265
educational practices and principles, 252–66; *see also* learning and teaching, methods of
eels, tuna, 19, 118, 124, 148, 223, 224, 232–3, 286
Ellis, Fred, 300; 115, 218, 220, 223–4, 302
Ereatara, Manukau, 26, 134
Evensong, 17, 197, 204, 216
exchange, of gifts, 124; *see also* reciprocity; utu
exorcism, 147
explanation/s, 25, 38, 40, 80, 139, 154, 166, 167; for tapu, 111; for gender differentiation, 183–4; lack of explanations 16, 24, 72, 81, 106, 110, 138, 182
eyes, use of, 89, 94

INDEX

family, nuclear/extended, whānau, 9–10, 212–15
farms, land development, 9–10, 11
farm work, *see* corn, kānga; fencing; harvest; horses; kūmara; milking; planting; ploughing; potatoes; shearing; weeding
father/s, 46–7, 276; as teacher, 55–6, 176–7; as storyteller, 212; *see also* parent/s; matua
fencing, 18, 29, 148
fire: for cooking, 10–11; how to light, 50; as light source, 147
firewood, 15, 119
fish, types of, *see* crabs; crayfish; kahawai; shark; snapper, tāmure; *see also* shellfish
fishing, 16, 18, 19, 38–9, 100, 148, 157, 254; diving, 37–8, 66, 136; line fishing, 136; netting, 69–70, 107–8, 136; tapu in, 76, 107–8
fishing grounds, knowledge of, 157; *see also* rua
flax, harakeke, 28, 66, 155, 180, 269
food, kai, importance and use of, 26, 88, 118–24, 233; *see also* corn, kānga; fish; greens, wild; kūmara; potatoes

games, 22–3, 57; *see also* sport
gardens, 16, 20, 31–2, 39, 41, 74, 118, 149, 255
gender differentiation, 74–7, 91, 93–4, 106–8, 183–8; explanations for, 183–4
generational differences, 35–6, 39, 90–3, 98, 100–1
giving, 107, 118, 119, 123–4; *see also* utu
Gregory, Ross, 300; 218–19, 224
grandparent/s, 10, 46–55, 81, 83, 87–8, 90, 144–53, 157, 174–6, 191, 206–7, 233; as storytellers, 213–14
gravedigging, 109
greens, wild, 15, 27, 29–30, 124
Grey, Sir George, 228, 302
grey warbler, riroriro, 39, 281
groups: learning in, 65, 66, 254–6; playing in, 10; storytelling, 213–14, 218; work groups, 20

haka, 257, 269
hapu, 209–10, 269
harrow, rakaraka, 20, 25, 280
harvest, 12, 21, 254–5
hīnaki, 19, 76
Hinenuitepō, 181, 270
Hohaia, Wiremu, 292; 25–6, 106, 107, 121, 180
holidays, hararei, 16, 19, 135–6
horses: packing with, 64; ploughing, 16, 20, 25, 118; racing, 23; riding, 69, 75, 78; drawing sledges, 16–17, 21, 146
hospitality, manaakitanga, 119, 123
houses, 10–11
households, 9–10, 15
housework, 16, 74
hunting, 18, 26

Hunkin, Liz, 292; 48, 60, 86, 87–8, 122, 123
humility, whakaiti, 175, 196, 288

imitation/copying, 23, 28, 29
initiation, 195
interviews (research), 2–6

Kaa, Jossie, 292–3; 28, 60, 71–2, 80, 117, 120, 135–6, 303
Kaa, Keri, 292–3; 24, 78, 104, 187, 212, 217, 220, 235–7, 302
Kaa, Wiremu, 293; 18–19, 31, 32–3, 39, 40, 44, 46, 50, 56–7, 62, 64–5, 66, 69–70, 74, 76, 78–9, 80, 82, 83, 87, 91, 107–8, 120, 121, 131, 132–3, 141, 240, 242–3, 251
kahawai, 69–70, 107–8, 120, 270
kaimoana, 19, 33–4, 37, 100, 119–20, 135–6, 146, 148, 255; *see also* fish; shellfish
kāinga, 9, 271
kai-karanga, 130, 159–62, 186, 271
kai-tiaki, 102, 112–14, 157–8, 271; *see also* taniwha
kai-tonotono, 131, 271
kai-whakauru, 3–6, 271
karaka, 26, 39, 271
karakia, 36–7, 41, 54, 96–102, 141, 147, 149, 198–9, 204, 229, 256, 271
karanga, 154, 159–62, 254, 256, 257, 259, 271
kaumātua, elders, 21, 43, 52–3, 125–6, 138, 195–6, 216, 220–1, 271–2; *see also* koroua; kuia
kāuta, 12–13, 272
kēhua, 115–17, 215, 223, 226–7, 272
kete, 20, 155, 272; *see also* flaxwork
kiekie, 226, 272
kinship terms, 46–7
kitchen, 10–11, 12–13
koha, 119, 236, 272–3; *see also* reciprocity; utu
knowledge: as taonga, 262; as group possession, 263; kinds of, 144, 262; handing it on, 179–83; holding it back, 112, 179–81; *see also* pūkenga
kōrero, 44, 182–3, 211, 212, 273; *see also* storytelling; whaikōrero
koroua, 261, 273
kōwhai, 39, 273
kuia, 25, 43, 261, 274
kūmara: cultivation, 20, 21, 26, 32–3, 65, 75, 87, 106–7, 256, 274; grading, 67–8, 149; sharing, 118, 121; storage, 68, 121, 149–50; tapu, 106–7, 134

landmarks, 37, 43, 138, 215–17, 221–2
learner/s, ākonga, tauira, 7; aptitude of, 71, 157, 256, 263; being chosen as, 144–58, 162, 189–90, 207, 254, 257; readiness of, 71–2, 114, 256, 260, 265; refused instruction, 156, 176, 181
learning and teaching, ako, 7
learning and teaching, methods of: demonstration, 23–6; imitation/copying,

INDEX

23, 28, 29; kōrero, 44, 182–3, 211, 212, 273; memorisation, 25–6, 172–3, 256–8; observation, 23–30; questions, pātai, 24–5, 35, 235, 278; reinforcement, 92, 261–2; repetition, 36, 172; taking opportunities, 28, 58, 71–2, 122, 137–8, 227, 261; use of approval and disapproval, 260; *see also* educational practices and principles

learning: about sex, 77–84; about sharing, 117–22; about tides, 27; as part of living, 14–142, 145, 253, 254; at different ages, 21–2, 64–73; by doing, 253–4; from catastrophes, 44, 114, 227; in context, 31–33, 43, 64–66, 70–1, 106, 127, 221–2, 234, 254; in groups, 65, 66, 167–8, 254–6; mātauranga Māori, 34–45; to read, 147; *see also* education; educational practices and principles; knowledge; 'Māori education'; school; understanding

learning, places of, 143, 178, 208–10, 212; on marae, 41–5, 70–1; *see also* context; school; wānanga

listening, 24, 44
love, *see* aroha; sharing
lying, 89

Maihi, Ani, 300; 78, 79
mākutu, 115–17, 225, 274
mana, 86–7, 129–33, 230, 274
manaakitanga, 119, 123, 274
manuhiri, 12, 274; *see also* visitors
mānuka, 274; broom, 10–11, 87–9; symbolism of, 235–7
Manukau, Priscilla, 293–4; 10–11, 15–16, 36, 79–80, 89, 110, 113, 118, 153–5, 180, 181–2, 213, 219
Maori Affairs, Department of, 11
'Māori education', 2
marae, 12–13, 21–3, 231, 232–3, 235–7, 254, 275; marae atea, 12–13, 174–5; marae atea and meeting-house, 183–8; as place of learning, 41–5, 70–1; tikanga of, 70–1, 130, 183
maramataka, 21–3, 33, 38, 41, 100, 275
Marsden, Maori, 294; 10, 17, 19, 29, 98–100, 121, 125–6, 191–205, 216, 220, 222–3, 245–7, 303, 304
Mataatua, 200–01
mātauranga, 8, 276
mātauranga Māori, 8, 34–5, 73, 144
Matete, Joe, 294; 12, 19, 28, 33–4, 39, 45, 52–3, 60, 62, 63, 72–3, 76, 97, 106–7, 109, 135, 156–7
Matete, Vi, 294; 28, 52–3, 62, 106–7, 156–7
matua, 276; *see also* father/s
Māui, 218, 220, 276
meals, 22, 34, 99, 197
meeting-house, 12–13, 21–3, 174–5, 187, 231, 276
memorisation, 25–6, 172–3, 256–8
menstruation, 75–6, 78–81
Mihaia, 174; *see also* Ringatū Church

milking, 15, 17, 69, 74, 99
modesty, whakamōwai, 132–3, 288
mokopuna taura, 144–53, 256, 277
money, 12, 117, 121; money tree, 236
mōteatea, 168–71, 277
mother/s, 47, 213, 232–3; as teacher, 56; as storyteller, 213; *see also* parent/s; whaea
Motu, Hera, 300; 213
mountains, 43, 215, 216, 221–2
music, 23; *see also* haka; singing; waiata
mythology, Māori, 248

Nepia, Moira, 300; 214, 219, 222
netting fish, 69–70, 107–8
noa, not tapu, 102–12, 154, 277
nursery rhymes, 51–2, 57

Ngata, Sir Āpirana, 11, 172, 240, 247, 304
Ngata, H. M., 267, 303
Ngātokimatawhaorua, 198, 200

observation, 23–30
opportunities, use of, 28, 58, 71–2, 122, 137–8, 227, 261; lost, 235

questions, pātai, 24–5, 35, 235, 278

pā, 9, 10, 19, 277
Pākehā, 1, 278
Pani, Cambridge, 300; 177–9
pao, 36, 278
Parekowhai, George, 295; 28, 34–5, 40, 54–5, 57, 63, 84–5, 90–1, 114, 128–9, 153, 157–8, 181, 182–3, 188, 212, 250
Parekowhai, Rose, 300; 182–3
parent/s, 34–5, 46–7, 55–8, 77–81, 90, 94, 260; *see also* father/s; matua; mother/s; whaea
pātere, 36, 279
pāua, 12, 19, 66, 136, 279
peers, *see* age-mates
Penfold, Merimeri, 300; 25
Pere, Rose, 295; 74–5, 81, 82, 92, 130, 151–2, 160–1, 207–8, 304
Pewhairangi, Wi, 168–72
pigs: domestic, 17; wild, 18; hunting, 223
Pihema, Ani, 295–6; 56, 58, 72, 116–17
Pirihi, Hone, 296; 15, 19, 22, 29, 30, 31–2, 48, 76–7, 86, 103, 115, 119, 124, 133–4, 135, 138, 139, 144, 158–9, 161–2, 215, 221, 223
Pirihi, Lena, 296; 22–3, 27, 30, 52, 109, 111, 112, 117–18, 122, 124, 144, 215, 223
place names, 138, 215, 217, 222
planting: of crops, 12, 15, 16, 25, 27, 32, 33, 99–100, 120–1, 255; by the moon, *see* maramataka
play, children's, 15–23
ploughing, 12, 16, 20, 25, 69, 255

307

INDEX

ponga, 10, 26
poroporoaki, 182–3, 279
Potae, Hapi, 296–7; 21, 22, 27, 30–1, 32, 35, 41–2, 44, 53, 61–2, 65 66, 67–9, 86–7, 95, 97–8, 111, 113–14, 116, 132, 138–9, 157, 161, 184–5, 186–7, 215, 225
potatoes, 15–16, 19, 20, 21, 26, 75, 256
pregnancy, 75–6
preserves, 17, 121
production units, 11
protection, 101–2, 116, 181
proverbs, whakataukī, 34–5, 39, 128, 179, 212, 288
puberty, 75
pūhā, 12, 27
pūkenga, repository, storehouse of knowledge, 8, 102, 127, 143–88, 261, 263, 280
puna, spring, 15, 101–2
Puketapu, Kara, 209–10, 304

radio, 146
rāhui, 33–4, 135–6, 280
Rākaunui, 33, 41, 280; *see also* maramataka
rātā, 26, 281
Rātana, 153
raupō, 10, 146, 147, 281
readiness, 71—2, 114, 256, 260, 265
rebellion, 73, 208
reciprocity, 122–24; *see also* utu
record-keeping, 193, 197, 203–4
Reedy, New Amsterdam, 297; 168–73
refusal to teach, 156, 176, 181
regrets, 71–2, 176
reinforcement, 92, 261–2
repetition, 36, 172
research, 1–6
resentment, 254
Ringatū Church, 101–2, 111, 135, 140, 142, 146, 176, 225, 148–9, 281; tohunga (ministers), 48, 145, 147, 176, 285
Roman Catholic Church, 96, 100–1, 129
rongoā, 17, 26, 30–1, 69, 134–5, 154, 236, 281
rua, 281; crayfish hole, 34, 53, 138; storage pit for crops, 68, 117–21, 149–50
ruru, 282; 113–14, 225, 282
Ryan, P. M., 267, 304

school, 95, 140, 238–51
scrubcutting, 66
secrecy, 80–81
seriation, 67–8
sex: learning about, 77–84; sex and marriage, 83
sharing: food, 117–22, 141, 204; correction, 84–5; responsibility for learning, 263–4; *see also* aroha; reciprocity; utu
shark, mako, 39, 113, 274
shearing, 12

shellfish, 17–18; kina, 19, 136, 272; mussels (kuku), 18, 136, 148, 274; ngākihi (limpets), 136, 277; pāua, 12, 19, 66, 136, 279; pipi, 148, 279; toheroa, 100, 285; tuangi, 100, 148, 286; tuatua, 100, 148, 286
siblings, 62–3, 81–2, 255
singing, 21, 23, 35–6; *see also* haka; mōteatea; waiata
smoking, 55
Smith, S. Percy, 190
snapper, tāmure, 148, 282
speechmaking, *see* whaikōrero
spirituality, 96–136
sports, 16, 22–3, 74–5
spring, puna, 15, 101–2
stars, 140
storehouse: literal, 150; metaphorical, of knowledge, 143–88
storytelling, kōrero, 34–6, 43–5, 115–16, 126–129, 147, 148, 211–37, 273; characteristic features of, 227–8, 231, 235
swearing, 56

Taiapa, Pine, 71–2, 168–9
Taha Māori, 7, 282
taha wairua, spirituality, 96–117
Tāne-mahuta, 43, 175, 217, 220, 282–3
Tāne-whakapiripiri, 174–5, 283
taniwha, 44, 112–14, 227, 231–5, 283; *see also* kai-tiaki
Tangaere, August, 297; 43, 44, 55, 57, 89, 112, 121, 141
Tangaere, June, 297–8; 20–1, 23, 44, 48, 88, 90, 103, 110, 111, 122, 131–2
Tangaroa, 39–40, 283
tangi, 162, 254, 254, 283
tangihanga, 44, 227, 231–5, 283
tapu, 36, 77, 101, 102–12, 284; meaning state of being, 103; referring to restrictions, 109–112, 134, 139; breaches of, 103, 226–7, 231, 234; *see also* kūmara; noa; sex; toilet facilities
Tarei, Wi, 176–7, 301, 304
taro, 124, 284
tauira, 7, 284
tauparapara, 163–4, 167, 228, 284
Tāwhaki, 43, 217, 220, 227, 228–30, 284
Te Paa, Ephraim, 298; 109–10, 205–6
Te Paa, Harriet, 298; 109–10, 214, 215, 224
teaching, *see* learning and teaching
teina, 157, 175, 236, 284
thanksgiving, 97–8
'third party', the, 31, 46, 59, 82, 93
Thompson, Ngaio, 301; 88
tides, learning to read, 27
tika, 77, 129–33, 285

INDEX

tikanga, 7, 47, 129–33, 285; breaches of, 44, 259; of the marae, 36, 41–2, 130, 174–5; of natural resources, 133–6, 174–6, 208; of valued knowledge, 158–9, 175–6
Tioke, Hurihia, 301; 266
Tioke, Tawhao, 298; 26, 134–5, 174–6, 213, 226–7, 244–5
tipu, *see* tupu
tohu, 40, 285
tohunga, 8, 48, 59, 145, 147, 176, 226–7, 228, 229–30, 285
toilet facilities, 12–13, 77, 104, 108, 109, 234–5
toilet training, 51–2
tokotoko, 43, 88, 233, 285
traditional, tuku iho nō ngā tūpuna, 9, 35–6, 100–01
translation, 6–9, 267
trees, sacred, 29
tuakana/tuākana, 72–3, 81, 126, 158, 285
Tuoro, Mavis, 301; 24
tupu, 65, 67, 118, 286
tūrehu, 226–7, 228, 286
Tu Tangata, 209–10
Tūmatauenga, 174–5, 286
Twelfth, Ringatu, 22–3, 86, 286

uncle/s, 9, 47, 58–62, 154, 157, 177, 178, 213, 219
understanding: achieving, 265; delayed, 34, 37–8, 40, 75, 102, 121, 127, 139–41, 254, 256, 257–8
utu, 122, 287, 303 (Metge 2002)

values, 53–5, 117–36, 253
visitors, 122, 147, 150, 223

waiata, 35, 36, 37, 71, 127, 173, 187–8, 219, 256, 258, 287

wānanga, 48, 139, 173, 189–210, 287; traditional, 189–90; Maori Marsden and Te Wananga o Tai Tokerau, 191–205; indirect reports on, 205–8; new meanings of, 208–10
water: finding in the bush, 26; carting, 15, 16, 21, 32; on the gardens, 32, 65; ritual use of, 101, 102, 141–2, 232–3, 234
weather knowledge, 37–8
weaving, 28, 66, 155, 181–2, 254
weeding, 33, 75, 254
whaea, 287; *see also* mother/s
whaikōrero, 44, 73, 75, 99, 100, 128, 156, 162–79, 204, 256, 259, 287
whakahīhī, 92, 132, 177, 259, 260, 288
whakaiti, 131–2, 256, 288; *see also* humility
whakamā, 86–7, 248, 259, 260, 288
whakapapa, 34–5, 73, 84, 124–9, 156, 162–79, 199, 207, 216, 259, 288; *see also* descent
whakataukī, *see* proverbs, whakataukī
whānau, 12, 20, 131, 288; wānanga, 209–10
whanaungatanga, 119, 289
whenua, 133–6, 290
Williams, Haare, 298–9; 49, 60, 61, 82, 83–4, 92–3, 101–2, 108, 112–13, 118–19, 126–8, 140, 141–2, 144–50, 213–14, 247–9, 266, 304
Wilson, Sonny Huia, 299; 42, 49, 51–2, 58, 59, 70, 77–8, 93–5, 104–6, 227–8, 231–5, 238–40, 240–2
Winiata, Maharaia, 200–2, 304
work and play, children's, 15–23
women: knowledge belonging to, 49, 184–7, 207–8; roles of, 152, 160, 185–8, 254

Young Maori Party, 247 fn